W9-CDN-311

Bloomberg

—— BY ——

Bloomberg

Bloomberg
—— BY ——
Bloomberg

REVISED AND UPDATED

Michael R. Bloomberg

WILEY

For general information on our other products and services or for technical support, please contact our Customer Care Department within the United States at (800) 762-2974, outside the United States at (317) 572-3993, or fax (317) 572-4002.

Wiley publishes in a variety of print and electronic formats and by print-on-demand. Some material included with standard print versions of this book may not be included in e-books or in print-on-demand. If this book refers to media such as a CD or DVD that is not included in the version you purchased, you may download this material at http://booksupport.wiley.com. For more information about Wiley products, visit www.wiley.com.

Library of Congress Cataloging-in-Publication Data

Names: Bloomberg, Michael, author. | Winkler, Matthew, author.
Title: Bloomberg by Bloomberg / Michael R. Bloomberg.
Description: revised edition. | Hoboken, New Jersey : Wiley, 2019. |
    Identifiers: LCCN 2018046908 (print) | LCCN 2018047878 (ebook) | ISBN
    978-1-119-55456-1 (Adobe PDF) | ISBN 978-1-119-55458-5 (ePub) | ISBN 978-1-119-55426-4
    (hardback)
Subjects: LCSH: Bloomberg, Michael. | Capitalists and financiers—United
    States—Biography. | Investments—United States. | Businessmen—United
    States—Biography. | Telecommunication—United States. | Mayors—New York
    (State) —New York—Biography. | New York (N.Y.) —Politics and
    government—1951– | BISAC: BIOGRAPHY & AUTOBIOGRAPHY / Business.
Classification:LCCHG172.B56(ebook)|LCCHG172.B56A32019(print) | DDC
    384.092 [B] —dc23
LC record available at https://lccn.loc.gov/2018046908

Printed in the United States of America.
V10005800_110218

To
Everyone at Bloomberg
who helped make the company what it is today,
and for making Bloomberg Philanthropies possible.

Preface

Two decades after *Bloomberg by Bloomberg* first appeared on bookshelves, so much has changed at the company. We have grown from 3,500 employees in 50 countries to 19,000 employees in more than 120 countries, and from 87,500 Bloomberg Terminals to 325,000, with Asia as our fastest-growing market. We've expanded to include a wide variety of products and services beyond the Terminal, including those that help companies manage their own operations and systems. News stories once published exclusively on the Terminal are now read by millions on the Web and social media platforms, with many syndicated internationally. And along the way, we became the first global news service to win every major journalism award in print and broadcast media, including the Pulitzer Prize.

What started in 1981 with four guys and a coffee pot—and not one customer—has grown beyond our wildest imaginations. And yet on the most important measures, Bloomberg has not changed at all. The culture that we created at the very beginning continues to define who we are: We are still a company that will outwork our competitors, take more risks than they will, serve our customers better, invest more in the long term, and place greater emphasis on transparency and teamwork. The design of our physical environment is still the same—no private offices. I have the same desk space as everyone else in the company. We have never stopped believing that our greatest asset is our own people, and we invest in them and reward them accordingly.

We remain deeply committed to using our success to benefit others. The vast majority of our profits go to support philanthropic causes—only now both our profits and ambitions are much larger than they once were, and the giving is managed by Bloomberg Philanthropies. Giving back has always been a big part of our company's identity, and as long as I'm in charge, it always will be.

The technology that we pioneered in the early 1980s has long been ancient history. But we never made the error that so many others have: mistaking their product for the device that delivers it. Executives at Eastman Kodak, for instance, thought they were in the camera and film business, instead of the photography business. The digital photography revolution passed them by, and after more than a century as one of the most innovative companies in the world, they filed for bankruptcy in 2012. At Bloomberg, we got out of the business of building physical computers as soon as PCs began taking off. We knew our core product was data and analytics, not hardware.

Look ahead or fall behind. We're still looking ahead.

When we started the company in a small room on Madison Avenue, we were refugees from Wall Street motivated by an idea that we could build something new that just might make a difference in the world of finance. People told me I was crazy to think we could overturn the status quo on Wall Street and challenge the giants of financial information. Maybe I was. But within a few years, we had our first customer. And from an initial bond product, we branched out into stocks, commodities, and news. We added magazines, radio, and television—all built upon the mountain of data and information generated by the Terminal and demanded by the world's most influential business and financial professionals. Before the Internet existed, we had created the world's most powerful intranet. And before the phrase "social network" came to be, we had created one for the financial services industry.

A few years after writing the first edition of this book, I stepped away from running the company to run for mayor of New York City—another idea that people thought was crazy. But it had been twenty years since we started the company, and I was ready for a new challenge. Besides, I've always believed that the next person can do it better. If a company can't survive a change at the top, the top person hasn't done her or his job. Talent development is one of a CEO's most important responsibilities.

The talented team of people who led the company in my absence—with Peter Grauer, Tom Secunda, Dan Doctoroff, and Lex Fenwick playing key roles—did an extraordinary job. They even managed to grow the business during the worst economic recession in decades. As most of our customers (those that survived anyway) slashed their payrolls, we found new markets by offering new services. Diversifying the business positioned us for a new era of growth. After twelve years in office, I returned to find the company stronger than ever, and resumed leading it.

This new edition brings the story of Bloomberg into the twenty-first century. It's my story, but it's one that thousands of Bloomberg employees have helped write. And that, truthfully, is the real story behind nearly every success: Teams make it all possible. Leaders get the credit, but the best ones are quick to share it. I've tried to do that throughout my career. I could fill a whole book acknowledging all the people who've played vital roles in our success, and I'd still miss some. But I hope everyone who has contributed to Bloomberg over the years takes pride in what we have been able to do together.

For all that we've accomplished, I still believe that tomorrow will be better than today, and the best is yet to come.

MICHAEL R. BLOOMBERG
New York, NY
July 2018

Contents

Preface   *vii*

Chapter 1   **The Last Supper**   **1**
  The Thrill of Getting Fired: Tarrytown 1981

Chapter 2   **Capitalism, Here I Come**   **9**
  School, Work, and Hard Knocks

Chapter 3   **I Love Mondays**   **39**
  Entrepreneurship: Vocation and Avocation

Chapter 4   **We Can Do That**   **69**
  Elementary Journalism, Not Rocket Science

Chapter 5   **"No" Is No Answer**   **93**
  Establishment Ignorance and Arrogance

Chapter 6   **Money Talks**   **113**
  Textbook Multimedia

Chapter 7   **Man vs. Machine**   **129**
  Technology: Politics and Promises

Chapter 8   **Management 101**   **153**
  The Bloomberg Way

Chapter 9   **Coming Up Next**   **177**
  America's a Wonderful Country

Chapter 10 **Out of the Office**   **189**
  Character and Consistency

Chapter 11 **Wealth, Wisdom, and Work**   **211**
  Philanthropy and Public Service

Index   *239*

1

The Last Supper

The Thrill of Getting Fired: Tarrytown 1981

So there I was, thirty-nine years old and essentially hearing, "Here's $10 million; you're history." One summer morning, John Gutfreund, managing partner of Wall Street's hottest firm, and Henry Kaufman, then the world's most influential economist, told me my life at Salomon Brothers was finished.

"Time for you to leave," said John.

On Saturday, August 1, 1981, I was terminated from the only full-time job I'd ever known and from the high-pressure life I loved. This, after fifteen years of twelve-hour days and six-day weeks.

Out!

For a decade and a half, I'd been an integral part of the country's most successful securities trading firm, even of Wall Street itself. Not just in my head. If my press was to be believed, in everyone's. Suddenly, though, needed no longer. I was a general partner. An owner rather than an employee. Nevertheless:

Fired!

I wasn't going to know what was happening, wasn't going to be making decisions, wasn't going to share in "my" company's profits and losses, wasn't going to be part of it at all. "We" had become "them and me."

"What do you think about us selling the company?" asked Henry.

"If I'm being thrown out, better now than later," I replied.

Of course, there was the $10 million I was getting. America's a wonderful country.

*   *   *

The Salomon Brothers Executive Committee had decided to merge the seventy-one-year-old partnership with a publicly held commodities trading firm, Phibro Corporation (previously part of Engelhard Minerals and Chemicals). We found this out on a hot, summer Friday night at a hastily called, "mandatory attendance, utmost-secrecy required," mysterious partners' meeting at the Tarrytown Conference Center, the former New York estate of society hostess Mary Duke Biddle. Security guards surrounded the complex, checking in each participant as he arrived. (Unfortunately, security missed seeing a Fortune magazine photographer who'd been tipped off and was hiding in a tree. So much for confidentiality!) For sixty-three of us, it was our last meeting as Salomon partners and the occasion when Gutfreund and Kaufman told me my time at Salomon Brothers was over.

We got together in a big conference room before dinner. Expensive lawyers and accountants, being paid at overtime rates, hovered to the side. Exchanging furtive glances, they oozed a nervousness, perhaps in fear that some prewritten script would go awry. Tables and chairs were arranged in rows with the Executive Committee seated in front, facing "the troops." At each partner's seat was a dark gray personalized leather folder. I sat at my assigned place and, though we had been told to wait, like everyone else I immediately opened the book in front of me. The first enclosures were financial projections for our company after a proposed merger with Phibro, this almost unknown oil, metals, and agricultural commodities dealer. Pro forma income statements, balance sheets, legal documents, and other corporate gibberish were attached. But the second presentation in the book was infinitely more interesting:

the effect of the deal on me as an individual. It meant millions of dollars in my pocket!

The pointless speeches went on and on. The Executive Committee was determined to sell the assets of the Salomon partnership. This transaction was a foregone conclusion: The process, a jury trial parody, where witnesses saw the accused pull the trigger, no mitigating circumstances are entered as evidence, and the judge instructs the jurors to deliberate. Everybody walks into the jury room and the foreman asks, "Did he do it?"

Twelve people instantaneously answer, "Guilty."

"Let's go back."

"We can't. We've got to give the accused some consideration. Let's sit around and talk for an hour."

So at Tarrytown we talked for sixty minutes. We were solemn. We were serious. Some asked about differences in corporate culture, others about earnings potential, a few about management structure and duplication of staff functions.

Irrelevant! The Executive Committee wanted this merger and could have voted it through on its own. Yes, we were presented with a fait accompli. But, make no mistake. There was 100 percent approval from the rest of the general partners. Nobody in that meeting gave a moment's thought to rejecting the sale, including me. It was such a lucrative deal for us, as owners.

By the time we sat down to eat, everything was said and done. We were all as serious and businesslike as we possibly could be while trying to stifle the enormous grins on our faces. Everybody attending this meeting was now wealthy beyond his dreams. Previously, partners' money had just been numbers in a capital account ledger book, "funny money." We could give it to charity, or retire, and wait another ten years to get at it. Other than that (and 5 percent interest paid out to us yearly), our fortune was only on paper. That was then. But this was now. All of a sudden, it was real. And ours. In our pockets. In cash!

We were told not to tell anyone until the public announcement the coming Monday. Nobody, inside the company or outside, had known that a sale was even being considered. (Still, my friend and partner Bob Salomon guessed, the day before, that whatever was brewing involved Phibro Corp. He showed me the company's symbol on his stock monitor before we drove to the Tarrytown meeting. Smarter than the rest of us!) The Executive Committee hadn't told the retired limited partners. Not even Billy Salomon, the grand old man of the company. He was informed personally in a much criticized surprise helicopter visit to his Southampton summer home two days later.

Strict instructions to the contrary notwithstanding, some partners did telephone their wives that Friday night. I thought it was nonsensical to make your spouse a possible leak suspect. What difference would it make if she didn't know for an extra day? Others didn't share my view. One partner called his wife while she was at their country club. She ran back into the club's dining room screaming, "We're rich, we're rich!" Fortunately, nobody paid any attention to her.

After the meeting, we ate greasy steaks and drank hard liquor. We shot pool, smoked Cuban cigars, played poker, and laughed uproariously. It was a great big wonderful fraternity party. Boozing and carousing into the wee hours. No thoughts of others. A moment just for us. We had worked for it; and whether or not we deserved it, we got it!

*   *   *

The next day, Saturday, with enormous hangovers evident all around, each partner sat down with two members of the Executive Committee. My meeting was with Gutfreund and Kaufman. Most of the sixty-three partners were asked to stay on as employees of the new company. Not me, though. A half a dozen other guys were pushed out at that time as well.

"Since you don't need me anymore, I'm going home."

There was no reason to stay for the meetings with the new owners. I wasn't going to be involved.

Was I sad on the drive home? You bet. But, as usual, I was much too macho to show it. And I did have $10 million in cash and convertible bonds as compensation for my hurt feelings. If I had to go, this was the time. I was getting my money out of the firm then instead of ten years later. With Phibro paying a merger premium, I was doubling my net worth. Since somebody else had made the decision, I'd even avoided agonizing over whether to stay at Salomon—a timely question, given my then-declining prospects in the company.

Still, it was unsettling that future discussions would be about someone else's company, a firm that until then had been mine. If they'd said, "We have another job for you"—say, running the Afghanistan office—I'd have done it in a second, just as I did at an earlier career turning point in 1979, when Billy Salomon and John Gutfreund told me to give up my sales/trading responsibilities and supervise the computer systems area. I was willing to do anything they wanted. It was a great organization and I would have been happy to stay. I'd never have left voluntarily: There'd be no reason to in good times, and I couldn't have abandoned them in bad times. Unfortunately (or fortunately for me, as it turned out), staying wasn't an option.

Afterward, I didn't sit around wondering what was happening at the old firm. I didn't go back and visit. I never look over my shoulder. Once finished: Gone. Life continues!

*   *   *

Although Phibro technically bought Salomon, Salomon soon ran the combined companies. The power shifted with record speed. Phibro took over when the transaction occurred, and Phibro became Phibro-Salomon. As the securities business boomed, the commodities business collapsed. Soon the entity became Salomon Inc., with Phibro Energy and Philipp Brothers as subsidiaries. The Philipp name went back to the obscurity it had had five years earlier. The acquirer never knew what hit it. The acquiree dominated almost from day one. A total mismatch.

With the merger, the Salomon partners got their freedom and their fortunes, but in the process they ended their own firm as it had existed for decades. By losing control of its key employees, Salomon destroyed its greatest strength. Until then, partners had a long-term, firmwide perspective insured by the golden handcuffs of a ten-year capital "lock-in." After the merger, everyone was just a hired gun. By the 1990s, at Salomon, as at Phibro, virtually all who were there at the time of the merger were gone. The then-partners may have gotten rich, but both old-line companies "lost" in the end.

*   *   *

I went to see Billy Salomon a week after the merger was announced. "So long, thanks for everything, and goodbye" was the purpose. He was not happy. He was, in fact, furious and embittered that "his" firm had been sold and that he had had no part in the decision.

"You screwed me," he said.

"Billy, these were your rules. You dictated years ago that nonexecutive general partners and all limited partners [as he had then become] had no say. You decided that the Executive Committee ruled absolutely. You personally picked every one of its members. Rightly or wrongly, they're your legacy. They made this decision to merge, not the rest of us."

I never thought Billy had a real complaint. One of style maybe, but not of substance. John and the Executive Committee had a responsibility to do what they thought was right for the firm, which is to say, for its owners. Billy had selected the people who made the decision. They followed the rules he had set. He just didn't antici-pate or like the results.

Although I did say "So long" to Billy Salomon, my recollection is that John Gutfreund didn't say goodbye to me. The next time I saw him was seven years later at the surprise fiftieth birthday party for Jack Kugler, our former partner. "Hello, young man, and how are you?" he said to me.

"Fine, and younger than you."

"You always were a wiseass."

That was it. Thanks, John. He had hired me as a fresh MBA when I needed a job, and he had fired me when my era there had really passed. In both instances, his timing was impeccable.

Even though my Salomon career ended involuntarily, I owe a great debt to William Salomon and John Gutfreund. They were my mentors. They taught me ethics, philanthropy, hard work, and to take care of others. They encouraged me to strive for success and supported me fully, even when I failed. They gave me the opportunity to prove myself, not to mention the chance to walk away with an almost unseemly fortune, which I used later to start my own firm. Given all the people Salomon Brothers employed over the years, there are myriad others who must feel the same about both of them.

Though their careers ended very differently, Billy (who retired voluntarily) and John (forced out when an underling cooked the books) both made their respective contributions. Wall Street is a better place because of their efforts—and I'm a smarter, better (and richer) person because of them. Billy died in 2014. John followed him a little more than a year later. It was not easy to speak at their funerals.

*   *   *

During the week after the Salomon partners' last supper in Tarrytown, I went to a furrier on Third Avenue and ordered a sable jacket for my wife, Sue. We had been married for five years at that point, during which time I was a Wall Street star. Unfortunately, from that Tarrytown dinner onward, when she met somebody in the street and was asked, "What does your husband do?" she'd be tempted to answer something like, "Well, he used to be a very important Salomon Brothers partner." The sable would be a surprise to get her mind onto something else.

I was never embarrassed to say that I'd been fired and was now running a small start-up business. I'm tougher than many others (or, perhaps as a psychological defense mechanism, I convinced myself not to care what others thought). But I was worried that Sue might be ashamed of my new, less visible status and concerned I couldn't support the family. A sable jacket seemed to say, "No sweat. We can still eat. We're still players."

I asked the furrier to stay open until 7:30 p.m. on my last day of work, September 30, 1981, and I put in my normal twelve hours. On the way home, I picked up the jacket. Sue was delighted. We drank a bottle of champagne, gave our daughter, Emma, a kiss, and went out to dinner. Next morning, I started Bloomberg, the company. The rest remains a work in progress.

2

Capitalism, Here I Come

School, Work, and Hard Knocks

It was a long way to that Tarrytown conference center from the place I began my journey. The child of hardworking middle-class parents—my father was an accountant at a dairy, my mother a woman of liberal views and independent mind—I wasn't exactly preordained from birth to make a big success of myself on Wall Street or anywhere else. But from them, as a child, I learned hard work, intellectual curiosity, and the ambition to strive relentlessly for the goals I set—all of which would serve me in good stead at school, during my capitalist education at Salomon, and in creating my own company later on.

The town of Medford, Massachusetts, was a blue-collar community outside of Boston. Its city-run high school (I was class of 1960) had 250 students in each grade. Very few went to college. Vocational training was the main mission. I was totally bored until my senior year, when the school started two "honors" courses—one in history and one in literature. For the first time, I was interested in and challenged by my studies.

The history teacher made current events come alive, especially those politically controversial events in America's past that he told

9

us had never before been taught in government-supported education. One event was the labor struggle in the 1920s, exemplified by the trial of anarchists Sacco and Vanzetti. He described how his mother went each day to the courthouse to listen, how some thought them heroes and others thought them the Antichrist. But by bringing his own family into it, the instructor made history real and relevant, not just something to read and memorize. Similarly with literature: The English teacher helped us analyze the world's great books instead of teaching spelling and grammar (two things I never did learn thoroughly). Discussing the meaning of the story versus memorizing the plot made the difference—fascinating versus boring. Both classes broadened my perspective: The exposure to history and culture opened my eyes to a whole new world. What a shame all the preceding time was partially wasted. It was an early lesson for me in how we, as a society, must find a way to better engage our children in the joys of learning.

Outside of school, in my early years, I remember reading *Johnny Tremain*, a novel about a teenage messenger and spy for the Yankee rebels in Boston in 1776. I must have read it a hundred times and often took the subway (the "T," as it's called) downtown to visit the Revolutionary War sites the story mentioned. I thought of myself as the hero patriot, sticking it to old George III—a maverick role I still try to emulate. I developed a sense of history and its legacy, and remain amazed at how little people seem to learn from the past; how we fight the same battles over and over; how we can't remember what misguided, shortsighted policies led to depression, war, oppression, and division. As citizens, we continually let elected officials pander for votes with old, easy, flawed solutions to complex problems. As voters, we repeatedly forget the lessons of others who didn't hold their chosen officials accountable. God help us if George Santayana was right and we're doomed to repeat it all again.

Being a Boy Scout brought together my sense of community with my ambitions of personal accomplishment. I loved it. I savored earning every merit badge, took pride in achieving every rank. I was one of the youngest Eagle Scouts in that organization's history. Boy Scout summer camp was the highlight of the year. I paid for my lodging there by selling our troop's Christmas wreaths door-to-door (my first selling experience). Accommodations were two-man tents under the stars for six weeks in the wilds of New Hampshire. A bugle blew reveille in the morning. We showered under ice-cold water. The food was hot dog and hamburger fare in a big mess hall where everyone took turns peeling potatoes, setting the tables, doing the dishes. I remember loving meals, particularly the grape-flavored punch called "bug juice." Daily, there were riflery, archery, rowing, canoeing, swimming, art, ceramics, and dozens of other games and skills. Hikes and river trips were the highlight of the week—and parents came to bothersome visiting days only once or twice in the whole summer. It was the time I learned both to be self-sufficient and, simultaneously, to live and work with others.

On Saturday mornings in the winter, I went to the Boston Museum of Science for lectures that introduced the natural and physical world in a way my school could not. Each week, for two hours, I sat spellbound as an instructor brought snakes, porcupines, and owls for us to hold; demonstrated the basic laws of physics with hands-on experiments; and quizzed us on every museum exhibit. All the kids—including me—tried to show off by having every answer. This competition taught the value of precise observation, attention to detail, and careful listening. Once the question concerned the age of a tree whose five-foot cross section was displayed in the museum upstairs. The exhibit had great historical events marked by a light bulb at each appropriate tree ring, from the current-day outside circle back to the tree's germination, centuries earlier, at the center of the display. The question was asked about "the redwood tree." We were suitably frustrated by an instructor who refused to accept what we all knew was the "right" answer, until someone realized the tree cross section was not from a redwood at all, but rather from a giant sequoia—a related but slightly different variety. Listen, question, test, think: Those instructors taught me the value of intellectual honesty and scholarship years before college.

*   *   *

While in high school, I worked after class, on weekends, and during summers for a small electronics company in Cambridge, Massachusetts. The technical genius of the company recommended Johns Hopkins University in Baltimore. I was interested in science, and she knew people at the school's Applied Physics Laboratory. Since I had to go to college someplace, why not? I sent in an application and was accepted in due course. The way things worked out, Hopkins probably isn't sorry it gave me a chance. And I was never sorry I matriculated there.

Academically, I was a mediocre student in college, more from a lack of motivation than natural aptitude, or so I hope. Mostly, my grades were Cs (average) in engineering, but during my senior year, I took double the normal course load and earned almost all top-of-the-class As. Nevertheless, I did little more than read the books, listen to the lectures, understand what was said, and parrot it back. Never did I think I could have gone out and originated the material. I hadn't the interest or intellect to be a real engineer, physicist, or mathematician. What I really liked doing—and what I was good at—was dealing with people. I became president of my fraternity, president of the Inter-Fraternity Council, class president, and all-around Big Man on Campus. I learned how to campaign for office while seeking elected school positions. I developed organizational abilities when I planned school dances and fraternity parties. I practiced building consensus and getting people to work together as I ran various school-related extracurricular organizations. All these skills helped me later in life, not only in running for office, but also at Salomon Brothers on Wall Street and with my own company.

When I began thinking about life after graduation, it was obvious that administration was the career for me. I probably would have looked for a job straightaway but for the fact that most people at Hopkins went on to get graduate degrees. Under this communal social pressure, I applied to business school. When the acceptance arrived, I was with friends in the campus mail room and noticed a large brown envelope from Harvard Business School in my mailbox.

"Great. Got in. Let's go get a cup of coffee," I said.

"Don't you want to open it?" someone asked.

"What's the point?" I responded. "They're not sending me a thick package if it was a rejection. That comes in a very thin letter."

*   *   *

My two years at Harvard were well spent. I learned the basics of accounting, marketing, production, management, control, finance, and behavioral science. Harvard's "case method" teaching honed my analytic skills and sharpened my communications abilities. There's nothing as educational as the instantaneous feedback of a hundred classmates shouting you down when you're caught unprepared or can't justify a position.

The academic standards there were superior, but not what I'd call outstanding. There were some very bright students in my class, some classmates I thought "not exactly intellectually gifted," and a few that I considered total frauds who could only talk a good game. As it turned out, those whom I thought were smart generally did well later in life; those whom I considered dummies did less well. The bull-shitters faded away. Street smarts and common sense, it turned out, were better predictors of career achievements after graduation than academic success. Given that I received average grades at "The B School," I don't exactly mind.

Embarrassingly, I remember being more impressed by whom I was matriculating with than by their abilities. As a kid from working-class Medford, never before had I met people as close to the limelight. Many were the sons of famous business leaders I'd read about in the newspapers. Did I think they'd rise to the top just because their dads did? (Generally, they didn't.) Was I secretly hoping for a career-enhancing introduction to their parents? (Few of their fathers' companies even survive today.) Was I looking for glamour by association? (Now, around our offices, celebrities are a dime a dozen.) In fact, although many Harvard relationships helped me, almost none were with those who impressed me so much back then.

*   *   *

Preparing to finish The B School with a Master's in Business Administration in 1966, I really hadn't pondered where my life and work would take me. Like most young men of my generation, I expected to go straight to Vietnam after graduation. Nobody I knew was actually in favor of the war, and I certainly didn't relish the idea of getting shot while walking through the jungle, but in those days the thought of rebelling against our country never entered our minds. Virtually no one went to Canada to avoid the draft—this was still 1966, before anti-war sentiment had galvanized. Home, school, Boy Scouts, sports, politics, newspapers—everything in life taught us duty, loyalty, responsibility, sacrifice, patriotism. As time went on, some marched, got riled up, and wrote about civil disobedience. But generally, Uncle Sam called, and we went.

I had a commitment from an army unit that would make me a second lieutenant after Harvard. Three months before graduation, I went for my standard-issue military physical. It was a pro forma thing; I was in perfect health. To my great surprise, the doctor told me, "You have flat feet. You're not going."

Now, not having to go and possibly get killed was good news. But I was given a draft classification that didn't disqualify me. Instead, it would let the government change its mind later if the war effort needed those of us with this dreaded podiatric deformity. And down the road, who knew what unit I'd be conscripted into or how my career would be going? So I tried hard to secure a lA classification that would get me into the military right away. I wrote my senators and congressmen for assistance, trying to do the right thing—serve my country—but also trying to maintain a measure of control over my own life. The legislators' offers of help were my first taste of politicians' promises that never seem to arrive. Other than the form letters written by staffers ("We'll try to help"), none of them ever appeared to intervene on my behalf. And as it turned out, even though in the mid-1960s everyone under age twenty-five was potentially marching off to war, I never heard from my draft board again. Eventually, we declared victory, and lost the war.

*   *   *

What would I do with my life? With twelve weeks until graduation, I had no plan for how I'd turn an expensive education into a living. I hadn't given it any thought, nor had I signed up for recruiting interviews. My good friend, Steve Fenster, a Harvard classmate who later would become a member of my company's board of directors (five years before he died of cancer), told me to call the firms of Salomon Brothers & Hutzler, as it was then named, and Goldman, Sachs & Co., and to say I was desperate to be an institutional salesperson or equity trader.

"Who are they?" I asked. "What would I be doing?" Busy as I was learning the details of Keynesian economic theory and the intricacies of textbook finance, I wasn't exactly familiar with the jobs and people of Wall Street. I had always assumed I'd go to work in general management for some engineering or manufacturing company, or perhaps even into real estate as my best friend from Harvard, Ron Burks, was doing. (Wall Street did not become the magnet for newly minted MBAs until the 1980s.)

"Don't worry about it," Fenster told me. "Just do it."

Steve had worked at the Pentagon as a Robert McNamara "whiz kid" and then at Morgan Stanley for a summer. My resident expert on both the military and the Street, he said I'd fit in and be happy at either place, doing either thing. Not having any better ideas of my own, I made the calls.

Fortunately for me, as someone who hadn't exactly hobnobbed with Rockefellers during his wonder years or had a mogul for a father, securities trading and sales were considered second-class occupations in those days. Relatively few Ivy League graduates wanted them. Unlike investment banking or research analysis, they were definitely not the prestigious jobs; not the kind of work that the more privileged kids would deign to do. Both involved getting your hands dirty by actually picking up the telephone and talking to customers. Forget the fact that almost all occupations have a big selling component—selling your firm, your ideas, yourself. Never mind that the deans of investment banking depend on their contacts as much as their analytical skills. Overlook the fact that a good trading mentality is synonymous with the ability and discipline to compartmentalize, focus, and compete for success. In those days, no self-respecting research analyst or banker ever thought of working the phones, actually bringing in business. Soliciting was undignified. Trading and sales jobs were going begging. The "swells" were heading elsewhere.

But I came from a background where none of those class distinctions mattered. I didn't know better, and I wouldn't have understood if someone had tried to explain the social niceties. I grew up with the civics-class traditional American ethic, with my parents as role models: Work hard, value education, and do things yourself, whether the labor was mental or physical. For me, with college loans to pay off, a good job was a good job. And, as I would learn later on in my life—at Salomon Brothers and in my own company— it's the "doers," the lean and hungry ones, those with ambition in their eyes and fire in their bellies and no notions of social caste, who go the furthest and achieve the most.

As a Harvard Business School graduate willing to go into the Wall Street trenches, I got an interview at both firms that Steve had suggested. Invited to New York as one of those relatively few MBAs wanting a Goldman Sachs sales/trading position, I was introduced to Gustav Levy, managing partner of the firm and a true legend. "Mike, this is Mr. Levy."

Standing in front of me was this ordinary guy, at once cordial and distant, whose circle of friends and acquaintances, while including world political and financial leaders, until then hadn't included me. I shook his hand and exchanged the usual pleasantries. Ignorant of his true importance, I wasn't as impressed as I should have been. Gus, as he was called, really was somebody and had done great things as one of the Street's top arbitrageurs and philanthropists. Decades after his death, he's still revered as an innovative banker, trusted adviser, and brilliant risk taker. I wish I'd had the smarts to ask him a few questions and, later in my career, spend some time with him before he died. But I didn't.

Then I trotted off to my Salomon Brothers & Hutzler interview. I was the only one at Harvard who'd signed up to meet the folks from this little bond trading firm that lacked the high-and-mighty profile MBA types typically sought. While being shown around by their personnel manager, Stuart Allen, I started talking to some man named Billy whose full name I didn't catch. We talked about school, New York, the weather, whatever. He seemed friendly, like a distant cousin at a family wedding.

"What did you think of Billy?" my escort asked after the guy had ambled away.

"Who was that?" I asked.

"Well, that was William R. Salomon."

I didn't know. He was just some easy-to-talk-to nice person. But since I was now on a first-name basis with "Billy," the managing partner at one firm, and I had encountered "Mr. Levy," the senior person at the other, I knew where I fit in.

My actual job interview at Salomon was not with Billy, but with three other people: the sales manager, Harry Nelson; the head of equity trading, Sandy Lewis (son of Bear Stearns's then–managing partner, Cy Lewis); and the number-two partner at Salomon, John Gutfreund. It took place in a windowless conference room that opened into the firm's Partners' Barber Shop, a standard owners' perk in those days. Equally impressive was the art (all rented, it turned out). I can still picture the massive famous oil color of the Dempsey-Firpo prize fight hanging in their lounge. I'd never seen real art outside of a museum before. It made an impression—and at Bloomberg, we've long featured art in our offices.

When I went back for the obligatory second interview with the same group, they offered me a job for $9,000 a year. In the meantime, I'd been offered employment at Goldman Sachs by its sales manager, Dick Menschel, starting at $14,000 a year—the going rate in those days for a Harvard MBA graduate.

"Look, I can't afford to work at Salomon," I told Nelson, Lewis, and Gutfreund. "I want to. I'd love it. But I don't own another suit of clothes." For those who sat back row in a Harvard class, the dress was jeans—called dungarees in those days—and your college jacket. "I don't have an apartment to live in. I have no cash in the bank. All I've got are outstanding National Defense loans I took for tuition when my part-time campus job as a school parking-lot attendant didn't pay enough."

"How much do you need?" Gutfreund queried.

Instantly, I decided asking for $14,000 would look greedy. Requesting less would get them to give me more. They'd obviously see that, with enough money, I could focus on the job rather than on paying for three meals each day.

"I need $11,500," I blurted out.

"Fine," said Gutfreund. "That's $9,000 salary and a $2,500 loan." He got up and left the room. So much for my trading ability.

"Well, that's done," said Sandy Lewis.

"But I didn't say yes or no," I protested.

"It doesn't matter."

And that was that. I signed the loan agreement (at least it carried no interest). The first year, my bonus was $500 forgiveness of the loan's principal, followed twelve months later by forgiveness of the remaining loan balance. In 1973, I would frame the note with Gutfreund's signature showing it had been paid off, along with the newspaper announcement of my entry into the firm as a general partner.

*   *   *

To say that I fit into Salomon and loved the industry is an understatement. I reveled in it, every minute of the day. In 1966, Wall Street wasn't the impersonal, corporate business it is today, where it's not uncommon for someone to change jobs six times in ten years. People then didn't move around. They were or quickly became a "Morgan Stanley type," an (A.G.) "Becker person," a "KL-er" (Kuhn Loeb), and so on. People were not only identified with their employers, but actually picked up the personalities of their firms, which ranged from haughty and pedigreed to breezy and disarming. The firms in turn were a collection of their staffs' characteristics. From the moment I was hired, no question, I was "Salomon." While many of the top firms coveted distinguished lineages, manners, accents, and Ivy League educations, Salomon was more of a meritocracy that prized go-getters, tolerated eccentricities, and treated both PhDs and high school dropouts disinterestedly. I fit in. It was me.

There was a reason each of us took on the protective coloration of our employer: What mattered on Wall Street in those years was not the individual but the organization. We never used the first person singular. (Billy Salomon once overheard a stock trader saying to a customer, "*I'll* buy 50,000 shares." In a very loud voice, Billy asked him how he got that kind of money in his personal account.) Today, with many companies having lost the family attitude, hiring and firing hundreds of people at a stroke, company spirit has disappeared and personal ambition is rampant. Employees are out for "Number 1." Everybody's a cowboy. Even the most junior-varsity assistant traders consider themselves individual, self-centered superstars. Today's Wall Streeters admit little value from their support people, their company's balance sheet, the franchise name, or their colleagues. Rather than join an organization, they "accept" employment. The company is merely a vehicle, something that offers them a venue for their irreplaceable (and always under-compensated) talents; they declare their free agency status almost on day one.

But when I began, if you could get into an investment banking firm—not an easy thing to do for a nondirect descendant of the founding family—you thought of it as a job for life. You would work your way up, eventually become a partner, and die at a ripe old age in the middle of a business meeting (that's how both Cy Lewis and Gus Levy left this world). You may not have liked all your coworkers and/or partners, but success was "joint and several." Their success helped ensure yours; your achievements abetted theirs. And when that important rule was forgotten by the end of the 1970s, the community that was "the Street" shattered. Charles Darwin told us what would happen: It may be survival of the fittest as nature meant it to be, but lots of good and worthy creatures die in the process.

*   *   *

The Salomon partnership was a unique organization. It didn't have the normal politics and infighting of the typical commercial enterprise. It was the ultimate "what you see is what you get" environment. Everyone important worked in the same room, sitting shoulder to shoulder, trading or selling stocks and bonds. Disagreements flared, as they did with any group of excitable Type A employees. People who were adversaries on an issue screamed at each other.

Then compromises would be made, and the squall was over. Alliances were formed anew. Enemies in the last battle would become allies in the next. Tempers didn't simmer behind closed doors, with staffs encouraging animosities and constructing barriers. Here, it was open, quick, and *now*!

Nor did so-called corporate democracy get in the way. "Empowerment" wasn't a concept back then, nor was "self-improvement" or "consensus." A managing partner presided at the top, with an Executive Committee below, followed by the general partners and everyone else. (The partners thought they had more power than nonpartners, but in reality, most didn't.) The managing partner in those days made all the important decisions. I suspect that, many times, he didn't even tell the Executive Committee *after* he'd decided something, much less consult them before. I'd bet they never had a committee vote. I know they never polled the rest of us on anything. This was a dictatorship, pure and simple. But a benevolent one.

The boss when I joined in 1966, William R. Salomon (WRS as we referred to him behind his back, or Billy as he preferred to be known), made the culture at Salomon Brothers special. He was decisive and consistent as a leader. If he ever harbored doubts after making a decision, I never saw it. And although he was easily approachable and willing to listen to everyone's views, when he said we were going left, we went left, and when he said right, right it was. We didn't have to prepare for both directions. He set the rules and even he conformed to them. Was it a rule to conduct one's personal affairs so as not to embarrass the firm? His own private life was exemplary. When he thought another's wasn't, we had an instantaneous partners' meeting to remove the offender—no matter how important that person was to the immediate bottom line. Did he decree each of us should be accessible to all? Anyone could come up to his desk, anytime. He was on a first-name basis with as many people at the bottom of the corporate ladder as at the top.

Did Salomon have a mandatory retirement for partners at age sixty-five? Billy retired voluntarily at sixty-three, when he felt he was slowing down. There was no different set of rules for him. He led by example. What he said, he did. And the rest of us did as well.

John Gutfreund was a great leader too, but I always thought he listened to too many people. The final guy to see him often carried the day. That was fine when I was desperately trying to save my career. As long as I saw John last and persuaded him of the virtue of my position, he'd back me versus the entire Executive Committee. But in retrospect it made running the firm much more difficult for him. Smart people prepared for both left and right when John succeeded Billy as managing partner. This event split resources and made it harder to lead when the going got tough. Unlike Billy, John consulted all interested parties before making a decision. No matter how noble the motive, that resulting apparent indecisiveness eventually destroyed his constituency and led to his downfall. Comparing John Gutfreund to William Salomon on leadership, I always thought John was as principled, as honest, as caring, more egalitarian, less effective.

The real difference between Billy and John was that John was smarter with securities, Billy with people. But I always believed the firm was best off when they ran it together. Each had different strengths. Without John, I think Billy would have had trouble running the financial engineering side of the company as the securities world grew more complex with derivatives, swaps, mortgage securities, and so on. And John certainly did have trouble running the people side of the business without Billy, when the organization ballooned to thousands of employees around the world. As a team, until Billy retired in 1978, they were the best.

After their partnership ended, as my career in running equities was waning and I needed something new to do, I tried convincing John that he needed an aide to tell him when the emperor had no clothes—someone to stand up and fight him a little. Someone to test his resolve and let him hone his responses. But he wouldn't sign on. Maybe John didn't think I was competent. Maybe he just didn't want someone looking over his shoulder. In any case, my proposal for a chief-of-staff, a gatekeeper—and me being it—didn't fly.

*   *   *

I got to Salomon's run-down building at 60 Wall Street in June 1966, and I worked my first summer there in "the Cage," physically counting securities by hand. It was a pretty lowly start for a Harvard MBA. We slaved in our underwear (it was virtually an all-male industry back then), in an unair–conditioned bank vault, with an occasional six-pack of beer to make it more bearable. Every afternoon, we counted out billions of dollars of actual bond and stock certificates to be messengered to banks as collateral for overnight loans. Then, every morning, when those certificates needed for delivery to customers were returned by a group of disheveled old men who blanketed the streets of lower Manhattan carrying "bearer" bonds and stocks door-to-door, we checked them back into the firm's inventory. By the 1980s, such practices would be as quaint as the horse-drawn carriage, eliminated by the computers of the information age. Not then, though.

Three months into my career, I was promoted to the Purchase and Sales (P&S) Department. One day, when good weather caused us to dawdle outside, the former longshoreman who was my manager explained at the top of his lungs (embarrassingly and deliberately, in front of the entire department) that a one-hour lunch didn't mean more than sixty minutes away from one's desk, even, or rather particularly, if one was an HBS prima donna. Working in P&S under this guy's eye was not much of a step up from working in my underwear in the Cage. There I was, a Johns Hopkins and Harvard Business School graduate, toiling in a slum with worn-out linoleum floors and broken wooden chairs, putting little paper slips in alphabetical order all day long, and getting berated by someone I probably should have respected, but didn't. When my friends asked what I was doing at work, to save face I told them I was "studying methods and procedures to simplify the work flow." After all, my friends were research analysts and investment bankers with lush, private, windowed, and carpeted offices, and I was what can only be called a clerk. Why didn't I quit? Too embarrassed.

Eventually, though, my big opportunity came. At the end of my first year, I got picked to be a real "Clerk" on the trading floor at the Utilities Desk. Here was where the action was—and the high-paying jobs. In this particular area, the bonds of electric and gas companies were bought and sold. It was run by two Salomon partners, Ira Lectman and Connie Maniatty. My main function was to keep the position book updated with our current inventory as we traded. After a partner signed each transaction ticket (big trades got both partners' signatures), I stamped them with a consecutive number and updated our records. The tickets then went zipping down the conveyor belt to the Back Office from whence I had just escaped. At last I had become an integral part of capitalism. Stamping and updating: I was so glad I'd gone to graduate school!

The execution of my only other Utilities Desk task proved to be my downfall—or my salvation, depending on your perspective. I was charged with the grave responsibility of having six sharpened No. 2 pencils in front of Ira and six sharpened No. 3 pencils in front of Connie each morning when they arrived—or maybe it was the other way around. Anyway, one day, to relieve the boredom and express myself, I deliberately gave them each other's pencils and broke off all the lead tips. Connie took it well. Ira, though, stood up and started screaming to John Gutfreund that I should be fired. Pencils were important to Ira.

John summarily removed me from that department (thus changing the fate of the utility bond business forever) and installed me temporarily in his Syndicate Department, but seated behind a pillar, alongside his second in command, Jay Elsas. From then on, Ira didn't have to have his field of vision ruined by my face. A little anarchy at Salomon in the form of a practical joke was fine, but I had pushed the envelope too far.

A month later, I moved to the Equities Desk and the rest is history. No more bonds. I was in the stock side of the business for good. The firm had just brought in Jay Perry, a glib, fast-talking salesperson from the St. Louis office, to build up our new block trading business. For decades, Salomon had been buying and selling thousands of bonds in single trades, away from any listed exchange, thereby avoiding sudden price fluctuations. For stocks, block trading fulfilled the same function, enabling big institutions to acquire or unload in bulk, without market disruptions. Salomon would become the biggest in this field. And I was part of it as Jay's right-hand man—or he as my left-hand man, as I was known to say on my more modest days.

Actually, Perry and I were a dynamite team. We could sell anything to anybody. If you wanted to dispose of a block of stock, we probably could have even convinced your spouse to buy it. Salomon wasn't a multifaceted full-service firm in those days, so we had to do without what our competitors had and took for granted—research, analysis, contacts. We just did what all great salespeople do: We presented everything we had, and then highlighted whatever facts enabled customers to convince themselves they were getting a good deal.

"It has a strong specialist behind it," I'd tell one buyer who might not have the slightest idea why the specialist mattered. (Specialists are people on the floor of the New York Stock Exchange who are obligated to buy and sell a company's shares, thereby ensuring an orderly market at all times.) "The chart pattern looks like a breakout," Perry would declare for those who believed. "The trend's my friend." I'd add, "Look at who the buyers and sellers have been," for the "misery loves company" crowd. Or, "You buy this and we'll help you sell that," we'd say, as if we wouldn't do either separately.

Often, when we worked on one of the big, critical, risky trades, Billy and John would stand over me, watching silently while I was on the phone with a customer, head down, totally focused on making the sale, talking, explaining, cajoling, pleading. I felt a great thrill when they saw I had closed the deal. "Done," I'd say matter-of-factly with a straight face as I hung up the phone and tossed the completed order slip to the trader with a studied nonchalance. And they'd walk away without a word. There weren't any congratulations. They weren't needed. I was the up-and-coming star. I was expected to make big trades. I (and they) knew!

And if our other strategies didn't work to close a deal, we had the ultimate weapon: the firm's capital and five smart guys with the knowledge and decisiveness to "pull the trigger" when needed. The two traders on the desk, David Healy and Robert Bradley (Perry and I called ourselves traders, but we were really just salespeople), along with Michael Meehan, David Kirkland, and Hans Kertess on the New York Stock Exchange floor, could always threaten to buy the stock for Salomon's own account. This would force the buyers to act, even if they wanted to wait. "Buy now or risk buying never" was the message. They always bought.

It was great. This mega trading was a new concept. We developed it as we went. Cy Lewis from Bear Stearns and Gus Levy from Goldman Sachs had started it—trading stocks like bonds. One large transaction going "over the counter" at a single price. It was an entirely revolutionary business compared to the old way of accumulating or disposing of many shares through small individual transactions executed over time on the stock exchanges. Through these pioneering efforts with block trading, we created a bigger, faster market for the gigantic new institutionalized money pools that were more and more coming to be stock market players: pension funds, mutual funds, hedge funds, and insurance annuities. In doing so, we changed the buy-side/sell-side relationship from the "old-boy" concept of doing business based on whom you knew to open, fair competition based on price. It was new, different, initially lucrative, and fun, and I was proud to be one of the young turks making it happen (along with contemporaries Ginny Clark, Bruce Hackett, and James Massey, who all became Wall Street luminaries later in their careers).

Over time, Billy and John, while not the hands-on traders Cy and Gus were, actually had more to do with making the concept fly than the other Wall Street leaders. Salomon and Gutfreund knew the value of consistency in customer service. They also knew the value of publicity, of getting out the word regarding Salomon's proficiency and aggressiveness in this new field. They encouraged us to do every trade, profitable or not. Before Billy ran Salomon, the bond partners invested in B&O Railroad bonds rather than Haloid stock (which eventually became Xerox). After Billy took over, equities dominated. Later, when the same Salomon partners complained that Perry was crazy, John excluded them and pushed block trading and stock underwriting as the firm's future. When they demanded that Salomon's capital—their money—not be jeopardized by nonpartners like this kid Bloomberg, John just ignored the lot and let us build a whole department of aggressive traders who would provide the service, take the risk, and get everyone together. "Never let the customer go down the street to another store—he might find they sell the same thing there and not come back," Billy always told us. "Do the trade today. Figure out how to make it profitable tomorrow."

*　　　*　　　*

I didn't love Wall Street just for the money, I also loved it for the lifestyle it provided. The Street promised vast riches—although few of the great fortunes have been made there. From John D. Rockefeller to Sam Walton to Bill Gates, great financial success comes from starting businesses with concrete products in the real world, building jobs, creating value, and helping people. But in those years, the practical comforts of prosperity, together with the delights of the job itself, kept me engaged and happy.

As a kid from the provinces, I had a lot to learn, not only about the Street, but about the amenities of high-style Manhattan living. I still remember the first time I went to a fancy New York French restaurant, La Côte Basque, in 1967 with Dave Osborn, a cosmopolitan salesperson who started at Salomon the same time as I did. (He became a general partner the same year as I, and got thrown out of the company, years later, on the same day yours truly met his demise.) I couldn't stop gawking. It was my first time in such opulent surroundings. A dozen people were seated around a table featuring the largest flower centerpiece I'd ever seen.

The woman seated to my right talked to me only when she had to, and in an accented English I couldn't readily understand. Her topics of conversation were equally incomprehensible, and certainly as inapplicable: Where did my family have vacation houses in Europe? In what country was our yacht registered? Where did we keep our plane? My late father, who never earned more than $6,000 per year, would have chuckled. And in front of me was more silverware per place setting than my family owned in total. I'd never seen forks and spoons set across the top as well as down the sides. Needless to say, I waited for others to start each course and just followed along.

In addition to showing me the life of high society, Osborn taught me about expense accounts. We took customers to the theater, to sporting events, to breakfast, to lunch, to dinner. We even took them to conventions, to golf outings, and to ski resorts out West, all on the firm's money. Everything was always first-class as we went about cementing those "vital client relationships." Yes, it was legitimate business, but it was whatever tickled our fancy, when, where, and with whomever we chose.

Sometimes, I thought I'd gone through the looking glass into another world. Once, we cruised uptown in a big black limousine.

The only other time I'd been in such a car was at my father's funeral. At our destination, someone tossed the driver fifty dollars—for what would have been a two-dollar ride in a cab! That amount of money would have covered my entire week's personal, social, and food budget. Funny world. Funny money. And different from everything I'd ever known.

*   *   *

Back in reality, I took the subway to work and read the office copy of the *Wall Street Journal* upon arrival, to save the fifteen-cent newsstand cost. I came in every morning at 7 a.m., getting there before everyone else except Billy Salomon. When he needed to borrow a match or talk sports, I was the only other person in the trading room, so he talked to me. At age twenty-six, I became a buddy of the managing partner. I would stay later than everyone else except for John Gutfreund. When he needed someone to make an after-hours call to the biggest clients, or someone to listen to his complaints about those who'd already gone home, I was the someone. And I got a free cab ride uptown with him, the No. 2 guy in the company. Making myself omnipresent wasn't exactly burdensome—I loved what I was doing. And, needless to say, developing a close working relationship with those who ran the show probably didn't hurt my career either.

I've never understood why everybody else doesn't do the same thing—make himself indispensable on the job. That was exactly what I did during the summer between my first and second years in graduate school, when I worked for a small Harvard Square real estate company in Cambridge, Massachusetts. Students would come to town just to find an apartment they could move into in September; they were always in a rush, eager to get back to their vacations as soon as possible. We ran generic advertisements in the newspapers for three or four different sizes of rentals; each ad would fit twenty of our apartment listings. Every day, the newly arrived would-be renters got up early, grabbed the newspaper at their hotels, looked at the real estate section, made a phone call, scheduled an appointment with "the next available agent" to see housing that sounded appropriate, and went back to bed. Later in the day, they'd go out and actually look.

I went to work at six-thirty in the morning. By seven-thirty or eight o'clock, all potential renters visiting Cambridge had called our company and booked their apartment-viewing visits with whoever was there. I, of course, was the only one who bothered to come in early to answer the phone: The adult "professionals" who worked for this company (I was "the summer kid") started work at nine-thirty. Then, all day long, they sat in wonderment as person after person walked into the office asking for Mr. Bloomberg.

It's said that 80 percent of life is just showing up. I believe that. You can never have complete mastery over your existence. You can't choose the advantages you start out with, and you certainly can't pick your genetic intelligence level. But you can control how hard you work. I'm sure someone, someplace, is smart enough to succeed while "keeping it in perspective" and not working too hard, but I've never met him or her. The more you work, the better you do. It's that simple. I always outworked the other person (and if I hadn't, he or she would be writing this book).

Still, I had a life. I don't remember being so driven or focused that my job got in the way of playing in the evenings and on weekends. I dated a lot. I skied and jogged and hit the town more than most. I just made sure I devoted twelve hours to work and twelve hours to fun—every day. The more you try to do, the more life you'll have.

Although I was serious about my career, I never had a "budget" for my future. Unlike so many of my classmates, I didn't set out to be a partner or vice president at age thirty, or a trillionaire at thirty-five, or president of the United States when I turned forty. Make a comprehensive scheme for the rest of my life? I had trouble filling out the part of the college application where you're asked to write fifteen hundred meaningless words about what you're going to do for the next ten years. Both at business and at home, I've never let planning get in the way of doing.

Life, I've found, works the following way: Daily, you're presented with many small and surprising opportunities. Sometimes you seize one that takes you to the top. Most, though, if valuable at all, take you only a little way. To succeed, you must string together many small incremental advances—rather than count on hitting the lottery jackpot once. Trusting to great luck is a strategy not likely to work for most people. As a practical matter, constantly enhance your skills, put in as many hours as possible, and make tactical plans for the next few steps. Then, based on what actually occurs, look one more move ahead and adjust the plan. Take lots of chances, and make lots of individual, spur-of-the-moment decisions.

Don't devise a Five-Year Plan or a Great Leap Forward. Central planning didn't work for Stalin or Mao, and it won't work for an entrepreneur either. Slavishly follow a specific step-by-step strategy, the process gurus tell you. It'll always work, they say. Not in my world. Predicting the future's impossible. You work hard because it increases the odds. But there's no guarantee; much is dependent on what cards happen to get dealt. I have always believed in playing as many hands as possible, as intelligently as I can, and taking the best of what comes my way. Every significant advance I or my company has ever made has been evolutionary rather than revolutionary: small earned steps—not big lucky hits.

And I stay "flexible." Long after Salomon had abruptly given way to my forming my own company, a reporter asked me what we at Bloomberg had failed at, as opposed to the successes that get all the attention. My answer, after some thought, was, "Nothing; but what we accomplished wasn't always what we set out to do." Often, in the process, things worked that we hadn't planned on; unforeseen uses arose for our products; customers appeared whom we hadn't known existed—and exactly the reverse occurred for those we had been dead sure of. Planning has its place; the actual thought process sometimes leads to great new ideas. But you can only accomplish what's possible when you get there.

Then, whatever your idea is, you've got to do more of it than anyone else—a task that's easier if you structure things so that you *like* doing them. Since doing more almost always leads to greater accomplishments, in turn you'll have more fun. And then you'll want to do even more because of the rewards. And so on. I've always loved my work and put in a lot of time, which has helped make me successful. I truly pity people who don't like their jobs. They struggle at work, so unhappily, for ultimately so much less success, and thus develop even more reason to hate their occupations. There's too much delightful stuff to do in this short lifetime not to love getting up on a weekday morning.

*　　*　　*

I expected to be at Salomon for a year or two while I looked for a job in manufacturing. Even though I thought I'd just date the company, not marry it, my romance with Salomon ended only when they threw me out after fifteen years. Thank goodness, every time another firm came to hire me away, I said no. I always found a reason to stay, some fresh outlook on my Salomon life that made me recommit myself to the firm. Maybe I lacked the guts to try someplace new. Maybe I possessed the resolve and foresight to ride with the best. In any case, in retrospect, staying was always the right decision—as I would find out in 1981, at the very end of my Salomon tenure, in a conference center in Tarrytown, New York.

Some young people starting their careers today are too impatient for current compensation, at the expense of continuing their education and giving their jobs a chance. Get back to work. Forget the money today. There's plenty of time for that later. Novices should go to the best firm they can get into—and then listen and learn.

The best example of reward for patience (perhaps the best in the history of the world) was when I wasn't made a Salomon general partner at the time I thought I'd be, and didn't quit over it.

Things were going great six years after I was hired. I was the fair-haired boy, the block-trading superstar in the most visible department of the trendiest firm on the Street. I was the pet of its two top executives. I greeted all important visiting customers, got interviewed by every newspaper that mattered, and had a great social life playing the role of Wall Street power broker to the hilt. More than "a legend in my own mind." When the other young turks sat around and predicted who would be anointed with the ultimate reward of a partnership, I was on the top of the list.

Money wasn't the issue. I'd long since paid off my loans and was living a respectable if not extravagant life. I took the subway to work, I went to free concerts in Central Park, and my most romantic dates were beer and pizza with a girlfriend late at night on the Staten Island Ferry (five cents round-trip, food and drink extra). I lived in the same one-room studio for ten years and didn't bother to own a car. I never spent a lot, but I also don't remember wanting anything I didn't just go out and buy. Good times, great friends, fantastic job, lots of cash: I had it all.

Still, the prestige of the partnership mattered more than everything in the world to me. It was the in-your-face statement to the world that I was the best, that I could go to the top in the most competitive environment there was. The B School kid had used his smarts and skills to work his way up the ladder. I'd earned this partnership, and now I wanted the public acknowledgment of my value once and for all, as a big fish in the big pond. Maybe it was all in my head, my private inferiority complex. But, no question—becoming a general partner in Salomon Brothers was my holy grail!

And then, the day came, in August 1972. The list of new partners came out—and I wasn't in! Everyone, just everyone else was on that list. All those people who deserved it less than I were there, even those who, according to company gossip, had no chance. I had been passed over and, with such a big group accepted, humiliated as well. It was so bad, there wasn't even anyone left with whom I could commiserate. I was devastated. No one ever explained why I wasn't chosen.

With tears in my eyes, I at first denied the truth. Then I thought up wild schemes of revenge. I searched for someone to blame. "I'll quit," I told myself, in the first of many crazy mutterings. "I'll kill 'em." "I'll shoot myself." How would I face anyone ever again? They would all be looking at me and laughing behind my back. I knew I shouldn't have been so arrogant. Damn it, I never learn.

Fortunately, after work, my normal evening jog alongside the East River let me take my anger out on the pavement rather than on management. The next morning, I went to work and did one of the largest trades the firm had ever done up to that time. I dotted every *i*, crossed every *t*. I focused. I worked. I smiled. I dialed. Was I stronger than everyone else? No one would come close. I would be as good at not making partner as I was at aiming to be one. "Screw 'em!"

Three months later, with no warning, the firm had an unscheduled partners' meeting in Billy Salomon's office. The participants came out stern-faced and silent. My boss, Jay Perry, walked over to my desk and stood behind me with his back to the others.

"What do those idiots want?" I growled without picking up my head.

"They're going to make you and Don Feuerstein general partners," Perry said.

He never could keep a secret. At that instant, someone yelled over to me, "Mike, Bill Salomon's secretary, Margarette Wilson, is calling on line one."

I picked up the phone. "Yes, Margarette?" Margarette always liked me.

"Mr. Salomon wants to see you."

"Does he want Feuerstein, too?"

"Oh, yes. How did you know?"

Billy never gave me an explanation for why they'd made me a partner then and not three months earlier. He was, as I have become, a member of the "never apologize, never explain" school of management. Asking him would not have been good form. And there was no chance I would have gotten an answer anyway. So when he gave me the good news, I didn't ask why they'd waited. I said, "Thank you," politely but not profusely. Even when I got what I wanted and deserved, I would be tougher than the rest.

*   *   *

Someone once said, "Be nice to people on the way up; you'll pass the same ones on the way down." I believe in treating associates well, but not for that cynical reason: Having been both up and down repeatedly, my experience says you pass different people as you go through the inevitable cycle.

From the high of the anointment as a general partner to the low of being fired in 1981, life at Salomon was a constant roller coaster. In 1973, my career was skyrocketing. I had just been made a partner. Next, I was given responsibility for all equities. It happened when Dick Rosenthal, the partner running the arbitrage department, and Jay Perry, the partner supervising stock trading and sales, had a fistfight. Perry was sent to run the Dallas, Texas, office; Rosenthal was ordered to an out-of-the-way area off the trading floor to "do deals," and I got promoted to run all stock trading, sales, arbitrage, and convertible bonds combined.

Although technically I was Jay's boy, nevertheless the three of us—Rosenthal, Perry, and I—conducted a multiyear battle for supremacy. Even Jay and I, who had worked together for years as one of the world's great sales teams, competed against each other, particularly in the last twelve months before his banishment to the Southwest. By then, he was having serious emotional problems. At one point, he became a recluse, actually not leaving his private office or taking any business calls during the day for weeks. Then one morning, while I was upstairs having breakfast with our two biggest customers, he stormed into the trading room and in a fit of pique over some imagined slight, emptied my desk drawers all over the floor before disappearing back into his sanctuary. Called out of the dining room by the desk clerk, I gave instructions to put my papers back before the meal was over. The clients never saw the embarrassing scene and Jay never mentioned the incident, ever. Nor did I. But one month later, after the famous Perry/Rosenthal brawl, I was in charge.

In 1979, my career at Salomon reversed its magical upward climb. Negotiated commission rates and increased competition had made the block-stock business unprofitable. While we were dominating the transaction volume on the NYSE, my administrative and trading skills were constantly being questioned. We certainly weren't making money. Then a surprise administrative message was hand-delivered to all employees, announcing that Richard Rosenthal would join the Executive Committee and from then on would oversee the firm's equity efforts. I walked over to John Gutfreund's desk, which was literally four feet behind me. Billy's was another ten feet away. "I need to see you both, now!"

We went into Billy's conference room. I held up the announcement. "I'm not going to work for Rosenthal, and he won't want me anyway."

"We know that," Gutfreund said. "We want you to go upstairs and run the computer area."

*   *   *

So I started what was to be my last job at Salomon, running Information Systems. This group was responsible for both keeping the firm's books and providing the analytical tools the traders and salespeople needed. I reported directly to Gutfreund in this position, as in the last; but from the beginning, the Executive Committee—particularly one member, my old nemesis, Rosenthal—made my life miserable. Dick, who constantly bragged about his business success in spite of never having finished Erasmus High School in Brooklyn, was jealous of anyone who had a college education, particularly someone who had added an MBA from Harvard. Rosenthal and I had started as friends in the mid-1960s. We stopped being friends around 1968 when I was assigned to work with Perry, who became my mentor and Dick's archenemy. Now, he was determined to keep his battle with Jay Perry and "Perry's boy" going.

So, even though I was out of equities, and computers weren't his area of responsibility, the guerilla warfare continued. It wasn't a fair fight. Truth never got in Dick's way. If the facts didn't fit, he just made them up. Over the next two years, he was an instantaneous expert on everything in my domain as well as his—and everyone else's, too. Determined, and armed with that great advantage lack of knowledge gives one, Rosenthal was a winner: Our rivalry was preordained to end in my divorce from the company.

Sure enough, by early 1981, he had persuaded everyone that I was incompetent. Many mimicked his ridicule of my insistence on one firmwide computer system to facilitate cross-department cooperation and multiple-product risk management. It didn't help my situation when I argued vociferously that the firm was going down the wrong path with the adoption of profit-center accounting I thought ill-suited to a complex, totally integrated business. Maybe I shouldn't have criticized the changing of our employment strategy away from promoting in-house producers to managers and toward acquiring outside, transitory, superstar "rainmakers" as department heads. It might have been smarter politically not to have focused computer development toward the newly fashionable minicomputers (which forced me to battle the entire IBM sales management team as well as Dick). Mythology also says I shouldn't have claimed I could run the firm better than the Executive Committee, although I don't remember ever saying that.

I had stirred the pot, lost the battle, and was paying the price. And though John Gutfreund supported me almost to the end, eventually the consensus in the Executive Committee would be unanimous. They won. I lost. It was time to go. The only questions left were when, how, and with what: I would receive all three answers unexpectedly at the 1981 "Last Supper" in Tarrytown.

*   *   *

Perry and Rosenthal have since died. Perry succumbed to leukemia after leaving Salomon Brothers and enjoying only modest success elsewhere. Rosenthal died later, and more quickly. On a rainy Good Friday in 1987, I was sitting in the car and listening to the radio while my family was shopping. A pilot from Briarcliff, New York, had been killed, crashing a new Beech Baron aircraft into a house on his approach to Westchester Airport. And I thought to myself, "I'll bet that's Dick Rosenthal." (Barons were very expensive twin-engine private planes. There weren't very many people who could afford them, and whoever it was came from the town where Dick lived. Too much of a coincidence.) They didn't announce the name until the next morning. Was I happy, or sad? After all the years of bitter fighting, I guess I'm ashamed to say that the right word was *ambivalent*.

I had nine great years at Salomon as a general partner, fifteen in total. I loved going into the office every single day for the entire decade and a half I worked there, even those days I knew would be tough. I made an unimaginable amount of money. I got some (but not all) of the acceptance and prestige I thought my due. And what I learned—not to mention the money I made—would provide the foundation for the company I created after I left.

3

I Love Mondays

Entrepreneurship: Vocation and Avocation

I had spent my first twenty-four years getting ready for Wall Street. I had survived fifteen more years before Salomon Brothers threw me out. At age thirty-nine, the third phase of my life was about to start. With whatever values my parents had taught me, $10 million in my pocket, and confidence based on little more than bruised ego, I started over.

A month after the 1981 meeting in Tarrytown, I realized that Goldman Sachs, the firm that had offered me my first job in 1966, wasn't going to call and offer me a partnership. If they had, I'd probably have accepted it just for ego reasons. But when they didn't, I had to knock on doors looking for a job, stay unemployed, or start my own company. The prospect of working for someone else wasn't exciting. Perhaps no one would hire me. Besides, I'd already done that. As to retiring, I've always been too restless. I'd go crazy just sitting around. So the last option, chasing the great American dream, seemed all that was left.

Resources weren't a problem. I didn't have to worry about feeding my family. That gave me the luxury of time. I had capital to fund a new business (thank you, Salomon Brothers). I knew how to manage and always thought both names on my old business card

(Bloomberg and Salomon) mattered. Thus, I could be an entrepreneur rather than an employee if I wanted to.

Did I want to risk an embarrassing and costly failure? Absolutely.

Happiness for me has always been the thrill of the unknown, trying something that everyone says can't be done, feeling that gnawing pit in my stomach that says "Danger ahead." Would it be nice not to have uncertainty, to sit back and "veg out"? When the phone rings constantly, when people keep demanding attention, when I desperately need time to myself, it seems an attractive notion just to "chuck it all." But then nobody calls, nobody stops by, and soon I'm nibbling my nails and getting irritable, and I realize that's not what I want. It sounds good. In reality though, I want action, I want challenge.

Work was, is, and always will be a very big part of my life. I love it. Even today, after toiling for 50 years, I wake up looking forward to getting in early, practicing my profession, creating something, competing against the best, having comradeship, receiving the psychic compensation that money can't buy. Whether you're in business, academia, politics, the arts, religion, or whatever, it's a real high to be a participant rather than a spectator. Not everyone gets the chance. But to have that opportunity and not use it? What a sin! (I was once quoted as saying, "Sunday night was my favorite because I knew when I awoke the next morning, I'd have five full days of fun at the office.")

Think about the percentage of your life spent working and commuting. If you're not content doing it, you're probably pretty miserable with the situation. Change it! Work it out with those next to you on the production line. Talk to your boss. Sit down with those you supervise. Alter what's in your own head. Do something to make it fun, interesting, challenging, exciting. You've got to be happy at your job. Sure, being able to feed the kids is the first focus. But when layoffs and promotions are announced, those with surly looks on their faces, those who always try to do less, those who never cooperate with others get included in the layoffs and miss the promotions. This big part of your life affects you, your family, society, and everything else you touch.

So, while finishing my last month at Salomon, I decided to be an entrepreneur rather than an employee. After a decade and a half as a loyal corporate soldier, I'd be my own general. Great. Enough of concept, however. Specifics pay the rent. Unfortunately, until I actually stopped working at Salomon, I didn't have much time to plan my next moves—or even to worry. I worked my usual 7:00 a.m. to 7:00 p.m. twelve-hour shifts right up to the last day and seldom discussed my next career with anyone. The only time I searched for office space in which to start my new venture was on weekends. No one could say I didn't give Salomon my all, even at the end.

Still, I did think about it while running. What would I do? Since I didn't have the resources to start a steel mill, I ruled out that possibility; in other words, I wouldn't go into industry. Having no musical abilities precluded starting a songwriting business; entertainment was out. Lack of interest in retailing excluded competing with Walmart; Sam Walton's investment was safe. My impatience with government kept me away from politics (at least at that point in my life); all elected officials could stop worrying. Should I start another securities trading firm and compete with my former colleagues? Been there. Done that. Maybe I could be a full-time consultant like so many forced-out executives. No. I'm not much of a bystander beyond watching my daughter Georgina ride horses. Doing rather than advising others is for me.

What did I have the resources, ability, interest, and contacts to do? The question led me back to Wall Street. It was obvious the economy was changing and services were taking a bigger share of the gross domestic product. My talents, my experience, my financial resources, the momentum provided by the American economy—everything fit. I would start a company that would help financial organizations. There were better traders and salespeople. There were better managers and computer experts. But nobody had more knowledge of the securities and investment industries and of how technology could help them.

All I had to do was find a value-added service not currently available. I conceived a business built around a collection of securities data, giving people the ability to select what each individually thought the most useful parts, and then providing computer software that would let nonmathematicians do analysis on that information. This kind of capability was sorely lacking in the marketplace. A few large underwriting firms had internal systems that tried to fill this need but each required a PhD to use and weren't available off the shelf to the little guy.

When it came to knowing the relative value of one security versus another, most of Wall Street in 1981 had pretty much remained where it was when I began as a clerk back in the mid-1960s: a bunch of guys using No. 2 pencils, chronicling the seat-of-the-pants guesses of too many bored traders. Something that could show instantly whether government bonds were appreciating at a faster rate than corporate bonds would make smart investors out of mediocre ones, and would create a competitive advantage over anyone lacking these capabilities. At a time when the U.S. budget deficit (financed by billions of dollars of new Treasury bonds and notes) was poised to explode, such a device would appeal to everyone working in finance, securities, and investments—combined, a very big potential market for my proposed product.

At great expense, each of the largest securities companies collected data independently. Worse (for them but not for me), they were practically relying on abacuses and slide rules, or the modern equivalents, such as small handheld calculators, to manipulate that information. I could provide a far more sophisticated system at a fraction of the price. Sharing expenses over many users would give me a distinct cost advantage. And if most firms used my data and analysis, I would be creating an industrywide standard, something which, for competitive reasons, the insiders themselves could never accomplish. Equally important, the advantage I had of not being a broker/dealer, of being beholden to no one, would give my product an independence others couldn't possibly claim. And best of all, nobody was currently doing it.

*   *   *

If you're going to succeed, you need a vision, one that's affordable, practical, and fills a customer need. Then, go for it. Don't worry too much about the details. Don't second-guess your creativity. Avoid overanalyzing the new project's potential. Most importantly, don't strategize about the long term too much.

Banks and venture capitalists can be the worst enemies of entrepreneurs. They create doubt in entrepreneurs' minds, with their insistence on detailed game plans before they lend. They want five-year projections in a world that makes six-month forward planning difficult, even for stable and mature businesses, and they insist on "revenue budgeting" when no one knows what the new product will look like or who'll buy how much. And worst of all, they think an originator will be helped by their oh-so-insightful views on how he or she should run the new business. Often, they kill off what's different, special, and full of potential.

In our early years, one venture capitalist who was on the boards of two successful companies came to see us. This guy was one of those self-entitled men who had been born on third base and thought he'd hit a triple. After telling us that everything we were doing was wrong, that we were too unstructured to survive and were stupid because we were unable to predict future growth with clairvoyant specificity, he left to advise his partners not to buy from Bloomberg. The reason? We didn't show much interest in his views on how to run our company. He sure was right on that account.

I once saw the classic cart-before-the-horse planning error during a presentation by a would-be competitor. He showed slides of his new company's shipping department. There were conveyor belts, packaging machines, truck-loading equipment, and a group of white-coated technicians ready to send out thousands of units each week. The only minor problem? They hadn't yet built the first unit. And they never did.

At Bloomberg, we've always built the product first. We think about accounting and shipping much later in the process, when those functions become important, at the point where we'd better stop and refocus or get into trouble. Selling is the only process we run simultaneously with development from the start. That gives us feedback as we build and makes the customers part of the evolution process (they come to believe it's their product). This strategy may not be without risks, but I've always thought it ridiculous to make the wedding arrangements before agreeing to the marriage.

The classic consultant's model for success dictates building in controls at the beginning, but that kind of premature preparation is counterproductive; in fact, it's usually diverting enough to preclude producing anything at all. You don't know exactly what you're going to deliver. You can't predict in what order things will be done. You have no real idea who will purchase it. Why bother gazing into the crystal ball? If you're flexible, you'll do it when it makes sense, not before.

Don't think, however, that planning and analysis have no place in achieving success. Quite the contrary. Use them, just don't have them use you. Plan things out and work through real-life scenarios, selecting from the opportunities currently available. Just don't waste effort worrying about an infinite number of down-the-road possibilities, most of which will never materialize.

Think logically and dispassionately about what you'd like to do. Work out all steps of the process—the entire what, when, where, why, and how. Then, sit down after you are absolutely positive you know it cold, and write it out. There's an old saying, "If you can't write it, you don't know it." Try it. The first paragraph invariably stops you short. "Now why did we want this particular thing?" you'll find yourself asking. "Where did we think the resources would come from?" "And what makes us think others—the suppliers, the customers, the potential rivals—are going to cooperate?" On and on, you'll find yourself asking the most basic questions you hadn't focused on before taking pen to paper.

As you discover you don't know it all, force yourself to address the things you forgot, ignored, underestimated, or glossed over. Write them out for a doubting stranger who doesn't come with unquestioned confidence in the project's utility—and who, unlike your spouse, parent, sibling, or child, doesn't have a vested interest in keeping you happy. Make sure your written description follows, from beginning to end, in a logical, complete, doable path.

Then tear up the paper.

That's right, rip it up. You've done the analysis. You've found enough holes in the plan to drive your hoped-for Bentley automobile through repeatedly. You've planned for myriad what-if scenarios. You've presented your ideas to others. You've even mapped out the first few steps.

But the real world throws curveballs and sliders every day, as well as the fastballs you practice against. You'll inevitably face problems different from the ones you anticipated. Sometimes you'll have to "zig" when the blueprint says "zag." You don't want a detailed, inflexible plan getting in the way when you have to respond instantly. By now, you either know what you can know— or you don't and never will. As to the rest, take it as it comes.

*   *   *

So, I wrote out my analysis and then ripped it up. I rented a one room temporary office on Madison Avenue. It was about a hundred square feet of space with a view of an alley, a far cry from my previous place of employment, Salomon's multi-acre forty-first-floor trading room overlooking the New York harbor. I deposited

$300,000 of my Salomon Brothers windfall into a corporate checking account. And fifteen years later, I had a billion-dollar business.

Of course, it took a little while to arrive at Bloomberg's current headquarters, on Lexington Avenue in New York. And I really didn't start out all by myself. At the end of 1981, I recruited four former Salomon protégés, three of whom are still with us today, nearly four decades later: Duncan MacMillan, who helped assess what our potential customers might want; Chuck Zegar, who created our software infrastructure; Tom Secunda, who wrote many of the first analytics; and one other guy. In our broom closet of an office, we celebrated our start on day one with a bottle of champagne.

Much to my surprise, on day two, the fourth guy came back to see me. "I'm more valuable than the others. I deserve more than they do," he told me.

"That's not true and that's not what we agreed."

"Yes, but I have kids to think about."

"This isn't about your children," I said. "It's you who has the problem."

"Mike, this is too much of a risk for me with too little a return. You're going to have to do better for me to join."

I had several conversations like this with different people after that as Bloomberg grew. They all ended the same way, before they started. Either people believed in me, trusted me, and were willing to take the risk that together we would deliver success, or they didn't. It was that simple. There was no haggling. I don't negotiate.

Years later, I told Sue I felt sorry for this guy because he hadn't swallowed his hubris and joined us back then as we got started. After leaving, he worked for multiple companies, never really making much of an impact or enjoying great success. Had he joined us, he would have done something important, had a great time, and become wealthy beyond his wildest dreams.

"Don't feel sorry for him," she said. "He didn't have the guts for it. The others ran risks. They alone deserve the rewards."

She was right, of course. At the same time, I do find myself more understanding, if not outright sympathetic. It's scary taking a chance. If l hadn't had the money from the Salomon sale bonanza, would I have made the leap? Funny, the older I get, the less simple life looks.

We rented a second temporary one-room office next to the original space and bought a small refrigerator for sodas and a coffee machine for survival. The first order of business once we were together was to go to our respective homes and make sure there were no papers there that arguably belonged to our previous employer. Since we'd all worked at Salomon, I worried someone would allege we were stealing software or ideas. That kind of accusation, however false, could make everything we were trying to do more difficult, from obtaining credit to building a reputation— the latter being especially critical, since our business was to be based on our collective reputation for probity.

Then, to maintain both the style and substance of independence and honesty, as we began getting some basic systems together and building the fundamental financial-information database, we took pains to differentiate ourselves from anything we had previously worked on. We used a different brand of computer. We wrote in a different computer language. We documented when and where we collected information. We even picked a different terminology and syntax for our entire system to use. After all that, it turned out that nobody ever questioned our honesty, but better safe than sorry.

The original four—Bloomberg, MacMillan, Secunda, and Zegar—got along pretty well from the first day (we still do). One time, though, I got annoyed at something they did that could have become a serious problem—so serious that I no longer remember what it was. It was infuriating enough that I stormed into one of our two office rooms and slammed the door shut behind me. I slammed it so hard, the catch broke. I was locked in. Having been an ass, I now had to humble myself and knock on the door until they came to let me out. They played with the handle for a while before it sprang open. I never asked whether the fumbling was deliberate or not.

In 1982 and 1983, we added some programmers: Tom Neff, Mark Purdy, Andy Wu, and Bob Ostrow, who worked on the Hubble telescope but claims no responsibilities for the incorrect curvature of its mirror—and who is still with Bloomberg today. Later, Nick Failla joined to run our nonexistent "Computer Room." Mac Barnes would become our customer liaison person, along with Susette Franklin, who took over administration—even though we had no customers and little to administer. In 1985, before we had a product to sell, our first salespeople came on board—Stuart Bell, Dana Neuman, and Curtis McCool—followed by programmers Lynn Seirup, John Punturieri, and Fred Mitchell, for whom we had no desks and no computers. We hired operators Rodney Brown, Brett McCollough, James Rieger, and, for London (our first foray overseas), Laurence Seeff. These are people who joined before we had much of a business and stayed through the tough times—and I'm glad to say several are still with us. That's the kind of loyalty that has always bound us together and promoted mutual respect—and it survives to this day.

*   *   *

Right after forming our company, we did some consulting. It brought in cash, gave us exposure, and helped provide us with Wall Street legitimacy that would later lead to work for more clients. And it brought our first sale: to Merrill Lynch & Co.

Three powerful members of that firm's Capital Markets Division—Sam Hunter, Jerry Kenney, and Gerry Eli—had convinced us to study Merrill Lynch's relationships with institutional customers. After a lot of traveling and research, our conclusions were the kind of insights we probably could have provided at the beginning based on just our Salomon experiences. Nevertheless, they seemed pleased with the report we wrote. We received $100,000 plus expenses for our six-month effort. That paid some real bills.

While Merrill was convincing us to undertake the study, we were told, "If you start to work for Merrill, you'll never leave." Well, the four of us didn't exactly dash back into standard-issue Wall Street life, but the comment was on target nonetheless. The contacts we made and the trust we built gave us our next big break: an introduction to the fellow running Merrill's Capital Markets Division, Ed Moriarty.

It was to Moriarty that I had to sell our proposed product. I finally arranged a meeting with him and his staff. It took place in an enormous corporate boardroom. At a forty-foot mahogany table, Ed was surrounded by accountants, lawyers, computer programmers, salespeople, traders, administrators—everybody in their company was represented. I went by myself, the way I always went into big negotiations, and was seated to Ed's left. Hank Alexander, who was running all their software development, was sitting on his other side. I spoke as confidently as I could, making it sound as if our company, Innovative Market Systems, as we were then known, had exactly what Merrill needed (I implied with perhaps some minimal embellishment that everything but the packaging was completed). I made my pitch.

"We can give you a yield curve analysis updated throughout the day as the market moves. . . . We can show you the futures market versus cash and graph it for you as it's changing. . . . For your traders, we'll keep track of every transaction as it's made and mark their positions to market instantly without any fussing." No one else had done any of these things—and neither had we—yet.

Moriarty turned to Hank Alexander. "Well, Hank, what do you think?"

"I think we should do it internally," Hank replied. "Build it ourselves."

"How long would it take?" Ed asked.

Then Hank made his fatal mistake. "Well, if you don't give us anything new to do"—which was clearly not a practical scenario—"we'll be able to start in six months."

And that was my opening.

"I'll get it done in six months and if you don't like it, you don't have to pay for it!" I practically shouted. "Since Hank can't even start for half a year, there'll be no time risk. And since you only pay if it works, no cost risk either."

Moriarty got up. "Well, that sounds fair enough," he said, and he left the room.

I don't think anybody had seen a decision made at Merrill that fast. Even I was surprised. But from Ed's point of view it was a "no-brainer." He didn't have any downside; it was win or break even for him. Hank just sat there, speechless, as did everyone else.

When I came back from the meeting with Moriarty, my colleagues were elated—until the reality of a six-month delivery for something that didn't exist began to sink in. As developers, we're magicians, not miracle workers. Fortunately, it took Merrill Lynch and Bloomberg two or three months to write a contract. That's when the six months we promised actually commenced—a little extra time to deliver something we hadn't yet started.

Month after month as we worked, our mood alternated between elation and a feeling of impending disaster. We weren't just putting out fires. We were adjusting to major earthquakes when some new software bug forced us to start over. But every day we got closer to building the machine we promised.

Our style then was pretty much the same as today. We took the problem and broke it down into little, manageable, digestible pieces. Then each of us took responsibility for the one we were best suited to do. We needed a proprietary Terminal to give us a technology and marketing edge; we hired an engineer, Ron Harris, to build it for us. We needed a central information storage computer; Chuck

Zegar analyzed which was the best and wrote a customized database package suitable for our specific application. We needed some data; Duncan MacMillan collected it, scrubbed it, and typed it in. We needed calculations; Tom Secunda sat at a workstation and did the programming. We needed customers; I went out and sold. We needed outside support; we retained a lawyer, Dick DeScherer, and an accountant/CFO, Marty Geller—both are still with us today. It wasn't elegant. It was laughably simplistic by today's standards. But we did it, and it worked.

*   *   *

Back then, most Wall Streeters didn't understand the language of general-purpose computers. It wasn't intuitive. A key labeled "Tab" on a regular PC didn't mean anything to average folks. Other buttons labeled "Ctrl" (Control) or "Alt" (Alternate) weren't salespeople's or traders' terms. To be better, from the beginning, we built things for real people. We changed "Enter" to "GO" on our keyboard. (Remember Monopoly? "Pass Go and Collect $200.") "Tab," "Alt," and "Ctrl" disappeared, though we brought them back when computer literacy improved. Function keys were labeled in English—no technical gibberish—for parts of the market that the Terminal has data on, such as "Equity" for stocks, "Comdty" for commodities, and "Muni" for information on municipal bonds. Making something practical ("user-friendly" in computerese) became our hallmark.

Merrill wanted its traders to be able to enter a transaction and automatically update the firm's positions themselves. That wasn't a big deal, you would think. But the only systems Merrill had for trade entry used massive, unreliable, and complex terminals that wouldn't fit on regular-size desks, much less in the typical, salesperson/trader's small cubicle. They connected these terminals to a single, large mainframe without backup. This wasn't what the market needed.

We built our own compact, low-priced workstations so we could give the reliability that a single-purpose, single-user machine provides. (PCs and mainframes have to do everything with everybody. By comparison, we, with our own "closed," custom-built hardware and software, could focus on a single task with perfect machine compatibility.) We designed our own color-coded, easy-to-use, small keyboard for the limited space our customers had in front of them. We built a customized square enclosure for the display screens we'd chosen, so users could stack them up vertically. We engineered our electronics to support keyboards and screens over great distances; that way, the actual computer didn't have to be at the user's cramped, dirty desk (the way PCs have to be), but could be kept separate, "down the hall," in a life-prolonging, temperature-controlled, and dust-free machine room. Desk space doesn't sound important unless you don't have any.

We made mistakes, of course. Most of them were omissions we didn't think of when we initially wrote the software. We fixed them by doing it over and over, again and again. We do the same today. While our competitors are still sucking their thumbs trying to make the design perfect, we've already gone through five rounds of testing. By the time our rivals are ready to begin development, we are on version No. 10. It gets back to planning versus acting. We act from day one; others plan how to plan—for months.

Then, as now, we had the resolve to see it through. We put together prototype after prototype and drummed up business again and again. We underwent a few very long years. In presentation after presentation, I guaranteed our product was going to happen. It was only a matter of time, I told the clients—and myself. Our efforts and my cash would carry the day.

Halfway through, I must admit I worried. I had committed nowhere near enough money to fund development. And it wasn't obvious that the customers would appreciate what we were attempting. In my own private world, maybe, just maybe, I questioned the wisdom of jeopardizing my wealth and our reputation. In fact, we were spending what would grow to be a $4 million investment of my $10 million Salomon Brothers windfall. Simultaneously, I was becoming responsible for the families of almost two dozen company employees. I had convinced these people to follow me, and if the venture had not succeeded, I would have failed them, their spouses, and their children, as well as our prospective customers. Fortunately, however, even had I wanted to leave this enterprise behind, there was no graceful way to exit (thank God for ego!), so we plowed ahead.

From the beginning, I was convinced we were doing something nobody else could do. Nor was anyone else trying. Our product would be the first in the investment business where normal people without specialized training could sit down, hit a key, and get an answer to financial questions, some of which they didn't even know they should ask. Over time, the Terminal evolved to allow users to run an ever-wider array of functions, developed by our more than 5,000 computer programmers and engineers. But it all began with a simple premise: putting more information at people's fingertips, more quickly and more accurately than they could otherwise get it. That's still the heart of our business.

So who uses a Bloomberg Terminal? Investment firms, regulators, security issuers, corporations, commercial and central banks, pension funds, universities, and other organizations and individuals.

It gives them the ability to select investments, do an endless number of "what-if" scenario analyses on their securities portfolios, and communicate over a private, secure e-mail and chat system (called IB, Instant Bloomberg) with their customers, suppliers, and associates. Money managers can buy and sell stocks and bonds and every other type of financial instrument. Foreign exchange traders use the Terminal to control exposure to risk and seize market opportunities based on fluctuations in the value of currencies. The Terminal lets them research information unavailable elsewhere. It gives them the ability to retrieve, store, calculate, graph, table, and share data, all customized around their needs.

The same is true for those in commodities—from cattle and coffee to soybeans and sugar—who use Bloomberg to stay on top of constantly fluctuating markets. Research analysts rely on Bloomberg for up-to-the-second, accurate data, news, and intelligence. And before the cloud ever existed, we had created one of our own. From the beginning, the Terminal has allowed customers to create and store as much of their own content from its myriad functions and data so that they can return to it, add to it, and amend it as they see fit. We write code, creating a never-ending stream of functions, but we also give customers the power to tailor those functions around their own individual and highly personalized needs and to keep those permutations in safe storage for future use.

Nearly every type of finance professional has a Bloomberg Terminal—or wants one. It's the hub of the financial community, an interactive network that processes about 80 *billion* market transactions a day, along with 15 to 20 million instant messages a day. It all occurs instantaneously and accurately. And it's available to subscribers 24/7, via the computer on their desk or the app on their phone. Wherever you need us, we're there. Bloomberg Anywhere, we call it.

Some people say we're like Google for the financial markets. The analogy works, up to a point. Like Google, Bloomberg collects, categorizes, and stores vast amounts of information that can be retrieved instantaneously—and it's something that people rely on every day. We employ thousands of people and sophisticated technology to make sure that the information and data we provide is 100 percent accurate. When our customers search on Bloomberg, they know they're not getting any fake news or phony data. They would never stand for it.

*　　*　　*

After the meeting with Moriarty, I was adamant we were going to deliver a product when we promised. It became a joke at Merrill: Bloomberg would deliver the first on-time software project in history. Yeah, right! What chance did we have when, in addition to writing software and collecting data, we had to build our own hardware? (There was nothing commercially available that could do real-time, computational analysis and still let us be profitable. In the early 1980s, we built a multiuser PC, something that took manufacturers more than a decade to replicate.) What chance did we have when no one had ever designed a real-time interactive system that was user-friendly enough for nonspecialists? Fourteen-hour days became typical at Starship Bloomberg. At one point, when nobody in our little electronics sweatshop could remember time off, the entire firm marched into a theater to see a movie and unwind together.

Finally, the day arrived. Almost. The six-month promise ran out on a Saturday, so we could postpone delivery until Monday. And Monday didn't necessarily mean Monday morning; it could be Monday afternoon. We were constantly having to fix the software, rewriting it again and again to deliver the consistency needed for reliable real-time analysis. "We're out of control!" I would shout, as each software bug surfaced. "We're going to be out of business if this continues!" (I still say the same things today.)

Late on that fateful Monday in June of 1983, Duncan and I got into a taxi on Madison Avenue. I carried the Terminal and Duncan carried the keyboard and screen. But it was hopeless. For reasons we couldn't understand, some newly introduced software problem kept the machine from starting up. Still, we took it down to Merrill while the others kept debugging the computer code. We installed the hardware in the office of the head bond trader, a smart, demanding guy named Danny Napoli. Everybody was standing around, astonished that the machine had actually appeared; nobody really expected delivery when promised. Were we going to be the first team in history ever to do so?

We plugged it in and turned on the power. As I talked, playing tour guide, I noticed out of the corner of my eye a flashing message on our screen saying "Loading Software." Instantly, I knew that the big software bug that had befuddled us all weekend had been fixed—*while we were in the taxi*. I could feel the tension ease out of me. It was going to work!

By that time, a bottle of champagne had been opened by a dozen traders. These guys were the friendliest people I had seen in six months. Everybody was laughing and slapping each other's back. I think we ran one function and the computer crashed. It didn't matter. It was the principle that we had delivered something on time (close to), something that worked (sort of), a machine that would be useful (somewhat). Then our entire staff went to a restaurant on the Upper East Side to continue the celebration.

When I saw that screen light up that day in the Merrill Lynch offices, I lost any residual doubt that Bloomberg could make it. We had picked just the right project. It was big enough to be useful, small enough to be possible. Start with a small piece; fulfill one goal at a time, on time. Do it with all things in life. Sit down and learn to read one-syllable words. If you try to read Chaucer in elementary school, you'll never accomplish anything. You can't jump to the end game right away, in computers, politics, love, or any other aspect of life.

*   *   *

The data we use in the analytical calculations we supply to our customers have always been dramatically better than anything the competition has. Long before we began developing sophisticated algorithms to collect data, one of the great contributions made to our success was by John Aubert, the man who started our data-collection facility in Princeton, New Jersey. When Mac Barnes introduced me to John in the Merrill Lynch cafeteria in April 1984, he was head of a three-person company consisting of himself, his wife, and his son. They collected sinking fund data (information about how companies and governments pay off the debt incurred from the sale of bonds) and put them into a book called *Sinkers*. As luck would have it, the day we met, John had just had a disagreement with his only customer and wanted to deal with someone new. We had a cup of coffee together, and by the time the meeting ended, a handshake. His company got absorbed into ours. He collected data better than anyone else and loved the process. His eyes lit up when he talked about information gathering. That's the kind of person we want in our company—people who love what they do.

John devised a way to give the data-collection process an analytical component. The clerical part became minor. Thus, we got much smarter people to "scrub," categorize, and store each piece of data where it truly belongs—not just where it's convenient to put it. They're not automatons on an information assembly line. They're traditional analysts who can provide a detailed contextual understanding of a market or industry based on current and historical information assembled from a multitude of sources.

Take our collection of income statements and balance sheets from companies around the globe. Many countries define depreciation differently. In the 1990s, we hired a consultant to teach us all the accounting systems in use around the world. That allowed our specialists to understand each standard. Thus, unlike other databases, ours knows the important distinctions. Companies can be viewed from different locations on a comparable basis. If one company depreciates assets one way, and another company a second way, we'll highlight the discrepancies up front. At Bloomberg, a problem spurs a solution. That's what makes us successful.

*   *   *

For our first product delivery, we built twenty-two Terminals, keyboards, and screens. Our plan was to install the twenty Merrill Lynch had ordered and then use the two others ourselves, for development and backup. Needless to say, we installed all twenty-two in their trading room. They wanted them. And who were we to argue? We needed the revenue. Of course, we had no reserves, but now we had the cash flow to build more machines for ourselves, for Merrill, and for other customers who would soon hear the good buzz on Bloomberg.

In the beginning, we had the inevitable reliability problems. But at least we had something. And that something was Merrill's system as much as ours. When we first installed it, Merrill assigned two traders to work with us. I thought they'd be real pains and second-guess us every step of the way. Was I wrong! It turned out both of them, Jack Delaney and Jack Meyers, were as responsible for our success as anyone. They were nitpickers, but not in a nasty way; they wanted us to succeed. When they said something didn't work, they could show us it didn't work, so we knew for sure it didn't work, and more important, to help fix the problem, under what specific circumstances it didn't work. Every day, our system got better as we fixed each problem they pointed out. I'd always rather have a smart, fair, honest, demanding client than a nasty dummy or an "I don't care" user.

The agreement with Merrill was that *if* we delivered on time and *if* they liked it, they would pay us $600,000, a onetime custom development fee, plus $1,000 a month per Terminal for two years. We would receive no money until the entire system worked reliably. So, although Merrill didn't fund our initial development, they were invaluable to our start-up. We just knew that if we could give them something useful, there was no way they'd walk away. And having one happy customer would lead to the next. For example, the Bank of England, one of the world's oldest central banks, became a customer within two years. (Bloomberg's London building, opened in 2017, is now just across the street.) The Vatican became a customer by the mid-1980s. (When their electricians seemed to take forever to install the wire needed for our Terminal, a nun in their funds' management office told us she'd have the Pope bless our cabling to make the installation process go more quickly. I don't know if he did, but the next day the installation was completed.) By the 1990s, the World Bank, the Bank for International Settlements, and every Federal Reserve Bank all became Bloomberg clients.

There was still a risk for Bloomberg after Merrill's first order. It was a long time before revenue exceeded expenses. But after building the machines for Merrill, we had money coming in and a product to sell. I remember calculating repeatedly on the back of an envelope, "Twenty-two Terminals at Merrill at $1,000 per month times twelve months per year equals $264,000, plus $600,000. We won't make a lot of money, but we'll cover our costs and stay in business." Today, that amount doesn't even cover our reception area's flower bill. But by starting small and working hard, we got where we needed to go, and Bloomberg was on its way.

Over time, along with the growth in our revenue, we hired more employees and became more specialized. Within about a decade, we had human resource professionals and accounts receivable and accounts payable people. We had a contracts department, a communications department, and an administration department. We employed controllers, lawyers, bookkeepers, consultants, accountants, tax advisers, and so on, just like any other big company.

Amazingly, for our first three or four years in business, I did all those functions. I also simultaneously worked full-time selling our services, negotiating all our supplier and customer contracts, and running the company. Never before or since did I have as much fun and as challenging a time in business.

Today, Bloomberg has the very best service and installation professionals. But back when we started, the original half dozen of us, after finishing our regular jobs, would go into clients' offices on weekends and do these functions as well. During the summer, with the air-conditioning turned off in those sealed skyscrapers, the heat sometimes hit 100 degrees Fahrenheit under the new customers' desks where we crawled to lay our cables. Amid old McDonald's hamburger wrappers and mouse droppings, we dragged wires from our computers to the keyboards and screens we were putting in place, stuffing the cables through holes we drilled in other people's furniture—all without permission, without giving any thought to any fire law or building code. It's amazing we didn't burn down some office or electrocute ourselves. At the end of the day, ten or eleven o'clock at night, we'd turn it on and watch what we'd created come alive. It was so satisfying.

We improvised everything as we went along.

Need to deliver the product? We transported the equipment in the back seat of a yellow taxicab. Import/export regulations? We just carried it into the next country in our luggage. Did we obtain passes to get computers and keyboards and screens into and out of buildings, past the security guards? "Hey, man. Going to get coffee. Want a cup?" They wave you through every time. Inventory tracking? "Did we install two or three at that last place? Beats me."

I used to write all the checks myself. I signed every contract. I paid every bill. I did the hiring and firing. I bought the coffee, sodas, cookies, and chips we nibbled on. I emptied the wastebaskets and dusted the window sills. I wrote and handed out the paychecks personally to each and every one of our employees working in New York City, thus giving me the chance to follow up on project and people development, to offer encouragement, or to "bust a few chops" if need be. By the 1990s, there was a specialist for each of these functions.

Those were the best days, the first few years in the early 1980s. We all were involved in every aspect of our company. I helped design furniture, select equipment, demonstrate our capabilities to prospective customers, order phone lines, collect data. I used a screwdriver as much as a pencil. As we grew and turned these functions over to newly hired specialists, I felt like I was losing a child to adolescence. Good for the kid, but painful for the parent.

Moving from "hands-on" to "hands-off" management was a gradual, and not all that pleasant, process for me. I like doing things myself, getting my hands dirty. If we were to grow and not be dependent on yours truly, turn it over I must. That doesn't mean I was happy about it, but the more we grew, the more I came to appreciate the importance of delegation. Anyone who tries to micromanage a large organization will fail in the end.

One of the growing pains small companies experience is when outside contractors are brought in who aren't invested in the company's success. Often, when we "farmed out" a project to others, I'd be reminded of the difference in Bloomberg's pioneering culture compared to others' standards, and I'd wish we'd done it ourselves. A consultant comes in to do something and stops at 5:00 p.m. Everyone "inside" works until 7:00, 8:00, or 9:00 at night, until the project is done. Once, we hired an electrician to "pin" (put plugs on the end of) a bunch of 25-wire, color-coded cables. It was one of those things that had to be done perfectly (i.e., red into No. 7, blue into No. 19, green and red stripe into No. 24, and so on, as specified on some highly detailed schematic drawings) or the computers would crash. The electricians' union shop steward assigned us an experienced guy who was hanging on until retirement, arguing that his age gave him the patience to do this tedious task without error. A month later, after tearing our hair out trying to find the reason nothing worked, we discovered he may have had lots of good qualities and work habits, but he was legally color-blind. Every single connector was wrong. The waste in computer programmers' time diagnosing the trouble was enormous. (The next electrician just cut off all the ends and did the job again from scratch. Needless to say, we had to pay for both electricians.) Outsiders at best do only what's asked. Insiders do what's needed.

Even today, when I watch a visitor throw a paper towel toward a wastebasket in the bathroom, miss, and just walk away, I want to scream. I react the same way when I see someone walking by a piece of scrap paper on the floor and ignoring it. Perhaps I'm compulsive, but I stop and pick it up, even at someone else's place. Your company is one of your families, and the office is that family's home.

*   *   *

America really is the land of opportunity and home to more start-up enterprises than any other country. In this country, banks, venture capitalists, and stock exchanges are all accustomed to funding new ideas. The United States has a culture that prizes innovation, its social hierarchy is primarily built around merit, and it rewards the risk taker. Low barriers that encourage trade, publicly funded research that spurs innovation, and favorable tax laws that encourage entrepreneurship have been critical to our nation's growth. Yet lately, Washington has been walking away from them and making us less competitive in the global marketplace.

Not all ventures succeed here, of course. Myriad other companies started at the same time we did, many with capital, enthusiasm, and potential. Some had transitory success. Like a balloon, they expanded rapidly and eventually exploded. We think those that lasted were the companies with philosophies and management practices that were appropriate for the time, well articulated to employees and clients, and consistently applied. Through both good and bad periods, staying power, we believe, requires team leadership in a constant direction, one that the organization understands and accepts. The winners have this kind of leadership. We hope we do!

Bloomberg philosophy may sound strange to "outsiders," but not to those who matter—us. We've always assumed that even if we're paranoid, they probably *are* out to get us. While you're reading this, we're thinking about how our competitors are plotting to take the food from our children's mouths. They must be attempting to beat our quality, provide better functionality, undercut our reputation, and mislead us as to their direction. And if they aren't, they should be.

To counter this attack (whether real or imagined) in every way, we've got to improve just to stay even. Each of us at Bloomberg has to enhance his or her skills. Every element of all our products must be improved. All our expenses need reexamination and our customer service should be enhanced. The basic assumptions behind our business must constantly be reassessed, off-line and out of sight. When we say we'll do A, we've got to do A, but internally we've also got to prepare for B and C in case the world changes or we've erred in our judgment. We really believe we won't die, but that doesn't mean we don't buy life insurance just in case.

The difference between stubbornness and having the courage of conviction sometimes is only in the results. Since the first twenty-two Terminals were installed at Merrill Lynch, we've developed into a global, multiproduct company with more than 300,000 subscribers. Sure, we're inflexible, if that means we don't react every time a news article claims a competitor's "to-be-introduced" product will be our downfall. But we change. We do things today we said "never" to years ago, and we no longer do other things that were our sine qua non then. Our customers, resources, and opportunities constantly shift. Our policies do too—when and at the speed we want them to, not just because we're being goaded by some outsider who doesn't have to deal with human beings, pay bills, or suffer the consequences of a hastily made wrong decision.

To run our organization, we've got to be consistent. But that doesn't mean we have to have the same consistency forever. What's appropriate in one part of our development isn't necessarily so in another. Henry Ford's infamous, arrogant statement that "You can have any color car you want as long as it's black" wasn't wrong. It worked for his company when he was the only large maker of autos. But he ultimately switched to a multicolor strategy when others came along with comparable vehicles and changed the competitive landscape. My job is to recognize that time in our business in advance and lead the organization into the new world.

For instance, one of our biggest growth areas has been what we call the "Enterprise" business. Virtually every financial firm is operating in a vastly more complex regulatory environment with many more requirements around transparency and risk management than existed before the financial crisis of 2008. That makes transaction processing and data management more crucial than ever, and it gives us an opportunity to offer our clients still more valuable services to support their information technology and operations. The kind of work that was long called "back office operations" has grown exponentially, into a world that is now referred to as "post trade services." For instance: The new regulations that forced more standardization of derivatives and clearing also created demand for new technology to support it. With the industry experiencing more and more electronification and automation, running large firms is a lot more complicated than it used to be. We help managers do it, by providing the state-of-the-art infrastructure they need to be efficient and keep pace with their competitors who are using our services.

Another tenet of Bloomberg philosophy is that our main asset is not our technology, our databases, our proprietary communications network, or even our clients. It is our employees. Improving the rest is far less important than the care and feeding of ourselves and the maintenance of our culture. Physical plant, compensation politics, personnel policies, promotion, training, and so on—all of these at Bloomberg are designed with our culture in mind. The prospect of losing our culture—open, nimble, innovative, driving, caring, cooperative, unafraid of risk—is a bigger threat to our company than any outside competitor.

Nevertheless, we also periodically face the fact that our competitors started out lean and mean too. They may be overstaffed today, but they didn't get that way deliberately. People at those companies never sat around trying to hire mindlessly. Every time they added someone, it was done with good reason. Likewise with us. But our world evolves, and people change. If we always add and never cut, why will we be different? We must have made some mistakes.

Infrequently we do have to face the issue of someone who just can't do the job. Very seldom do we have the stomach for the process. But that's what management's all about. What are we doing with the bottom 10 percent? Do we as managers have a plan to improve those employees' productivity? Are there better places for them in our company? Have we sat with them and attempted to address their problems, improve their attitudes, provide counseling, discover personal problems we can help with, retrain them? And if nothing works, after all that, while we're doing well and can afford to be generous, no matter how distasteful facing the inevitable may be, have we exercised our responsibility to upgrade our staff? Management's obligation is to all of us in the organization. We sink or swim together, and when someone's not carrying his or her weight, everyone in the company suffers. It's painful, but nature is filled with examples of extinct species that didn't improve the breed. We don't want to be one of them.

Most companies never upgrade until they are forced. When you read of a management's "decisiveness" in making large sudden layoffs, ask yourself what they've been doing all along. No change in labor requirements happens suddenly. If they'd been minding the store, they'd have stopped additional hiring years earlier, retrained their excess workers for other positions, and improved everyone's productivity so as to avoid the downturn and layoffs.

*   *   *

Doing things differently has been basic Bloomberg from day one. If the world's going left, we often go right. In football, going around the line when you are a light running back usually makes more sense than going up the middle through the heart of the other team's defense. For us too. If our competitors' strength is their balance sheets, we try noncapital-intensive strategies. If they concentrate on one part of the world, we focus on another. Letting them define the rules is a sure way to come in second. And in life, unlike in children's games, second place is first loser!

We will survive if we can control our own destiny. We've come a long way since Merrill's first order, but the challenge is still fundamentally the same. What's in our interest? Who's going to take us there? And most importantly, are we taking care of the current clients who got us this far?

Bloomberg has always treated its existing customers at least as well as its new ones. Not everyone else does the same. The next time a magazine subscription comes up for renewal, watch what happens. The first request asks you to pay full price. Don't sign. The second's at a lower price. Don't sign. The third's better still. Let it expire and they'll practically pay you to subscribe again. Why some companies give a better deal to their worst customers, I've never understood. What's the incentive to be a good client? Treat your customers well and they'll stay with you forever.

Our pricing policy for all our products tries to reward the best clients over those not so good: the five-person firm with five Terminals over the thousand-person firm with one hundred Terminals. Size isn't everything. Intent matters, too. Sure, we want the giant orders, but we don't forget that the Big Guys are with us because we're the small ones' champion.

The same with pricing. Want a special deal? If we give it to you, how could you be sure we're not giving your competitor an even better one? To publish one price and then negotiate secretly with those you want to favor or those who complain the loudest—that just encourages confusion, dissent, uncertainty, and unpleasantness, not to mention what it says about the seller's ethics. Favor one client over the other and, when the roles reverse, the favored client forgets and the initially disadvantaged one remembers.

At Bloomberg, we have a published price for the Terminal and generally stick to it. If we do make an occasional exception, it's usually for the small shop on the verge of bankruptcy. My sympathies have always been with the struggling up-and-coming firm anyway. We were once like that, and to this day I remember who helped us and who didn't. Besides, if a company chooses another's product over ours because of small price differentials, we don't have a long-term customer.

*   *   *

From unemployed to having my own growing business was a lot of work. I loved every day of my fifteen years at Salomon Brothers. I was just as ecstatic "doing my own thing" building Bloomberg LP. In both venues, I worked six-day weeks and twelve-hour days. In both, I cared about the company and other people there. In both, I've strived and thrived. And in both, I knew when it was time to leave. At Bloomberg, I don't want any manager here to do the same thing for too long, and I shouldn't either. That's why I left to run for mayor.

Before I entered City Hall, people always asked which I liked better: working for others or working for myself. Many assumed the answer was the latter. But I was not sure. Certainly, I made much more money being an entrepreneur, but I remember every day at Salomon as being just as challenging and just as much fun. Let's leave it that I'm a lucky guy. I had two careers—and together, they prepared me to pursue a third, in public service. More on that later.

4

We Can Do That

Elementary Journalism, Not Rocket Science

I first met Matt Winkler when he called me one afternoon at our New York office while I was making popcorn. I love popcorn and often made some in our food court, to share with our customers and staff (an easy way to take everyone's temperature while we nibble together). A reporter for the *Wall Street Journal* who enjoyed the intricacies of the bond market, Matt was the first person in the news media to analyze the Bloomberg enterprise. Winkler was trying to figure out why we were actually starting to challenge Dow Jones & Co.'s dominance of financial news. He was to become a pivotal character in making Bloomberg a major contender in journalism and would help us not only to expand the utility of our online computer Terminal, but to wrestle a way into news dissemination by other means as well.

Matt and I share a glass-is-half-full outlook, and that initially brought us together. When he called in February 1988, he said he was working on a story about me for the *Journal*.

"Come on up," I said. I liked the idea of getting interviewed for a story in the flagship enterprise of a future competitor.

Unbeknownst to me, Winkler had already come to see Bloomberg as a major threat. I would find out later, to my great pleasure, just how many of his Wall Street contacts, who were also my close friends and customers, agreed with that view. He was a well-connected reporter. In his ten-year career, he had written about financial markets for all the big Dow Jones media platforms—*Barron's*, the *Wall Street Journal*, and Dow Jones News Services.

It was as a *Wall Street Journal* reporter in London in the mid-1980s that he first learned of the Bloomberg Terminal—then a beige box with a small amber computer screen that flashed "what if" scenarios for the bond market. He was interviewing Merrill Lynch trader Mark Cutis, who had a rare ability to explain which bonds from the United States, Japan, or Germany were cheap or expensive on any given day.

"Mark," he asked, "Where do you get all this stuff? Nobody has all this information in his head."

"Oh, that's easy," he replied. "We get it from Bloomberg."

Our computer-based information Terminal that let users determine the relative value of debt instruments based on their yield and price histories was by that time installed on fifteen hundred Merrill Lynch desks around the world. In the 1980s, bonds were coming to new prominence in the financial market, totaling trillions of dollars. Deregulation of the housing finance and the thrift industries, the repeal of withholding taxes worldwide, soaring budget deficits, and the high interest rates required to bring down inflation—all these events helped transform the government and corporate bond markets into Wall Street's hottest growth industry. Suddenly, the world's biggest fiduciaries were buying and selling junk bonds and Eurobonds. They invested in bonds created out of mortgages and car loans. Becoming the rage were "structured" securities that enabled borrowers to exchange the cash flows from bonds sold in different markets and different currencies. Although not as visible to the general public, to businesses debt had become bigger than equities. And for a firm like Merrill Lynch, doing everything it could to expand its offerings beyond service to individual investors, the Bloomberg system was indispensable.

In May 1987, after returning to New York to cover Wall Street and revise the bond tables for a new money and investing section, Winkler learned to his horror that I had just convinced the *Wall Street Journal* and the Associated Press that Bloomberg should be their sole supplier for daily U.S. government bond prices, instead of the august Federal Reserve Bank of New York. For decades, the Fed had been the authoritative, impartial source for U.S. Treasuries. The daily prices of United States Treasury bonds and bills help determine every company's borrowing cost, everyone's personal finance interest rates—and the perception of the United States as a strong or weak country. Every stock and bond trader around the world pays attention to U.S. Treasuries. Bloomberg, then a five-year-old company with less than 150 employees, would become the definitive source for the key market that told all the other markets what to do. That, needless to say, made me very happy.

We'd been able to beat the Fed at its own game by becoming a benchmark for yield information. The New York Fed had procrastinated for years on its promise to automate the delivery of its daily U.S. government securities price list. Each afternoon, a runner would show up at the New York Fed's downtown offices and be handed two or three legal-size sheets of paper with prices and yields on the front and back. The runner would rush uptown through end-of-the-day traffic to the Associated Press office in Rockefeller Center. Upon arrival, he'd hand the price sheets to some tired wire operator poised to type the prices under intense deadline pressure so newspapers could get them in time for the next day's first edition.

It was essentially the same pony express method in use for more than one hundred years. The fury of meeting the deadline with so many numbers with decimals invariably created typographical errors in the next day's newspapers. Readers complained. But Bloomberg could deliver, with perfect accuracy, more timely prices (reflecting the trading that continued after the runner left the Fed) in five seconds, at 5 p.m., electronically. We could even provide prices of zero-coupon Treasury bonds, a burgeoning new market—numbers that the Fed itself couldn't supply.

Matt, who at the time hadn't met me and whose "blood ran Dow Jones red" (something he would remind me of again, and again, and . . .), believed no one in his company understood that suddenly the *Wall Street Journal* was running a full-page, daily, free advertisement for Bloomberg, a direct competitor of the Telerate electronic bond information terminal, the only product of a company Dow Jones was in the process of acquiring for more than one and a half *billion* dollars. In a single stroke, this arrangement had made Bloomberg-delivered financial information the daily source for the most important market in the world. Freshly returned to New York, he wasn't in a strong position to convince anyone at the *Journal* that, from their point of view, this was a bad idea.

Further, to him at least, a Bloomberg-provided broadsheet-size page of the most important bond data from Merrill Lynch, a securities firm that sold bonds and actually set the prices we were reporting, was problematic. "How can we do this?" he asked his colleagues.

Because it was efficient and expedient and because no reader ever complained, he was told. But as long as Merrill was in the business of selling securities, commodities, and other forms of money to people, Matt thought, this arrangement where Merrill was pricing those same securities presented a potential conflict of interest.

*   *   *

The alliance of Bloomberg and Merrill Lynch was mutually beneficial. Merrill, which lacked a long history of institutional relationships, needed credibility with the biggest investment institutions, such as central banks and pension funds. It got a customer-service edge by putting its information on the Bloomberg system. Bloomberg needed real-time prices to provide timely analysis. Merrill, because it managed hundreds of billions of dollars and sold securities to several hundred thousand investors daily, had better, more accurate prices than anyone. A truly symbiotic relationship.

Merrill also assisted Bloomberg and its own cause by helping Bloomberg rent as many Terminals as possible to Merrill customers. That way, the Terminal users would have firsthand knowledge of what Merrill (as opposed to other securities firms) and Bloomberg (as opposed to other information systems) could do for them.

By 1987, Merrill was poised to become the world's top under-writer of stocks and bonds, something Wall Street couldn't have imagined ten years earlier. We helped Merrill get there. And, by giving Bloomberg data, Merrill made it possible for us to enter the news business years before we wrote a single word.

Overnight, and over Matt Winkler's vociferous objections, and thanks to the generosity of two giant companies—the largest daily newspaper in the United States, the *Wall Street Journal*, and the Associated Press, whose stories hundreds of other newspapers used—both Bloomberg and Merrill had achieved an importance to die for.

Within a few years, we built Bloomberg to the point that we were receiving price feeds not just from Merrill Lynch but from hundreds of other sources in the securities industry. Then any conflict issue would disappear. (And Dow Jones would eventually look elsewhere for bond prices as its competitive instincts strengthened.) Now, however, Matt was worried that the *Journal*'s integrity might be questioned. Unbeknownst to me, he argued in vain with *Journal* bigwigs to have the decision to use Bloomberg nullified. It also annoyed him that Dow Jones's product, Telerate, could have provided similar bond prices and yields and was being snubbed by the authoritative flagship publication of the same parent company.

His perspective would alter later. While eating a sandwich one day in his firm's cafeteria, Matt almost choked on his chicken salad when a colleague, Michael Miller, a technology writer, asked, "Have you ever heard of this outfit Bloomberg?"

"Have I heard of Bloomberg?" he yelped. He went on to give Miller an earful about the U.S. Treasury prices being published in the newspaper they wrote for—the legal-size sheets of prices, the runners, Merrill Lynch, Telerate, the importance of the bond market, the geriatric wire operator at the Associated Press office, the pony express . . . Miller stopped him. "Sounds like this guy Bloomberg is doing to financial information what American Airlines and United Airlines electronic reservations systems have done to the travel business: become influential by getting everybody hooked onto their data."

When I heard about this conversation later on, I had to chuckle. At last, somebody in the media—besides me—was thinking like a late-twentieth-century information entrepreneur. Fortunately, by the time Winkler, Miller, and my potential competitors were figuring out what we were doing, we'd already done it.

*   *   *

Although Miller didn't know much about bonds, luckily for Bloomberg, Winkler realized that he had identified a story no one had yet reported—a story that was bound to get bigger with every blink on the digital scoreboard that recorded the astronomical rise of the U.S. national debt. So the two of them agreed to write an article about a man and his machine that no one outside the securities industry had ever heard of.

When at last Matt and Michael arrived at my midtown office, I offered them the same speech that I used to convince people to take jobs with us.

"We've got the best people in the world working here. All of them think they walk on water. All of them are workaholics. Once they come, they stay for the rest of their lives because they love it. They've built the better mousetrap. They're doing something important. Giving the little guy the information he needs to fight. Having fun. Staying ahead."

Of course, like all cynical reporters, these guys weren't easily swayed by my silver tongue. So I stalked out of the room and returned carrying a two-inch-thick computer printout.

"Here," I said, dumping the paper into Matt's lap. "Here's every customer we have, by name, by firm, by phone number. Call them yourself!"

Among the first people Matt phoned was investment specialist Robert Smith, who in 1988 was managing $5.5 billion for the state of Florida's retirement system. "I'm working on a story about information technology on Wall Street and why money managers are using the Bloomberg system," Matt said to him. "I understand you have a Bloomberg Terminal. What's so special about it?"

Smith told him what everyone he asked would tell him, that the Bloomberg Terminal did a great job of doing what no other system did—letting him see which bonds were cheap and which bonds were expensive, without having to rely on the calculations and spiel of a bond salesperson with a vested interest in which securities he purchased. Believe it or not, until we came along, buyers were stuck paying the price set by sellers—and the smaller the buy-side firm, the more they were at the mercy of sellers. Sure, buyers could shop around. But that takes time. And they had no negotiating leverage because they had no independent benchmark for knowing real-time pricing. That's what Bloomberg provided.

This independence gave Smith greater confidence as he traded financial instruments in the Florida portfolio, something he did a dozen times a day. Matt was stunned, he later told me, because this brief explanation from a little-known money manager in Florida potentially represented a seismic change in the investment industry. If the "buy side," the big custodians of wealth—pension funds, central banks, mutual funds, insurers—were no longer dependent on the "sell side," the underwriting and trading firms, for essential financial and commodity market information, a very fundamental power shift would occur. The securities industry would no longer dominate the investment industry. And if Bloomberg provided that indispensable information, it would become the fulcrum to the world's most important fiduciaries. Once the buyers depended on a particular system to help make decisions of relative value, then the sellers would have to use the same system too, or risk the potential disadvantage of not knowing what the customers knew.

In short, Bloomberg disrupted the relationship between the sell side and buy side by empowering the buy side with information that previously had been almost entirely in the hands of the sell side. The sell side wasn't too happy with us, to put it mildly, because we provided accurate historical and real-time data to their customers, who could now refuse to pay inflated prices. As a result, Bloomberg cut into the spreads (commissions) sellers could make on trades. In other words, by making an opaque market transparent, we made pricing more accurate and trading more efficient, driving spreads down— and making the cost of a financial transaction less expensive. On one hand, that cut into the profits of the big investment firms, but on the other, they benefitted from faster and more efficient trading— volumes soared—and a more transparent marketplace. They came out ahead, just as the smaller firms did. And we did, too.

"What did you use before you had a Bloomberg?" Winkler asked Smith.

"Telerate."

"What did you do with it?"

"I got rid of it," Smith said.

Matt had used a Telerate throughout his career at the *Journal* and considered it an essential electronic bulletin board for price quotes supplied by the three dozen or so securities firms that did business directly with the Federal Reserve Bank of New York, the agent of the U.S. Treasury. At one point, before the Bloomberg Terminal, everyone needed Telerate's prices. Yet Telerate's prices weren't really Telerate's. They were prices posted by a broker, Cantor Fitzgerald

& Co., which in turn acted as the middleman between securities firms. Telerate was nothing more than a vehicle of convenience for this broker and its customers. And it wasn't even unique: Depending on what was "fashionable" that month, there were three or four other equally important interdealer brokers whose prices mattered as much and who distributed their data separately.

What was worse for Dow Jones, Telerate couldn't show, the way the Bloomberg did, yield calculations based on many varied reinvestment assumptions—a function money managers coveted because it helped them do their jobs better. It couldn't show the total return of bonds: the income, price, and currency changes that determined how much money a bondholder made or lost, however long he or she held the bond. All it did was transmit an image of a page of quotes. It had no ability to *do* anything with the data being shown. Moreover, Winkler's Telerate froze too often. (Matt once told me he pleaded with a Dow Jones technician to help get his Telerate working again. The technician, a Russian immigrant, made myriad phone calls to different voicemails at the Dow Jones service department. After the last one, he slammed down his phone and screamed, "This is worse than the Soviet Union!")

The industry was ripe for disruption. If we hadn't done it, someone else would have. We just saw it before anyone else—and we gave it a harder shake than anyone else dared.

The *Journal* article on Bloomberg ran September 22, 1988, right-hand column, picture "above the fold"; it was more flattering than I would have had the nerve to make it if I had written it myself. Even though Dow Jones then owned more than 60 percent of Telerate, the *Wall Street Journal* editors, in a page-one story, let Robert Smith of Florida extol the Bloomberg system and diminish their own product with an unflattering anecdote to more than two million readers worldwide.

*　　　*　　　*

Even in its embryonic state, the Bloomberg system was already a news machine. Although it provided only numbers, graphs, and charts, it delivered the most valuable news a money manager could use: prices, relative values, and trends. And that news wasn't coming secondhand from any wire service, newspaper, magazine, or electronic broadcast: It was presented as it happened. By contrast, by the time anyone read a newspaper report on the price and yield discrepancies that create investment possibilities, it was too late. The buying or selling opportunity had probably vanished.

I had already decided, however, that Bloomberg should become something more than a niche information provider to a group of bond-market-data junkies. Our competitors provided business news, real-time stories with real text. In fact, we carried their newswires on our Terminal. But if we were successful, as the Bloomberg Terminal became more of an indispensable analytical tool for money managers and the securities industry, the competitive threat we posed would tempt them to stop letting us do so. Worse, for all practical purposes, there was only one real-time news organization in the United States for textual financial news—Dow Jones. There was only one news organization in Europe for following those markets in prose—Reuters. And both of them competed with us to put computer terminals on the desks of financial professionals.

We had two choices: Be nothing more than a small specialist in the information industry and always vulnerable to Dow Jones cutting us off, or challenge the giants. So, a little more than a year after I first met him in 1988, I phoned Matt Winkler—the reporter for our competition, who had impressed me with his understanding of our business and his mastery of his own.

"Hi, it's Bloomberg. I need some advice."

Matt waited several seconds before speaking. "You?" he asked, familiar enough with me to wonder why I would ask advice from anyone, let alone a reporter for the *Wall Street Journal*.

"I want to make our Terminal indispensable to stock as well as bond traders. Should we get into the text news business?" His answer wasn't what I expected, although it encouraged me to keep the conversation going.

"Mike," he said, "you and the people who work with you have created a Terminal that explains more about why bonds fluctuate each minute, day, and week than any collection of reporters ever could. You already provide charts and graphs that influence the major debt-trading decisions worldwide. Add text to that information and you'll have something that doesn't exist anywhere else. No one in debt or equity will be able to live without it."

He was free for lunch that day, so we met in a Japanese restaurant across the street from the Bloomberg office. Since I hadn't gotten a direct answer over the phone to my question, I asked again, as he contemplated a bowl of miso soup. "What does it really take to get into the newswire business?"

He started answering with a rhetorical question that put me on the spot but obviously, for a journalist, was a litmus-test issue to him. It would tell him whether I was serious about becoming a publisher.

"All right," he said. "You have just published a story that says the *chairman*—and I mean chairman—of your biggest customer has taken $5 million from the corporate till. He's with his secretary at a Rio de Janeiro resort, and the secretary's spurned boyfriend calls to tip you off. You get an independent verification that the story is true. Then the phone rings. The customer's public relations person says, 'Kill the story or we'll return all the Terminals we currently rent from you.' What do you do?"

"Go with the story. Our lawyers will love the fees you generate."

"Good," Matt said, pleasantly surprised that I was willing to choose journalism over commerce.

"Now, what does it really take?" I persisted, because he hadn't told me the cost yet.

"Five reporters in Tokyo, five in London, and five in New York," he said, still not giving me a real budget. (Before long, we would have over 3,000 journalists and analysts in more than 120 countries. So much for Matt's planning abilities.)

That was it for the money and operations talk that day. Until he brought up the subject, I certainly hadn't thought about the ethical conundrums we might come up against, particularly those created by the fact that we had by then let the world's largest broker/ dealer (Merrill Lynch) make a 30 percent passive investment in our company. (It's now zero percent; we bought them out in 2008, after the financial markets collapsed.) In fact, our first conversation dwelt almost exclusively on that topic rather than on how to build a financial news business. Unless our news was impartial, free of any outside influence, and not tied to some hidden agenda, then no amount of money or talent would assure us success as journalists. I understood that much. Our customers at that point were loyal because they considered our data to be untainted. Customers for our news would expect no less.

History shows that any gutsy entrepreneur (Joseph Pulitzer, William Randolph Hearst, Henry Luce, B.C. Forbes, Ted Turner, Rupert Murdoch, and Oprah Winfrey) can enter the news business anytime. And, Bloomberg being Bloomberg, we had some advantages those others didn't. When we started, there were lots of very competent reporters looking for jobs. In the face of the looming 1990 and 1991 recession, the news industry was cutting back exactly when we were expanding. People wanted to join us. We had a reputation as an exciting, innovative place to work. In the Bloomberg Terminal, we had a distribution device par excellence. Best of all, we had revenue from Terminal rentals, which meant we didn't have to worry about a news service paying for itself as a stand-alone product— one heck of an advantage.

Fundamentally, at Bloomberg we're builders, not buyers, so it never occurred to me to acquire a news organization as a starting point. It's always more fun to create from scratch, and a lot less risky. And when Matt came along—someone I could connect with, particularly after our ethics discussion—I knew I had the right guy to help us start.

"We're going to do it," I told him as he chewed his last piece of sushi. "I want you to run it. When can you start?"

When he realized I was serious, he said he would call me the next day with an answer. Twenty-four hours later, he did: "Fine. Let's do it."

Basically, a handshake between Mike Bloomberg and Matt Winkler was all it took to get going in news. That kind of informal, informed decision making is something that most companies find very difficult to do. How it was going to fit in at a tactical level we'd figure out later. Strategically, it made sense. We weren't paralyzed like others that have the business school/accountant desire to quantify and predict everything before proceeding. Sure, you can count numbers and compare scenarios. But generally, projections regarding new, untried businesses are meaningless. The noise in the assumptions you have to make is so great, and the knowledge you have of strange areas so limited, that all the detailed analysis is usually irrelevant. We saw a need. We went ahead and filled it. If we had tried to come up with a detailed business plan, it never would have gotten going.

A public company would have had an even more difficult time than we did. Public companies typically must have specific goals and declare exactly where they'll wind up, or the securities analysts have a field day, and the investors, heart attacks. If public companies change what they're trying in midstream, everyone panics. In a private company like Bloomberg, the analysts don't ask, and as for the fact that we didn't know exactly where we're going—so what? Neither did Columbus. The truth of the matter was that we were moving forward.

*　　　*　　　*

The Bloomberg Terminal, our first and greatest strength, was providing information that the other news companies weren't—even before the Bloomberg News service produced a word of text. From our first day in business, Bloomberg was making news, with numbers.

Some journalists derisively labeled those numbers "agate," even though that agate took up more space in the daily newspaper than any reporter's column. But as I would come to realize, media people are often both ignorant and contemptuous of financial news in general. In the field of journalism, business and finance have never been the subjects of choice. None of the journalism schools taught reporters how to cover business. For a long time, none of the reporters and editors most visible to the public had any experience covering financial markets. On their way up the career ladder, no top news anchors for the networks had ever written earnings stories. No executive editor running the *New York Times*, the *Washington Post*, or the *Los Angeles Times* had ever edited financial markets stories day in and day out; the ambitious rushed to cover war, revolution, or riot. Even at the *Wall Street Journal*, it was rare to find top editors who included among their accomplishments daily stints covering stocks and bonds.

When Matt Winkler told editors and reporters at the *Journal* he was leaving, most of them shrugged, not knowing much about Bloomberg and caring less. To journalism's insiders, Bloomberg wasn't on anyone's radar screen. Even the *Journal*'s Washington Bureau Chief at the time, Alan Murray, asked Matt a month after he joined Bloomberg, "How does it feel to have sold out to . . . who's that firm?" That prevailing attitude became our opportunity.

Our timing was right. When the Berlin Wall came down in 1989, there was no question who had won the Cold War. Capitalism had triumphed. The forty-four-year-old battle of the superpowers had ended—and gone, too, was journalism's top tale. Money, in contrast, was emerging as the big story that needed telling at the end of the century—where money was, where it went, who made it, and who didn't. The demand for information about money was burgeoning everywhere. By the end of the 1980s, Bloomberg already had about 300 employees in New York, Princeton, London, and Tokyo, many of whom had Wall Street experience. To create a news operation, all we needed were the journalists who could translate that knowledge intelligently and communicate it as informative, concise, cogent prose.

Fortunately for us, the late 1980s were only slightly less kind to Communism than they were to newspapers and wire services. By 1990, United Press International, a once-proud wire service that had produced bylines from William Shirer and Neil Sheehan, was stumbling from bankruptcy filing to bankruptcy filing. Cities with two news dailies were becoming one-newspaper towns. McGraw Hill, after spending three years and about $30 million, killed its nascent financial news wire just as it was about to get its first big customer. Conventional wisdom was that you couldn't compete with Dow Jones and Reuters, the two entrenched powerhouses, and if you tried, you'd end up in the poorhouse.

Until the 1980s, few newspapers even had a business section. The size of the sports staff always dwarfed the business staff. And yet, though not everyone cared about athletics, almost all people had their livelihoods at stake in the world of commerce. How people earned, saved, and spent their money helped determine prosperity, economic depression, wars, and elections. Readers might not have realized it to start with, but here was a hole. I knew Bloomberg could fill it.

*   *   *

From the beginning, we tried to be different. We built a unique product: We combined text and analytics with computer-driven tours that let readers automatically see the calculations and graphs of what we wrote about. We gave an illustration to complement what we told in words, then followed up with words to expand what the illustration showed. Our policies were not the same as at other news organizations: We made sure every company's earnings were reported as soon as we had them, instead of using the big-companies-first pecking order that was customary among wire services—and left shareholders of smaller companies in the lurch during earnings season. Thus, we had some content long before our competitors. At the end of each story, we gave our reporter's name and phone number. Unlike everyone else, we built customer access to our people rather than protection from our clients. We used customized standards. We banned the term profit-taking when we wrote about a market in decline. (How can everyone make money if the market lost value?) We insisted on two independent sources for important new facts. When you read our copy, it really was more accurate and better written than the competition's. Small items, but all things that we thought would differentiate us.

There are other practices that separate Bloomberg from the conventional, old news services. For some stories, we don't use human writers or editors at all. When we describe a market's value at a given instant (as opposed to why it had moved there), only speed and accuracy matter—and they are not most people's strengths. But what device did I make my career creating and managing since Salomon days? What instantly does exactly what you've asked it to do every time?

Beginning in the 1990s, we programmed our Bloomberg computers to "write" periodically a series of stories informing readers of the current state of the market. At the start, the stories were basic. For example, the machine would take the predefined phrase "The Dow Jones Industrial Index is" and add the word "up" or "down," based on calculations of all 30 stocks' moves from the previous day to that millisecond. It then added the appropriate numbers—for example, 1 point, 2 points, 3 points, and so on. Then it printed the words "The most active stocks are" and, from continuous trading volume monitoring, automatically translated the appropriate ticker symbols to company names (e.g., Procter & Gamble, General Electric, Walt Disney). It then added them to the sentence. A sample result: "The Dow Jones Industrial Average was 1.09% lower at 3:01P.M. Eastern time, down 62.14 at 5650.24. The stocks that contributed most to the average's fall were Procter & Gamble Co., which lowered the Dow by 5.55 points; General Electric Co., 5.18 points; and the Walt Disney Co., 4.07 points." A story created and "written" in microseconds—and one of many done the same way every hour.

Today at Bloomberg we use algorithms we developed to detect anomalies in data, such as a stock that's rising in an unusual way or a category of stores in an economic report with slow sales. We automatically turn those findings into news stories, which are written and published by computer without involving human hands. At first reporters were concerned that this kind of machine learning, or artificial intelligence, might take their jobs away. But they came to embrace it as they saw that the computers actually freed them to do the kind of reporting they wanted to do—not merely transcribing, but more in-depth writing and analysis, using their knowledge and skills to help readers understand data and events. The computers are sparing them some of the drudgery of their jobs—exactly what computers have done in so many other industries—and allowing them, and us, to cover even more news.

No group of humans could as specifically and as quickly, around the clock, write these stories from markets worldwide. (There are thousands of indexes investors follow, with hundreds active enough for a textual description.) Our reporters, from the start, have been too valuable to be assigned to mechanical tasks anyway. Understanding and reinventing how news should be produced and delivered, as opposed to doing it "the way it's done," lets us beat the competition back in our early days, and it's the strategy we've stuck to since.

*   *   *

When he showed up for work at 8 a.m. on February 5, 1990, Matt Winkler was already late. Bloombergers were at their desks by 7:30. That's the hour when most of our customers sit down at their desks. (Someone from a *small* software house accosted me once at a convention, alleging that we overworked ourselves with this start time. The fact that he thinks it strange to be at work simultaneously with one's customers says he'll always be small.)

"Nice of you to show up," I said. He told me 8 a.m. was early in the newspaper world. I pointed out he no longer worked in that domain as I led him to his new desk in the middle of a room filled with people. After that, he began coming in at 6:30 a.m. Today, as editor-in-chief emeritus, he allows himself to come in late: 7 a.m.

At the end of his first month, Matt received his first paycheck and found out what his compensation would be. We had never discussed his pay before he joined Bloomberg.

I handed him a three-page list of what Bloomberg Business News (later shortened to Bloomberg News), as we agreed to call it, should be doing. Our purpose was to do more than just collect and relay news; it should also, ethically, advertise the analytical and computational powers of the Bloomberg Terminal by highlighting its capabilities in each news story. This would make each story better and, at the same time, make it easier to buy more Terminal subscriptions (total subscriptions were then about 8,000 worldwide). With our Terminal functions included, each of our news stories would be more informative than the competition's, and more people would want access to them. More retrievals meant more rentals, which meant more revenue, which in turn meant we could afford more reporters and have more news, and so on.

One important, immediate business-development task was to prevent any Bloomberg customer from canceling a Bloomberg Terminal if Dow Jones grew wary of the new kid on the block and stopped distributing its newswire over our system. That was unlikely right away since Bloomberg was a large Dow Jones customer. Bloomberg customers paid Dow Jones to receive the Dow Jones newswires on the Bloomberg Terminal, and Bloomberg itself paid a Dow Jones subsidiary millions of dollars annually to help install and service Bloomberg Terminals throughout the United States.

Who knew how long this arrangement would last if Bloomberg, equipped with Dow Jones news, continued to displace the Telerate terminal equipped with Dow Jones news. Fortunately, even after Matt arrived, there wasn't anyone at Dow Jones (or any other news organization) who thought we had a realistic chance to compete with the century-old news service benchmarks. Thank God they never told me that. Ignorance is bliss.

Even so, I was asking for trouble if I didn't believe that the perception of our company could change in a second. Low-key may not have been our normal style, but for a while, we would try it. We agreed to make the relationship with Dow Jones as friendly as we could; we decided not to hire anyone else away from it. Our news formula would provide as much information as fast as possible about anything that might affect the price of a stock, bond, currency, or commodity, but without making waves. I would initiate no public relations effort to tweak the establishment's nose. With a little luck, we could build a credible news service before the inevitable confrontation with the giants, and after it was too late for them to retaliate successfully.

In August 1990, two months after the first Bloomberg Business News story crossed the Bloomberg Terminal, Dow Jones said it would no longer install or service Bloomberg Terminals and would no longer distribute its news via Bloomberg when its contract with our customers expired twelve months later. So much for avoiding a showdown. Dow Jones reported the announcement on its newswires and in the *Wall Street Journal*, declaring war with a competitor. Since most people still hadn't heard of our news service, a story in the nation's largest newspaper saying that Dow Jones considered Bloomberg's service a competitor, a threat—well, that was advertising we couldn't have bought. I was thrilled that the battle had been joined that way.

On the other hand, we had less than a year to convince our Terminal customers that our news was good enough to offset the loss of Dow Jones news. People find all sorts of ways to become motivated and creative when they're threatened with extinction. And that's the way it was with our fledgling news organization of two dozen reporters and editors at the end of 1990. It was a similar situation with our service and installation people. When Dow Jones ended its service contract with us, it only hurt itself. It forced us into an expensive conversion to start doing ourselves what we had hired it to do. But that was good for Bloomberg in the long term. Because we installed all new equipment as we moved our communications sites in every city from its offices to ours, we improved our product vis-à-vis theirs. We came out better; it lost a revenue source and contact with all our customers.

Few analysts gave us any chance to succeed independently with our own news, so we exceeded expectations when it became clear we weren't going to lose customers if Dow Jones was no longer available on the Bloomberg system. The verdict from some of our customers was even more encouraging. In March of 1991, H. Ross Perot & Co. sent us a copy of a letter it had written to Dow Jones, explaining that it wouldn't need Dow Jones news on the Bloomberg because "We get everything we need at no extra charge from Bloomberg News." Our own news was an example of how Bloomberg could add value, save customers money, and make them more reliant on the Bloomberg system.

The big surprise came a month later. If Dow Jones news disappeared from the Bloomberg system, Bloomberg's Merrill Lynch customers might need to get their financial news some other way—which was exactly what Dow Jones hoped—and thus, the appeal of the Bloomberg Terminal would be limited. So Merrill, without our knowledge, created its own set of criteria and decided to compare Bloomberg news to Dow Jones news, point by point. On four days during a three-week period, both news services were scored for accuracy and timely reporting on financial markets. When the test was completed, we were told we scored well enough that Merrill was no longer worried. The Bloomberg without Dow Jones news was as good as the Bloomberg with!

Of course, once it became clear we wouldn't lose any customers, Dow Jones changed its mind and decided to renew our contracts. To this day, you can subscribe to Dow Jones news on the Bloomberg Terminal. (If this sounds strange and antithetical to the basic American idea of healthy competition, remember that big companies have lots of different divisions. You compete with parts. You buy from some, you sell to others, and you might not even notice that additional ones exist. Those kinds of conflicts and the tolerance of them are just the way the world works.)

*   *   *

As an entrepreneur, I've learned to know what I don't know, get access to the people who do know, and then study hard. When we started Bloomberg News, I relied on professional journalists for our editorial policy and the management of our newspeople. I always worried that, in the rush to succeed, we might confuse fact and opinion. Facts aren't always what they seem, or what you want them to be. Inaccuracy and incompleteness can make yes into no and vice versa. Errors can ruin reputations, destroy companies and their employees, even start wars and kill people. Writing news stories takes time and requires restraint. As an organization, we have to take care not to err, even if it sometimes means coming in second in the race for headlines. The balance among speed, accuracy, and aggressiveness is an issue we must grapple with continuously, keeping our demand to be first from overcoming our insistence on being right.

Getting that balance right is more important than ever. At Bloomberg, we have never sought eyeballs at the expense of accuracy. Other media companies have turned to clickbait headlines to attract readers, and the advertising that follows them. But we have never been dependent on advertising. We've always been subscription-based. In 2018, we moved our Web content to a subscription model, too, by moving much of it behind a paywall. People will still pay for quality journalism. And the more that other news organizations acquire a reputation for tilting left or right, the more valuable our reputation for playing it straight—and getting it right—becomes.

But why did Bloomberg News rival Dow Jones and the British wire service Reuters so quickly? No big company thinks a little start-up company will ever become a major competitor. Invariably, by the time the big guy catches on, it's too late. The customers have grown used to having a choice. And playing catch-up isn't easy. In this case, major company complacency was furthered because Reuters and Dow Jones were growing at the time Bloomberg came on the scene; at first we were barely a distraction to either behemoth. Moreover, both of those established companies possessed a large status quo infrastructure with a vested interest in convincing management it was doing a good job, doing everything right, covering all the bases. So what management heard internally were reassuring feelings, not facts. I have always worried when our people tell me that we're doing great, that all is fine. As the "emperor" of Bloomberg, I need someone to tell me when I've left my clothes at home.

Bloomberg found niches that Dow Jones and Reuters news didn't fill. From the start, it was easier for us to add to our basic product what they provided, than for them to add what we built to theirs. Although they were unable to replicate our analytics—the computational answers to all sorts of "what-if" scenarios in the financial and commodity markets—we started matching them story for story, interview for interview, scoop for scoop (and unfortunately sometimes, error for error). They made a dramatic mistake by not paying attention; at Bloomberg, as we keep on growing with time, we've got to be sure we don't do the same.

In fact, we would have had a much tougher time had we entered an industry that had lots of small, scrappy competitors. But we went against giants, and giants are usually easy to beat. Remember the Germans and then the Japanese versus Detroit's "Big Three" automakers? If you have to compete based on capital, the giant always wins. If you can compete based on smarts, flexibility, and willingness to give more for less, then small companies like Bloomberg clearly have an advantage. The world changes every minute, and you forget that at your peril. Ted Levitt at the Harvard Business School, in his famous *Marketing Myopia* paper, argued that the railroads failed because they should have realized they were in the transportation business rather than running trains. If they'd caught on to that idea, they'd have grown up to be General Motors, Boeing, and American Airlines, he argued. I'm not sure that's true, but I know this: Those enterprises that see new needs and react more quickly, win!

That has certainly been true in our industry. Nearly all of our original competitors have either failed or been part of a merger or acquisition. After buying Telerate in the late 1980s, Dow Jones sold it for about $1 billion loss in 1998. Another early giant, Quotron, was acquired by Citgroup in 1986, when Quotron had more than 60 percent market share. After losing money and customers (largely to us) for nearly a decade, Citicorp *paid* Reuters more than $100 million to "buy" Quotron. Reuters used the acquisition to create a data and analytics unit to compete with Bloomberg, but eventually decided to get out of the business: Blackstone bought the unit in 2018. Thomson, an early rival, merged with Reuters in 2007. Other competitors also came and went. Standard and Poor's, McGraw Hill, and Knight-Ridder all started financial news services to compete with us. All folded long ago.

All the firms that were the heavyweights of the industry in the 1980s have been have been acquired, devoured, eviscerated, or otherwise exterminated. Bloomberg, the smallest of the bunch back then, is the only one the still standing in its original form. And we still punch above our weight. No one knows the future, and we certainly face great competitors and all sorts of business risks, but to the extent that we can shape our future, hard work, constant innovation, and a focus on customer service is the recipe we'll continue to follow.

5

"No" Is No Answer

Establishment Ignorance and Arrogance

Once we had the Bloomberg News service, it never occurred to us that our access to the events financial journalists covered, such as economic indicators briefings, would be denied by anybody. We were wrong. Journalism is no different from any other profession; it's not exempt from the lessons of George Orwell's *Animal Farm*: Some are more equal than others. And we were about to have some real barnyard battles to get fair access.

We started the news service with no plans to cover politics and policy, or Washington, D.C.—not, at least, at the start. We wanted to focus our resources where our needs and strengths resided: in the financial markets. Of course, every statistic about the economy—and every public policy tremor—can drive the bond, stock, commodity, and currency markets into turmoil. So, early on, we decided we needed to include coverage not only of the numbers, but also of the people who produced the numbers, and the politics behind these people. Either we had to pay someone to give us that, or we had to provide it on our own. We decided to do it ourselves, naturally. And we met more resistance in getting ourselves credentialed that we had ever imagined possible.

*   *   *

One afternoon, just as we were getting started, Winkler happened to be telling Mary McCue, an official from the Securities and Exchange Commission, about Bloomberg's plans to expand coverage into Washington, D.C. She interrupted him. "I'm not sure I can talk to you," she said.

"What do you mean?" Matt asked.

"I'm not sure I or anyone else who works for the government can talk to you in any official capacity."

Matt was astounded. "Mary. I've known you for twelve years now and you're saying you can't talk to me?"

"You're not accredited. We can only talk to accredited news organizations."

"What the hell does that mean, I'm not accredited? Hundreds of bylines in the largest U.S. newspaper during the past ten years isn't good enough?" By now, Matt was shouting.

"Look, Matt, the only way we can talk to journalists is if the House/Senate Standing Committee of Correspondents says they are journalists. Unless you have credentials from the Standing Committee, you can't get any of those economic numbers you were talking about, or even talk to me. No offense." At this point, Mary McCue's tone changed. "But you are in luck. The chairman of the committee is Jeffrey Birnbaum of the *Wall Street Journal*. He must know you."

"Thanks, Mary." Even if McCue was being ironic in mentioning his onetime employer, Matt didn't think for a minute that a *Journal* reporter would cross another *Journal* reporter, even a former one, over a matter as seemingly mundane and bureaucratic as obtaining a visa into Washington's duchies of access. Journalism was a club. Members took care of one another. Of course, we were wrong again.

The House/Senate Standing Committee of Correspondents consists of an annually elected group of five newspaper or wire service reporters who decide who is and who isn't a journalist. Their high and serious intention is to keep the halls of government from being littered with lobbyists, investment bankers, economists, brokers, and other "influence peddlers" posing as journalists. Elected officials, wary of interfering with the Fourth Estate, long ago decided to let journalists themselves decide who's fit and who isn't. The standing committee meets and holds hearings in government chambers. Its rulings have the effect of law among government employees in Washington, D.C.

*   *   *

Matt admits now that he was hopelessly naive about his colleagues at the competing news services. He thought the whole issue of credentials for Bloomberg News in Washington, D.C., was a formality to be resolved among civilized people over lunch at the American Cafe across from the Capitol. He and a couple of colleagues met Birnbaum, who had started at Dow Jones & Co. about the same time Matt did, a decade earlier. Matt explained that Bloomberg was starting a news service to cover financial markets, and its two reporters in Washington needed to follow the economic indicators. These are numbers, such as the Gross Domestic Product (GDP), the Consumer Price Index (CPI), and the Producer Price Index (PPI), that are released by government officials in a quarantine-like setting so no one can trade on advance information. All serious business reporters need credentials to be in the "lock-up" where journalists get the releases before the general public does. In this sealed room, they write their stories before the publishing time, and all release these news flashes at the same instant. Not being included with the other reporters would mean reporting the numbers too late in the day for traders to act, and not having a competitive news product to sell.

After the ritual greetings and introductions, Matt got to the point. "So, Jeff, how do we get these dog tags that let us report on GDP, CPI, PPI, now that we're starting this news service?"

"What are you?" Birnbaum asked, inspiring no confidence that Winkler's request was routine.

"We're an electronic newspaper," Matt said. Birnbaum's skepticism persisted. "Who reads you?"

Matt, proud of his new professional home, replied: "Every central bank in Europe, and there are thirty of them; most of the world's biggest commercial banks, institutional investors, pension funds, and securities firms."

Birnbaum still wasn't impressed. "Where are you published?" he asked.

"On desks around the world via a dedicated computer Terminal," Matt said, providing an answer that would be the zeitgeist to all journalists around the world by 1995, but was obviously obscure to all but the cognoscenti in the spring of 1990.

"What newspapers publish you?"

"Hundreds via the Associated Press, which prints our complete list of government bond prices and yields daily," Matt said. He was referring to the data we were supplying to the *Wall Street Journal* and to the AP and hundreds of its members—electronically instead of pony express style.

"Where are your stories published?" Birnbaum asked.

"On desks around the world," Matt said again.

"What newspapers publish your stories?" Now, Birnbaum was coming back to what for him was the crux of the issue. Whatever Bloomberg News was, he would require that it look like something Gutenberg produced instead of a computer derived from the Numerical Integrator and Calculator—the father of the PC.

No problem, Matt thought. "Well, if you give us the dog tags so we can cover the numbers, we can probably get published in newspapers somewhere," he said.

"I'm sorry, Matt. We don't have criteria for you," Birnbaum replied.

Matt was stunned. That was it? "We don't have criteria for you."

"Hey, Jeff. Let me get this right. You're saying just because Bloomberg News is born in 1990, instead of 1900, and because it's digital instead of married to a printing press, it has no right to cover GDP, CPI, PPI?"

"I'm sorry, Matt," he said. "That's right. I don't make the rules. We don't have criteria for you."

"Well, that's the biggest pile of shit I've smelled in a long time," Matt said as he excused himself to pay the check.

While he was gone, Birnbaum turned to Matt's colleagues: "Whatever you do, don't let him go before the House/Senate Standing Committee." Talk about waving a red flag in front of a bull!

*   *   *

Birnbaum's reaction was just the beginning of the stonewalling we encountered. Within a month, a new slate of journalists had been elected to the committee, including a new chairman, the defense correspondent for United Press International (UPI), Elliot Brenner. We had no luck convincing him either. "We can't give you credentials because Bloomberg is owned by Merrill Lynch," he misinformed us.

Our Washington reporter tried patiently to explain reality to him. "Merrill is a passive minority shareholder with 30 percent of Bloomberg L.P. Mike Bloomberg owns almost 70 percent."

"Right," said the chairman of the committee. "What if Merrill called in its loans to Bloomberg?"

"Merrill is a passive equity shareholder."

"Right. What if Merrill called in its loans?"

"No. You see, there are no loans. Merrill is a passive equity shareholder."

"Yeah. What about the loans?"

Now, here was a good reason for Bloomberg News to exist. The chairman of the committee that decides who's fit to cover the big and little stories of the day in the capital of the world had never covered a financial market in his life. He didn't know the difference between debt and equity and yet he was deciding who should cover stocks and bonds. Ignorance and arrogance are a deadly combination. They run riot in the profession of journalism, and this guy had them both.

We later learned that all sorts of folks had credentials to cover the economic numbers. They included Tass, the news agency of the old Soviet Union, and the Iraqi News Service, whose dispatches depicted Saddam Hussein as one of the world's greatest humanitarians. Reporters for the Haitian News Service, the house organ of a brutal dictatorship during much of the twentieth century, could cover Federal Reserve Chairman Alan Greenspan giving his semiannual testimony to Congress, and Bloomberg News could not.

Frustrated, we decided to accomplish by indirection what we couldn't make happen head-on. In addition to providing the Associated Press with bond prices for several years for free—a service for which AP was in turn charging its newspapers—Bloomberg was also paying AP millions of dollars a year to have AP news on the BloombergTerminal. We figured that when you're dealing with a bully, you'd better get someone bigger on your side, and AP was the logical someone.

We asked the Associated Press, which, with three thousand reporters and editors, was the largest news-gathering organization in the United States, to ask the House/Senate Standing Committee of Correspondents why it objected to giving Bloomberg News the credentials. The AP, being a great journalistic organization of impeccable integrity, didn't have any objection at all to Bloomberg's writing about the Gross Domestic Product. When Chairman Brenner received a phone call from an AP correspondent who was wondering why the Committee was giving Bloomberg such a hard time, he said there had been a misunderstanding and Bloomberg should just "chill out"; they would get the credentials, just shortly *before* hell froze over.

So, even after the AP's investigation, we were still meeting resistance. One of the journalists on the Committee told us, "All you guys up on Wall Street are corrupt anyway." We sweated through two hours of testimony in a Senate chamber in front of him and four other reporters, none of whom could define a Collateralized Mortgage Obligation (but probably wouldn't have gotten their own home mortgages if CMOs didn't exist), all demanding to know why we thought we were fit to write about housing starts. Bruce Harmon, the Washington bureau chief of Knight-Ridder Financial News, went so far as to tell the Committee, in a letter on Knight-Ridder stationery, that allowing Bloomberg News service into the Labor Department to cover employment statistics would open the possibility of insider trading. This, of course, is impossible where information is given to all journalists simultaneously in the same sealed room. Besides, if there was some way we could, so could his company.

*   *   *

Every problem is an opportunity, as the saying goes. Just as we were tangling with the journalists' commissar committee in Washington, Matt was asked by former Dow Jones colleagues who were now at the *New York Times* if they might be able to get a Bloomberg Terminal for free. They wanted the same instant information about companies, stocks, and bonds that the money managers they were writing about now had. "We can't afford to rent your Terminals. We don't have enough money for everything," said Diana Henriques, a *Times* reporter, half in jest. I believe no customers are more equal than any others, so the idea that we would give the Terminal away was a nonstarter. We could, however, provide Bloomberg Terminals to people who provided us with something equivalent to the monetary value of the Terminals. News companies often barter, so we weren't exactly inventing a new form of remuneration. We told the *New York Times* that if we provided them with news items that they decided were fit to print, just like any other news-service stories the *Times* published, we might be able to get them a Terminal.

At that time, the credibility gained from having Bloomberg News stories published in the *New York Times* was worth more to us than any cash payment. It would directly counter the argument of those who were reluctant to recognize Bloomberg because we weren't "published" in the old-fashioned way. The agreement would be simple enough to avoid any conflict of interest: The *New York Times* would decide what it published, as it always had. But when it published one of our stories, there would be the Bloomberg News byline and the Standing Committee's problem would be solved.

When Max Frankel, the *Times* executive editor, agreed to our suggestion in 1991, Bloomberg had its first newspaper customer. Within a year, every major newspaper in the United States asked for the same arrangement. By 1995, Bloomberg News was published in more American newspapers than any other news service, after the Associated Press. We provided what so many newspapers had in short supply: an army of reporters and editors who do nothing but report and explain money, markets, companies, industries, and the economy. The newspapers, in turn, provided what we needed: access, distribution, credibility, and recognition for us and our products. Selling news for cash we would do, but to the ultimate users, not the intermediaries.

I am very proud of how hard we fought, what we produced, how fast we grew, and how we became a news inevitability. Yet we might never have considered newspapers as customers if the journalists in Washington hadn't created the predicament that forced us to include print media in our distribution. In 1995, the *New York Times*'s own newspaper syndicate, received by 700 newspapers around the world, asked to include Bloomberg News. It happened because someone told us, "We don't have criteria for you." Oh, and of course in the end, over a year after we first asked, we did get our dog tags.

*   *   *

In Japan, we had an even tougher time getting our reporters the access and credentials they needed. Our problem wasn't with the government. Once again, it was with a self-appointed group of journalists trying to protect their cozy fiefdom. Since we weren't Japanese reporters with a Japanese news organization, the home-town press kept us from reporting on the economy and corporate earnings in the most timely way by not allowing us into the *kisha* (reporter, in Japanese) clubs where all government and corporate press releases are distributed. Thus, we couldn't get information when it was first made public. Well, economic and corporate news was our business and we had to protect our franchise—even if it meant doing what no foreign news organization had ever done before: confronting our opponents in the Fourth Estate directly and demanding equal access for our customers, a growing number of whom were Japanese.

In 1991, Bloomberg News shouldered ahead of all the other cowed and overpolite foreign media to demand equal treatment for foreign news organizations. We made it clear we would not shut up until we got it. Our threat was dismissed with a combination of half bows and condescending giggles. Even our non-Japanese competitors were leery of rocking the boat and declined our invitation to stand together publicly on the issue.

The Japanese *kisha* clubs consist of reporters from Japan's elite news organizations. The clubs control the newsrooms at all government agencies. The *kisha* clubs decide who gets desks, who gets to ask questions at news conferences, and who gets advance copies of news releases. *Kisha* club members also are given preferential treatment when it comes to background briefings with Japan's top policymakers.

The prejudice against *gaijin* (foreign) journalists in the post–World War II era meant that no overseas news organization ever had a desk inside a Japanese government newsroom. When the almighty *kisha* clubs stooped to allow *gaijin* to attend news conferences, they did so only with the proviso that we not ask any questions.

Our loudmouthed campaign to end this system made us the most hated news company in Tokyo. Each week brought a new snub. We got a telephone call from Clay Jones, president of the Foreign Correspondents Club of Japan and correspondent for the *Christian Science Monitor*. He passed on the bad news that Bloomberg would not be invited to a dinner hosted by Japan's own Publishers and Editors Association staff. The association wanted to talk with foreign journalists about *kisha* clubs. But they didn't want us there. That marked the second time the Publishers and Editors Association had hosted a dinner at which access to the clubs was the topic and had spurned Bloomberg despite our intense involvement in the issue and an appeal from Mr. Jones that we be invited.

At stake was our ability to cover a global financial and economic story. Japan was the world's second largest economy. By denying us equal access to the figures that measured the performance of Japanese companies and the economy, Japan's news organizations were also depriving shareholders and bondholders (our customers inside and outside Japan) of news they had a right to know. It was an explicit move by one group of journalists to deprive another group of journalists of the information both needed.

At first, we tried the normal route. We applied for membership in one of the clubs. We were turned down. The official reason given was that we didn't meet the criteria for membership, though the criteria were never defined. In reality, we didn't get in because we weren't a Japanese company. To press our case, Matt Winkler and David Butts, then our Tokyo bureau chief, met Osamu Asano, the secretary general of the Publishers and Editors Association, in February 1992. They were ushered into a paneled conference room and seated on one side of a twenty-foot-long table. Under the gaze of a gallery of the association's past secretaries general, the negotiations began. We said that many of our worldwide subscribers were both employees and shareholders of such companies as Nissan, Sony, Honda, and Toyota: We demanded equal access to the news that mattered to them. At the same time, we said we considered it appalling that Japanese journalists—who ostensibly share our freedom-of-speech views as members of the Fourth Estate—should maintain a system that blatantly discriminated against non-Japanese journalists.

Dave Butts, a native Texan, did all the talking for us. "We'd like to join the club," he said.

"You can't join because you have to speak Japanese to be a member," said Asano.

When Butts reminded him (in his fluent Japanese) that all our Tokyo correspondents speak Japanese, Asano paused. "Oh well, there aren't enough desks in the club rooms for foreigners."

To which Butts countered, "You have more than one hundred desks in most clubs, many are empty, and there are only four or five foreign organizations that would want one of them."

Then Asano smiled and said, "Right. Well, it is not really up to us to give you membership. Membership is decided by the individual clubs, not this association."

Butts persisted: "We asked the clubs to admit us and they said they can only do so if we are members of your organization first."

Asano shook his head. "Is that true?" he asked. "Well, we don't give membership to companies just because they want to join." That response was typical of the entire discussion.

*   *   *

A year later, in March 1993, the association took the bold step of setting up a subcommittee to study the issue. Matt and Dave once again met the man in charge, Yoshio Murakami, senior editor at the

Asahi newspaper. They didn't exactly hit it off with him. This time, the conversation was in English, and his English, after a ten-year tour of duty in the United States, was probably better than Matt's.

By now we were too familiar with disappointment to pull our punches. No self-respecting journalist ever likes to be rolled. If we could make the point that journalists restraining other journalists is shameful, maybe we could finally puncture the veneer of politeness that led us nowhere. Matt suggested that by limiting foreign press access to government agencies, Japanese journalists had become puppets of the politicians and bureaucrats. During the next fifteen minutes, Matt uttered the phrase "puppets of special interests" about a dozen times. The *Asahi* editor, a model of composure to everyone who knew him, suddenly snapped. He now told us what he really thought.

"You can go to hell!" he said, leaping from his chair and spilling his green tea.

After so many polite rebuffs, this outburst was just the kind of reaction we wanted. "Now, you know how we feel," Butts said. "Will you resort to violence?" the *Asahi* editor asked in the frankness of the moment.

Butts said simply that he *hoped* it wouldn't come to that.

Two months later, we were back hammering at the stone wall once again. We asked the *kisha* club at the Tokyo Stock Exchange to let us have news releases at the same time they were delivered to club members. "No way" was the club's answer. So we decided to try a little civil disobedience.

Reporters from our Tokyo bureau stood by the club's mailboxes, outside the entrance to the club, and insisted that the public relations folks from the companies who regularly visit the club give us each release as it was distributed. To protect us, we had our lawyers there with their books defining "trespass," and even invited the TV networks to have the cameras rolling. The club members rose to protect their turf. They surrounded us, preventing the corporate crowd from getting close, and they "asked" us to leave. This is one of those confrontations that made the evening news: Journalist bites journalist. The commotion and subsequent publicity created was more than the club could bear. Under threat of repeated visits from us and the possibility that journalistic access could burgeon into a "free trade" issue at the level of Japanese automobile imports to the United States, the club promised to set up a fair system for the distribution of releases.

The Publishers and Editors Association finally followed up in a June 1993 statement: "The *kisha* clubs, as a matter of principle, should grant full membership to foreign correspondents who wish to join." The statement should put an end to foreign criticism of Japan's *kisha* club system, said the host at yet another dinner from which we were excluded. Still, to his credit, the host, Yoshio Murakami, offered to help Bloomberg; his newspaper agreed to sponsor Bloomberg for membership in the stock exchange reporting club.

But our single-minded efforts to open up one Japanese market were even now not yet successful. The *kisha* club voted to admit one of our competitors, Reuters, and keep Bloomberg out. The club's off-the-record explanation to friends who asked on our behalf was that Bloomberg might expect to get in by October 1993, if it showed more deference to the club. That meant we had to be quiet and do nothing that might be interpreted as casting an aspersion on the club. Our competitor's bureau chief, when asked by Bloomberg to wait until the doors were open to all of us, demurred.

"We used the back channel and quiet diplomacy," he said.

"Bull!" As a publisher, I was furious.

This other non-Japanese news service had done nothing. Bloomberg had done it all. Their Tokyo office had never tried to gain *kisha* club access. They never even took the trouble to report releases as soon as they were available, much less try to get them more quickly. They always published earnings and other time-sensitive stories only when they got around to it. Not being "in" had suited their customer-be-damned laziness just fine.

The Fourth Estate has a long, proud history of never letting commercial competitive interests override its integrity. Reporters *always* stand together on matters of journalistic freedom. And real journalists never stoop to using a back channel to talk to each other. They would not be journalists if they did. No reputable news service would permit it, nor would any quality journalist want to be associated with such behavior. It was a sad episode in the history of that other news organization whose journalistic standards were once legendary. Either they cared about their earnings more than their ethics, or, more charitably, perhaps their main headquarters on another island six thousand miles away had no idea what was taking place in Japan.

After a twenty-four-month battle, in October 1993, the *kisha* club finally let us in. The vote was unanimous. A year later, our reporter was rotated into the club's presidency.

*   *   *

Six years after we started our news service, the issue of credentials had become history. One of our editors, Pulitzer Prize–winner Monroe (Bud) Karmin, was elected president of the National Press Club in Washington—and more of our reporters have been elected president since. One of the rooms at the Club has proudly carried the Bloomberg name as its major sponsor for more than twenty years. Knight-Ridder Financial News, whose Washington bureau chief went out of his way to hurt us in our infancy, was sold— a casualty of inadequate returns to its parent. In Japan, many newspapers subscribe to Bloomberg News and carry the news our reporters write. Our Japanese-language news service is used by Japanese speakers worldwide.

By the 1990s, the New York Stock Exchange had three "official" news organizations: Bloomberg and two companies that were well over a century old, Dow Jones and Reuters, each of whom was designated as providing sufficient distribution for exchange-listed companies to fully inform their shareholders. No other group of journalists but these three could say that, and lots tried.

*   *   *

Was starting a newswire, and building it into a global media business, worth the effort? After all, in the 1960s, Marshall McLuhan, in *The Medium Is the Massage* (no, not "message") and *Understanding Media*, wrote that we were never going to read again. Books, magazines, newspapers, and other "hot" media would cease to be influential. "Cool" media, like television, which are "extensions of our senses," were the future. In the pop culture of the information age, distribution would triumph over content.

The 1990s had a similar "everybody knows." We were told all would be "on the Net." The computer was supposed to eliminate the drudgery of thinking. Research would be "touch a button" automated browser output. Contextual software would replace analysis. The mind's eye would die. Modern simulation would show all: imagination, an antiquated concept. Thinking would no longer be required. It didn't quite work that way. But McLuhan's famous line that "the medium is the message" (no, this time not massage) has proven partly true. He argued that the transmission device was an extension of ourselves—and when you see people with their eyes glued to their phones, it's hard to argue with that. But media devices—Who remembers the iPod? And beepers before that?—come and go. And that's been true for computer hardware, too.

When we first began, we manufactured computers and keyboards because we had to—personal computers didn't really exist—in order to deliver our product. But we never made the mistake of believing that we were in the hardware business. We are in the business of producing and distributing the world's most accurate, reliable, comprehensive, up-to-the-second information and analysis. That has been our mission from Day 1, and it has never changed. The story and its message—not the medium that relays it—is what has always mattered to us.

To us, presentation is important, but substance is paramount. It may take too much time for the world to beat a path to your door if you lack a slick format or a lot of bells and whistles, but if you have the better mousetrap when the world gets there, then you are more likely to survive and thrive. Substituting "how" for "what" is a strategy many adopt, but that's not Bloomberg's plan. Sure, we want to provide every medium, but not as a goal per se. For us, it's a means, not an end. We think timely, accurate news stories that are well researched and well written will be in demand for a long time. Technology will continuously revolutionize distribution. But our product is content. It remains consistent.

Much of that content sits behind the media world's most expensive paywall. A subscription to Bloomberg costs about $22,000 a year. That works out to about $88 per work day. When customers complain that it's expensive, we tell them: If you can't make $88 a day using Bloomberg, you have a bigger problem than our bill.

The paywall doesn't stop us from distributing news globally. Our 3,000 journalists and analysts produce more than 5,000 stories every day. Some of the biggest stories are published on Bloomberg .com, which also features an opinion section offering commentary grounded in data—from the left, right, and middle.

While Bloomberg publishes and broadcasts in countries around the world, more and more people are using their phones to watch video. So we created the first global video news network streaming live and designed for mobile phones, called TicToc. Mobile phones are displacing TV and PC screens as vehicles for video—another example of hardware coming and going. And partnerships with social media platforms found on mobile phones give us access to an audience we might not otherwise reach. And since social media communication is two-way, we can learn more from our audience, which helps us break more stories, which benefits our customers.

Media distribution is constantly changing in ways that groups like the House/Senate Standing Committee of Correspondents and the Japanese Publishers and Editors Association members won't ever be able to anticipate.

*　　　*　　　*

When I first wrote this book, in the 1990s, it was clear to me that the transmission of all forms of media (including radio, television, and the Internet) would become increasingly personalized, allowing users to tailor their consumption of news—from sports and weather to stocks and politics—both around their interests and their availability. Here is how I saw it back then:

"Technology is beginning to allow each of us to listen to whatever we want, where and whenever we want it. The more people can specifically select what to hear, the more demands there will be for our diverse group of short 'wire service' reports, and the more value we'll get from our far-flung journalists generating multiple stories each day. Better radio means more Bloomberg.

"And TV? The only difference between television and radio is the amount of bandwidth needed for transmission. If we can tailor radio to suit you exactly, television is close behind. It's already got a name: Video on Demand, or VOD. At reasonable cost, it's a few years away, but it's coming fast. It's the infamous 'Killer Application' for the Internet: what you want, when and where, convenient and independent of others' demands."

And so it has been. We now live in an "on-demand" world where consumers are breaking free from the programming timetables set by broadcast executives.

What's been gained is clear: greater freedom and flexibility for the consumer, an indisputable benefit. What's been lost, however, is increasingly coming into focus. No more do Americans gather to watch "must-see TV" at a set hour on a set day. And no more do we discuss what the "big three" anchors say on the evening news. As the media landscape has fragmented, so has society. The less we have in common as media consumers, the harder it is to speak a common language around the biggest issues facing society.

There is no turning back. Media fragmentation will continue—and it will continue to bring benefits, by providing people with an ever-wider array of choices. But these choices will also pose challenges to social cohesion and national unity, by allowing like-minded people to construct their own realities, often influenced by conspiracy theories and partisan paranoia. And the harder it is to find and trust "real" news—news reported according to the highest standards of professional journalism, with facts backed by data and reporting free of partisan or ideological bias—the more valuable it will become, and the better Bloomberg will do.

The late New York Senator Daniel Patrick Moynihan once said, "You're entitled to your own opinions, but not your own facts." That didn't used to be a controversial statement, but that was before "alternative facts." Some elected officials just ignore data when it conflicts with their beliefs—or they attack the motives of the groups that produce the data.

This breakdown in an accepted basis of fact has coincided with the rise in partisan media and the segregation, by political beliefs, of the American public. Pundits talk past one another, and people gravitate to news outlets that will confirm their preexisting beliefs—and the more bombastic the pundits, the more popular they are, and the more money their employers make. For nearly all of history, from Socrates to Cronkite, news was written, organized, and disseminated by the educated and wealthy. People didn't always like the news, but they mostly believed what they were hearing and reading. They trusted news organizations to deliver facts and truths. That world is gone.

Today, anyone with a blog or social media account is a publisher, capable of disseminating news and views to millions of people. But what's real and what's fake? What's been fact-checked and what hasn't? What's gossip and what's been verified by multiple sources? For most of history, we didn't have to worry much about those questions. Today, millions of people still don't worry much about them—and that's a problem. People believe what they want to believe and block out, dismiss, or minimize conflicting evidence. Social scientists call it "confirmation bias," and it's one of the biggest challenges facing democratic societies.

*   *   *

Technology has disrupted every aspect of the media industry. So many newspapers and magazines have folded. Broadcast outlets are struggling to compete with on-demand streaming services, which have reduced their audience size and revenue per show.

What's required for success in these businesses? Why do some companies like Bloomberg, charging about $2,000 per month for electronically delivered information, keep growing when others can't keep customers even when charging only pennies—or nothing at all? Simple: *supply and demand*. If you're not providing something unique, you have no ability to impose charges. Most of what's available electronically on one website is available on many others simultaneously. Most broadcast TV programs are just copies of earlier or other successful shows. No uniqueness: *too much supply*. Hence the success of original shows on on-demand services.

Then there's the question of utility. Whether it's television sitcoms or hecklers online, most entertainment programming is only marginally more desirable than other alternatives or no programming at all. (The definition of entertainment is just that—nice but not necessary.) If there's no great value added, the public's smart enough to find alternatives like reading a book, watching something else, or going to bed. No great need: *low demand*. Much supply and little demand equals low prices.

But if you are selling something no one else has—say, breaking news stories or a heavyweight prize fight that's the talk of the town—buyers have little choice. Those who can't earn a living without having the information, or face their fellow sports fans without having watched, will pay whatever the provider asks. Pay-per-view for Mayweather vs. McGregor in 2017, which cost $100, made a fortune. Bloomberg never loses a customer to competitors that undercut our price. *Limited supply* and *great demand* equal high prices. The economist Adam Smith did know what he was talking about.

*　　　*　　　*

As happens time and time again in this world, distribution changes rapidly. Content evolves slowly with cultural advancement. Creative people become even more valuable as their reach increases over difficult venues. The more choice the reader/listener/viewer has, the more demand there'll be for Bloomberg's product—independent, quality journalism—and the more important it is to fight the credentials battles everywhere in the world where access is denied to the people's only true representative: the free, unfiltered, intelligent, investigatory press. And at a time when the free press is under attack by those in Washington and other capitals around the world, the fight isn't just about gaining credentials. It's about preserving democracy.

6

Money Talks

Textbook Multimedia

Every decade has its personalities. In the 1980s, people on Wall Street started appearing on society pages. All that money from bull markets and deregulation turned both the players and the scorekeepers of yields and P/E ratios into superstars. Louis Rukeyser made stock-picking a hot Friday night television show. When hostile takeovers and junk bonds became the rage, bond traders became "Masters of the Universe." My former partner, John Gutfreund, was anointed King of Wall Street. Until then, there hadn't even been a Prince. Michael Milken graced magazine covers by uprooting corporate boardrooms for better and worse from his perch in tony Beverly Hills. T. Boone Pickens, Carl Icahn, and Ron Perelman moved from page 41 to page 1. Gossip columnists Liz, Suzy, and Cindy pounced on a new set of glitterati: the financial moguls and their wives, who, with jewels and couture, moved from middle class to aristocracy at a speed only new money and a good PR firm could deliver. Even Ivan Boesky joined celebrity status when he said a little greed was good—just before he went to jail.

*   *   *

I was not yet part of all that. I wasn't in the newspapers. It had been years since I'd left Salomon and was quoted as the definitive expert on stock market direction. Entrepreneurs in the booming 1980s were

113

commonplace. My company, still using our initial catchy moniker, Innovative Market Systems, was small and virtually anonymous. Our product, the market data Terminal that we were selling to Merrill Lynch and called Market Master, could have been confused with a kitchen appliance. No one knew us. No one cared about me.

But by 1984, this was about to change. Those were the days when Ronald Reagan proved how marketable ideas could be when they were peddled with charisma. You needed a spokesperson for mass appeal. Consumers and the media identified products and policies with people who pitched them: Chrysler Corporation's comeback was built around Lee Iacocca, the person. Nike didn't just make sneakers, it pushed them with a mystique that could come only from Michael Jordan. To have the best mousetrap wasn't enough; success was delivered by people promotion.

If we were going to build our business, we, too, needed a personality. The obvious choice? Me. Our competitors' founders, Messrs. Dow, Jones, Reuter, Knight, and Ridder, were all dead. I, on the other hand, was alive and out making speeches and sales calls every day in city after city around the world, turning my name and work into a great weapon that others in the financial news and market data businesses couldn't match. And since I'd spent so much time demonstrating our product, people had begun to mentally interchange me with the Terminal. It was only a matter of time before traders and salespeople began referring to the black box on their desks as the Bloomberg. "Jack," some trader might say to his boss, "I'd like one of those, what do you call them? You know, the machines Mike Bloomberg sells, one of his 'Bloombergs.'"

When we had an opportunity to change company names (a potential trademark conflict arose with the Market Master name), I acquiesced to a decision the marketplace already had made. Henceforth, the product and the company itself would be "Bloomberg." As my friend Harvey Eisen said, "An ethnic name—and all the more memorable for it."

So, just as my old partner Billy Salomon ran Salomon Brothers as *his* company, with *his* name and *his* reputation on the line, now it would be me and my name at risk. I would become the Colonel Sanders of financial information services, the target for clever barbs from acerbic columnists, but simultaneously the one whose company and product would be on everyone's lips. I'd delegated day-to-day company management to trusted lieutenants so I was free to travel. I was good at giving presentations and, from my Salomon days, already had years of practice representing a company. As the owner, by definition, I spoke with authority. And to make good copy, I gave the press a colorful personality to focus on. I was Bloomberg—Bloomberg was money, and money talked. Perfect!

Of course, no one does it alone. Telling your own story is only part of getting great press. In the quest to get Bloomberg recognition, our competitors deserve some credit too. Reuters let it be known it was developing a new system its executives haughtily dubbed the "Bloomberg Killer." Journalists love such stories and gave it maximum play. (While there are advantages to running an eponymous business, sometimes there are unintended effects on your family. My young daughter Georgina burst into tears when she saw a framed article with the headline "Bloomberg Killer!" She thought that her Daddy was the target of assassins. "No, George, not me; just the company.") Henry Becher, a Dow Jones vice president, told *Forbes*, "You tell that fella [Bloomberg] I'm gonna get him." Thanks, we needed that. Then six large banks and brokers formed a market data consortium named the Electronic Joint Venture, or EJV, for short. It was positioned by their people, and by me every chance I got, as targeting us. Another Bloomberg Killer. Spare me.

Journalists are just like you and me—well, sort of. They try to do their jobs and get home to the kids. If you make filling inches and minutes easier for them, they'll help you every time. What more of a layup could our competitors create? David versus Goliath! Murder threats in computerland! Ganging up on the little guy! It's hard not to feel sorry for the old giants. No wonder we became everyone's favorite.

Today, new entrants to the market have tried to flip the script on us, positioning themselves as David to our Goliath. The press always loves the story: "The new Bloomberg Killer!" But at least so far, it always ends the same way. And as long as we continue to be driven by our forward-looking culture, instead of looking over our shoulders and following what the competition is doing, we'll be fine.

*   *   *

The next step to notoriety was Bloomberg's expansion into broadcasting. Radio and television were the furthest things from my mind at the end of 1991, when I got a call from Jon Fram, a fast-talking executive bearing a faint resemblance to Groucho Marx. Jon was an employee of the Financial News Network (FNN), a television channel whose parent was in bankruptcy. He told me I should buy FNN in its entirety. "Mike, what you really need to do is television. It will create synergies with everything else you're doing."

"What a dumb idea," I said, cutting him off. My operating principle has always been build, don't buy. Besides, what did we have to do with television?

"Look, just give me five minutes in your office. It won't cost you a cent and I can show you a great opportunity."

I've always had sympathy for a guy with an idea or two who doesn't take no for an answer. So Fram came over for a cup of coffee. A total waste of time. We weren't going to spend $200 million or whatever it took to buy TV distribution, no matter what he said. Dow Jones and General Electric could battle each other for that privilege. After a courtesy listen, I told Fram we had nothing further to talk about and made it clear he was leaving.

Fram called back the next day as if we were now old friends. This time he suggested that instead of buying a network, we needed someone in-house to develop audio and video programming at Bloomberg. Actually, he said we needed three people: himself; one of the on-air talents at FNN, Bob Leverone; and a young producer, Janet Weinberg. Once again, I said television and radio made no sense for Bloomberg and hung up the phone.

A few days passed, then I got another call from Fram. This time he rattled off a whole bunch of reasons why Bloomberg Financial Markets was made for TV. As I listened to a longer version of the pitch he'd made a few days earlier, it occurred to me, "One of us is stupid—and it isn't him!" So I hired the three of them that day, and we took our first steps into the world of sound and pictures.

First, we bought a New York City radio station, WNEW, 1130 Kh on the AM dial. For decades, WNEW had been the closest thing to your father's radio station. I guess that's one of the reasons it was for sale. Much to the annoyance of its loyal but dwindling listeners, we had no intention of playing Frank Sinatra and Bing Crosby into the millennium. The $13.5 million we paid (an amount that constituted one-third of its market value twelve months later) provided us with the station's broadcast license and a 50,000-watt transmitter —not their studios, not their record collection, not their people, not even their call letters. Our programming would be an extension of our other news coverage: politics, diplomacy, lifestyle, science, business, markets, the economy, war, and peace. We would not do sensationalism. Our general standard would be: If I wouldn't want my children listening to it, it's not suitable for us to broadcast. Those wanting "all crime, all the time," the staple of much news radio, could go elsewhere.

We started day one by ignoring the fundamentals of conventional radio: no murder and mayhem, no prima donnas. Gone were the breathless on-the-scene reporters stumbling over the usual banalities, the self-important producers, and the separate on-air anchor talents whose only talent was reading others' copy and whose egos never quite get enough massaging.

We built technology for both efficiency and creativity: Our people had capacities and capabilities the competition could only dream of. Instead of using traditional audiotapes, we were completely digital and computer-based from the beginning. Reporters recorded their voices on a PC in a manner little different from writing text. The computer then fed the sound to the transmitter at exactly the time we wanted each story to be heard. Moreover, we could use the same prerecorded piece in multiple shows. Independent radio stations that became affiliated with us around the world could insert discrete Bloomberg-supplied stories into their lineups, or take our programming in a different order from the one we broadcast in New York. They just told the computer which story they wanted, when, and where—and out it came. Recording segments into a computer also enabled reporters to write, voice, edit, produce, and introduce pieces on their own. They could even go from radio to television and back several times during the day, using almost the same scripts for both media.

Bloomberg was breaking and remaking all the rules. For the radio industry, we were more than a little strange. We were crazy. I liked that.

*   *   *

Our first venture into television was to produce a daily thirty-minute morning show, *Bloomberg Business News*, for Maryland Public Television. Syndicated throughout the United States, it was a hit from the beginning. While Bloomberg didn't make any money distributing over Public Broadcasting, as with our contributions to National Public Radio, we got notoriety, and the audience, which included our clients, appreciated it.

People often asked me why Bloomberg ventured into radio and TV. Was there some hidden motive—for example, an executive who moves his company closer to the golf club and then declares, "The labor force is better there"; or a mogul who buys a film company for its "communications value," when his secret urge is to associate with movie stars?

Other companies make money in radio and TV—lots of it. Why shouldn't we? We have the necessary information and the technical know-how, so broadcasting's an easy extension of what we do elsewhere. Radio and television provide our company with instant visibility. The media like nothing better than writing about themselves. The more exposure Bloomberg has to the Fourth Estate, the more they'll promote us to the general public. To reach potential customers who don't yet subscribe to our print products, radio and TV help us get our message through. The people who lease our Terminals are part of radio and television's masses. They need news while jogging, showering, driving, or sitting at home, and we've got to give them what they need. Last, our competitors do radio and TV. That doesn't require us to do it too, but the fact that we do shouldn't surprise anyone. For some time, we'd been offering letters, numbers, sound, and pictures over our Terminals to financial and investment professionals, selling a worldwide news service to newspapers, and publishing a magazine. Radio and television simply became other delivery mechanisms for the same content. Politicians, entrepreneurs, sports stars, celebrities, company officials, and business leaders interviewed for one Bloomberg media form get distribution via all the others as well. The more exposure the interviewees get, the happier they are to answer our questions, the more they make themselves available, the more product we have for all our ventures, and the more we can sell. Radio and TV enhance the appeal of our Terminal and our publishing—and vice versa.

Bloomberg offers two kinds of media: *broadcast* communications, where many consumers get the same information simultaneously; and *narrowcast* communications, for small groups. Most people use both daily. Many watch or hear the day's key sporting event live, or view a new movie when it's released. Many at the same time: broad consumer interest, as with traditional television or radio broadcasting. Some watch less popular programming or they view the popular content at a different time from everybody else: narrow demand, since there are very few receiving it at any one instant. Another narrowcast media form used daily is interactive electronic communications, involving only one party (you, via your smartphone, to and from a database) or two individuals (you, having a telephone conversation with a friend). Bloomberg, albeit with a serious focus, must deliver both kinds of "casting" or risk leaving its customers unsatisfied.

At Bloomberg, the most customized narrowcast product using the phone system is our Help Desk. Thousands of our customers call with requests for technical help each day. They all get to interact (the technical term for two people talking) with a human being. Depending on the day and time, the helper's accent may be different, but the service isn't. On the East Coast, call Bloomberg anytime. In local daytime, New York answers. Call late in the evening, and Singapore or Sydney will take that same call as if they were across the street. You don't know the difference. Call Hong Kong during their nighttime hours, and Frankfurt or São Paulo may have the honor of providing assistance. That's what internationalization is really about. That's what service is all about. That's what useful technology can do.

We also offer instantaneous help through the Terminal. Click HELP on the Terminal and get immediate access to the Global Customer Support team, which provides help on general inquiries, and our Analytics Help Desk, which provides expert support in the most complicated and arcane financial areas. Each team has more than 1,000 employees—and users can chat with them instantly to solve problems or find answers. Customer service isn't just a catchphrase for us. It's the whole shebang.

*   *   *

As a true capitalist, I've always believed in the markets' (rather than central planners') ability to make efficient selections. In many of our new ventures, we don't appoint a manager at the beginning. We simply throw everyone interested into the deep end of the pool, as it were, and stand back. It becomes obvious very quickly who the best "swimmers" are. We just watch who people go to for help and advice. And later, when we formalize a management appointment, no one's ever surprised.

The leverage we gain from employing creative people and letting them do their own thing is incredible. Our open office design encourages innovation, and our flat management structure guarantees a well-functioning meritocracy. Our New York headquarters has thirty floors, but everyone who enters the building, whether they are an employee or a visitor, takes an elevator to the sixth floor, to what we call the Link. That's where we have snacks and drinks, as well as standing tables where people can gather to chat or hold impromptu meetings. This way, everyone in the company—no matter what unit they're in—mixes and mingles. That helps information and ideas spread across units—"cross-pollination" in management lingo. So whether someone works in the basement or on the twenty-seventh floor, we all go to six to start and end our day—and very often, for a snack or soup in the middle of the day. Collaboration starts with dialogue. And dialogue depends, in no small part, on design.

Fortunately, for us, others do it differently. Typical company politics elsewhere stifle most free-thinking employees, impede collaboration, and discourage risk taking. The accounting oversight in most corporations prevents trying in a year the diverse creativity we encourage every day. Thank goodness. We've got enough competition as it is.

Of course, not everything we try works. One project was our year-and-a-half experiment publishing a monthly Sunday newspaper financial insert, *Bloomberg Personal*. The initial concept came from our salesforce, which thought large advertisers with an upscale focus would be interested. After listening to a presentation, I signed on immediately. It was a great idea, I thought.

Unfortunately, in the end, it really wasn't. We had planned on distributing through the most prestigious Sunday newspapers, but could not get many to carry us. (They thought of us as competition for ad sales rather than as a valuable supplement.) The resulting less attractive distribution meant fewer advertisers: We never sold more than one-fifth of the space we had budgeted. Then, when the cost of newsprint almost doubled, ensuring large losses every month, it was obvious we had a problem.

We had a dynamite team of writers, artists, and editors. They tinkered with the insert every issue, but it was hard to improve on something that was excellent from the start. The salespeople gave it all we could ask. Try as they might, we just couldn't make ends meet.

After eighteen months of overly optimistic ad sales projections and runaway costs, I pulled the plug, converting the concept into a subscription-based product. This would be our second magazine. We had the skills for this format in-house. We kept the title *Bloomberg Personal*, the creative people, and the salesforce from the Sunday newspaper insert. We just gave the content a different delivery form. It still meshed with our *Bloomberg Personal* website and our weekly *Bloomberg Personal* television show (TV stories relate to magazine articles relate to computer data). It still capitalized on our cross-branding policy of naming everything Bloomberg where recognition for any one product spills over onto all others. Contributions from people throughout our company were still incorporated, so we had the very best ideas. Technology we already had in place was still employed, giving us dramatic cost advantages. All vintage synergy. All vintage Bloomberg.

The new magazine was an instant success. We sold more ads for the first 100,000-circulation subscription version than we did for the last 7,000,000-circulation giveaway Sunday newspaper insert. And we went from paying others to distribute our publication to receiving subscription fees that covered our mailing and printing costs. Here a simple change of format saved the project. Generally though, deep pockets and a strong stomach help when trying new things. Few innovations are accepted right away. You must bring changes along slowly, improving them over time, building an audience with persistence and repetition. But with just as much resolve, when you find something not working, after giving it a reasonable time, you've got to take a deep breath, bite the bullet, and stop the carnage. The embarrassment of failure can't be allowed to kill the company.

The day we turned off the insert's life support, we made sure everyone worked extra late on the new venture, the subscription version of *Bloomberg Personal*. More important than any publication is our organization; we didn't want people to feel their jobs were in danger, or that they would be penalized for conceiving of or working on a "failure." At Bloomberg, all we ask is that they come up with as many new ideas as they can think of (no matter how "crazy"), and do their best on the projects we assign. If a concept is flawed, the blame and pain rest with me. The credit for whatever's right goes to them.

The success we had with *Bloomberg Personal* led us to create additional magazines, like *Bloomberg Markets*—and even to buy one: *Businessweek*. I've never been big on acquisitions. Why buy something when you can build it yourself? But *Businessweek* was a strong brand with a readership among executives and up-and-comers in a wide variety of industries. It was a great audience for us. Plus, it came cheap. McGraw-Hill put it on the block in the midst of the Great Recession. We bought it, rebranded it as *Bloomberg Businessweek*, brought it into the digital age, and injected new life into it by tapping into our deep pool of talented reporters and analysts—and of course the Terminal's wealth of data. It's been a big success.

*　　　*　　　*

When we bought the radio station, we hired ten or so radio reporters, all with at least a few years' experience, and gave them new-world tools never seen before. For the first few months, they struggled to become accustomed to our advanced proprietary technology, which in all fairness really didn't work very well. As usual at Bloomberg, even after installation we were still developing. These reporters were convinced it never would work. "This just isn't the way radio is done." "It's not possible." "You don't understand broadcasting." One reporter even wanted to bring his manual typewriter to work. Today, no one questions our use of such techniques. Is it accepted? Our people act like they reported news this way all their lives. They produce more great minutes of programming per capita than any other group. And, on balance, they get paid more too. They deserve it.

With what we've developed, we routinely do things that no one else would attempt even as a demonstration—from financial reporting to weather news. We began separately recording every temperature, every sky condition, every form of precipitation, all possible market moves, all sports scores: the basics of what you need to know in twenty seconds. Then, all day long between stories, a computer automatically checks with the National Weather Service and our Bloomberg Terminal and combined the appropriate prerecorded pieces: "At 3:12 p.m. outside, it's 50 degrees, cloudy skies with light rain, the Dow's up 3, and in baseball the Yankees lead the Orioles 6 to 5 in the 3rd." All this vital but routine information presented without a single person's involvement. Today, this is routine. Back then, it was revolutionary.

Think about having someone in front of a microphone twenty-four hours a day, seven days a week, in multiple cities where Bloomberg broadcasts, just doing routine stuff. It's mindless work—and expensive. The new economics of media don't let you stay in business if all your production is done manually. Nor will the people asked to do trivial tasks survive the boredom in this day and age. Industries other than media figured this out fifty years ago. We get more from each person by reducing the drudgery and enhancing creativity. Then we hire more people since each person now is a greater contributor. Work doesn't expand to fill capacity—opportunity does!

Eventually, large broadcasters began to do things our way and old-line practitioners felt threatened. "There's got to be something wrong," they told me. Why? "I don't know, that's just not the way it's always been done." (Where had I heard that before?) Technology makes our jobs different but more productive and more interesting. Technology frees us to do more creative work. And it has been an important force for freedom in the world.

Television, for instance, has been a great enabling technology, as powerful as Gutenberg's press. When television was first invented, politicians and social reformers screamed that the poor could never afford to own the "hardware" and would be denied equal access to ideas and educational opportunities. Well, everybody's got television today, including on their phones, and it hasn't exactly raised education levels. But it has proven to have other benefits.

Television brought down the Berlin Wall and, in turn, the whole Soviet Union by broadcasting ideas and pictures from the West that showed a better way to live. TV opened up China. Television has drawn people around the world closer together with pop music, comedy, and drama—and the serious kind of information that Bloomberg provides. Today's mobile phone technology is doing similar incredible things for society, while also presenting new challenges that society must confront—including increasing levels of partisan isolation and polarization, and all of the attendant difficulties that they produce for democracies, which we see playing out in Washington's extreme dysfunction.

*   *   *

Bloomberg was one of the first, if not the first, true multimedia companies. We use every available medium—the Terminal, television, print, radio, telephones, web, social media, podcasts—to deliver useful information to our customers. During Winkler's twenty-five years as editor-in-chief, Bloomberg became the only news organization to receive every top award in every form of news media, including the Pulitzer Prize, the Emmy for television, and the National Magazine Award. Today, all of our media is overseen by a single editor-in-chief, John Micklethwait. After returning to the company in 2014, I hired John away from running the *Economist* and put him charge of overseeing all of our news content—no matter what medium delivers it—as well as our research arm, Bloomberg Intelligence. Never before had all of these teams reported up to the same person. By breaking down internal barriers, we've been able to make better use of our expertise and enrich the quality of content that we can deliver. The value of clear and direct communication can never be underestimated.

Why use all media forms rather than focus on just one? What business are we in? Some companies declare themselves to be "in radio" or "in television" or "in newspapers," and so on. We have a greater vision. Bloomberg is in the business of giving its customers the information they need, no matter what that information is, where and when they need it, in whatever form is most appropriate. We don't shoehorn programs into less-than-optimal presentation formats, or deliver them at inappropriate times and places. With all methods at our disposal, we do better. We give our customers what they need, not just what we have. When there's a difference between the two, we create or adopt a new medium—we don't ask our customers to accept less.

At Bloomberg, just as our content is tailored to what's best for the story, it's also made for what suits the user best. What's our customer doing when he or she needs news? Where is he or she? One can't read print or watch television when taking a shower, jogging in the park, or driving to work. One can't read a whole in-depth report when one has only two minutes to get caught up. If one's traveling, one can't receive local content easily. By having all forms of media, we can focus on utility, not just our own commercial interests.

Most companies pay lip service to multimedia, but few actually deliver. They may make minority investments in each other to get "experience" in the field. But when they buy another firm, they usually run it separately from their own, with separate people, content, culture, and profit centers.

Some find external reasons for why they can't expand into new communications and technologies. Some blame the laws (prohibiting cross-ownership of TV and newspapers in the same market, or Federal Trade Commission anticompetition restrictions). Some blame the unions. (While there are exceptions, unions are not irrational. If management can make what it wants to work in the union members' interest, management will get the best possible ally.) Some cite analysts' demand for short-term results. (Investors generally aren't that stupid, and management should be worrying about its business, not its stock price. In these cases, the executives have no guts and no vision. They're afraid to take risks or accept responsibility. "Blame anyone else. I don't want to screw up before I retire" is the subtext.)

At Bloomberg, we don't resist multiple cross-product responsibility. We don't have problems blending short-term performance with long-term growth and development. And so far, we're not obsolete because the difference between those timid, failing companies and Bloomberg is people—from top to bottom.

7

Man vs. Machine

Technology: Politics and Promises

$\mathbf{M}$y education in the 1960s and 1970s era of horse-and-buggy computer systems formed the basis of what I did more than a decade later, when I brought the Bloomberg Terminal to financial desks worldwide. The hardware and software had advanced eons, but by today's standards, it was still incredibly primitive and basic. Yet what I discovered then about data management, and people management, still serves me well today: people have a need for information; and once confronted with it, they can exhibit bravery, jealousy, adventurousness, and fear of the new. No matter what systems we create in the next decades, these two statements will remain true.

My first experience using computers came early in my Salomon career. In the late 1960s, not too long after I was sorting slips of paper in the Purchase & Sales department and sharpening pencils for Connie and Ira in Utilities, I found myself staring at stacks of *Wall Street Journals*. They were our source of historical stock prices. Nearby, we had dozens of loose-leaf notebooks that contained public stock ownership lists. Piles of papers crammed with facts about the companies behind those securities littered our desks. Each night, a clerk would painstakingly go through the day's transactions and, like Bob Cratchit, manually update all of our trade history records.

This mid-twentieth-century information-gathering operation was in the tradition of the Dickensian quill pen nineteenth century, but it was the only way we could get the information we needed to conduct our trading business.

And we at Salomon weren't alone. Wall Street, up to its eaves in paper, was peopled by thousands of clerks who catalogued details by hand, year after year after year. Near the end of the "go-go" market of the 1960s, the paper deluge became so difficult to manage that the New York Stock Exchange shortened its workweek; for a while, it actually closed on Wednesdays. Many securities firms couldn't cope with the avalanche. In the end, Francis I. DuPont, McDonnell & Co., Hayden Stone, Goodbody & Co., and Loeb, Rhoades, were among the casualties brought down by too many forms.

As a Wall Streeter in the late 1960s, I experienced firsthand the paper-driven shakeout and the frustration of not having what you needed, accurately, easily, and when it was useful—not to mention the damage done when a cup of coffee spilled over your only copy of some important document. A solution existed, however. From what I had read, computers were good at storing information. You entered your data at night when the market was closed and you had lots of time. During the day, when you needed facts and numbers quickly, you hit a button and they would come back instantly. The computer makers told us that all we had to do was buy a machine for every desk, stick in the information—and voilà, problem solved.

I approached John Gutfreund and Billy Salomon about changing an information collection and retrieval process that hadn't been altered much since the firm was founded in 1911. "We should automate this," I said to them. "I'm told it won't take long or cost very much. We'll get instant access to the data we collect manually in all those books and even to those 'inaccessible' records stored on the company's mainframe computer."

My bosses were open enough to explore the idea. I was directed to Joe Lombard, the Salomon partner who ran our Boston office and who always found time to humor young kids with crazy ideas. After much discussion, I convinced him, and in turn the administrative partner, Vince Murphy, that computer workstations for the salespeople and traders were the future for investment firms. We already had a big IBM machine to handle bookkeeping, so extending its use to the trading floor made sense. One computer or another computer—they all seemed the same. We would just wire them together and get what we wanted. It would be simple and noncontroversial, and I would be doing Salomon a big favor. Or so I thought.

Murphy and Lombard went to the Executive Committee and made my case. While they probably never envisaged the producer/overseer data integration of today, they were way ahead in letting accounting information be used by those who generated it.

The answer from the committee wasn't what I expected. "They've agreed to let you do the automation," I was told. "But you can only work on it part-time so it doesn't get in the way of your main responsibilities, selling equities."

Fair enough. I didn't want to give up my block trading power base anyway. It just meant I now had to do my regular day job with stocks and simultaneously develop a computer system in the evenings. No sweat. What I hadn't counted on, though, was the committee's insistence that I create something for fixed income as well as equities. That directive shouldn't have surprised me actually, as bonds were Salomon's first love. Since the beginning of the century, Salomon Brothers' primary business had been making markets in government and corporate debt. During the First World War, Salomon Brothers & Hutzler was one of the biggest sellers of the Liberty Bonds that financed our military. Decades later, when there were still few firms in the fixed-income market, Salomon traders liked to say a bond wasn't worth its purchase price unless it received a bid from SB&H.

Nobody really knew how the computerization I was proposing would wind up affecting our business, nor how debt securities fit into my suggestions for automation. But Salomon traded bonds just like it traded stocks, and Salomon had bond data just as it had stock data. So why not build one simple system for everything?

*   *   *

What we eventually created at Salomon we called the "B Page" (no, B Page did not stand for Bloomberg Page, but I didn't mind if that's what people thought). When it finally worked, by coincidence, its very first message sent to all users was the announcement of my general partnership appointment after the December 1972 special partners' meeting in Billy's office.

It all began when the firm assigned me a junior computer programmer, Jessy Gerstel, who was willing to work nights in addition to his regular daytime job (for no additional pay). I bought Chinese food for the computer room operators, to get our software testing moved to the top of their queue. I bribed the data collection department with beer and pizza to gather and enter the securities information we needed. Together, in 1970, Jessy and I began building Salomon's initial online information system, parts of which survived for decades.

The project was not just to write some computer code. One task was to find the right display device to put in front of the traders and salespeople. (Desktop personal computers didn't exist in those days.) On its equity desks, Salomon already used one that flashed stock quotes, a machine called "Ultronics," manufactured by General Telephone & Electronics, later GTE Corporation and eventually, Verizon. But it was cumbersome, not suited for the bond markets, and technologically impossible to employ for the data distribution we contemplated.

The author, age 3.

At Boy Scout Camp in 1955. Always industrious, always prepared.

With his proud parents and sister looking on, Mike becomes an Eagle Scout.

As president of his class at Johns Hopkins (second from right), with the three other class officers, 1964.

On the trading floor at Salomon Brothers. Mike was Salomon's field commander for multimillion-dollar mega-stock trades, a role that required strong nerves, decisiveness, and quick thinking. *(Copyright © Edward Hausner, NYT Pictures)*

With the co-founders of his new company. Their friendship endures to this day. From left to right: Mike Bloomberg, Chuck Zegar, Tom Secunda, and Duncan MacMillan. *(Copyright © Fred R. Conrad, NYT Pictures)*

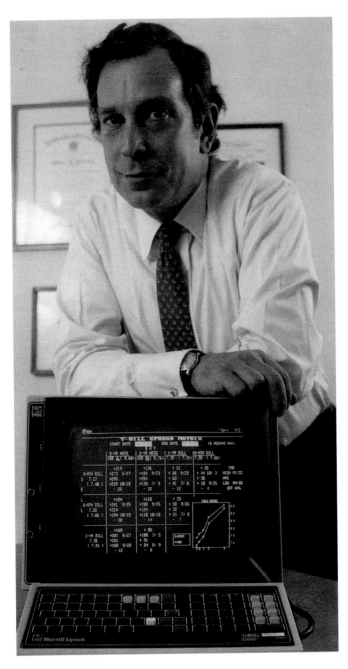

With an early version of the Terminal, 1986.

Being sworn into office on a Bible held by his mother, January 1, 2002. (*Courtesy of the City of New York*)

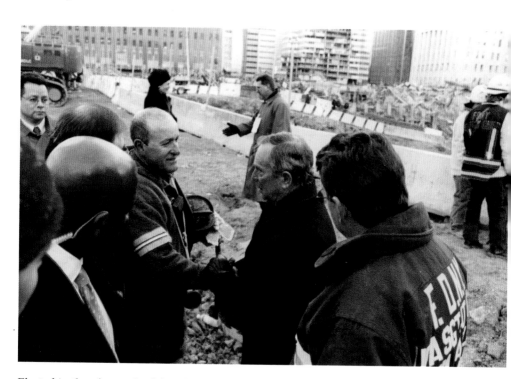

Elected in the aftermath of the 9/11 attacks, he visited emergency personnel on his first day in office on January 1, 2002. (*Courtesy of the City of New York*)

Piloting a police helicopter over Manhattan. Flying is one of Mike's favorite activities.
(*Courtesy of the City of New York*)

Receiving the endorsement of the United Brotherhood of Electrical Workers,
in Times Square, during his 2005 reelection campaign.

Campaigning for reelection, 2005.

Celebrating his 2005 reelection victory with Magic Johnson on election night.

At his desk in the City Hall Bullpen surrounded by his senior staff. Mike brought the company tradition of an open office to city government. (*Courtesy of the City of New York*)

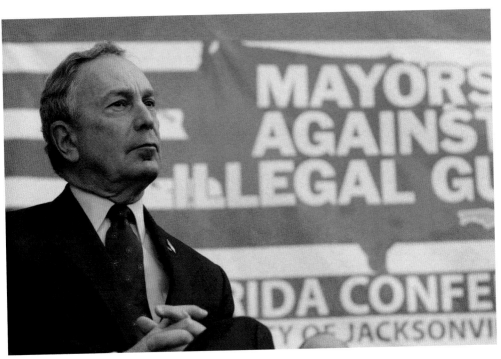

Mike and Boston Mayor Tom Menino co-founded a bipartisan coalition of mayors who supported common-sense gun laws. (*Courtesy of the City of New York*)

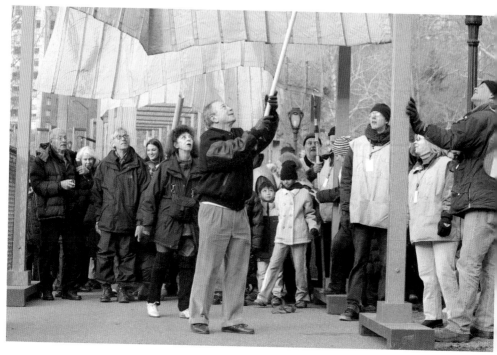

Mike supported more than 500 works of public art throughout the city as mayor, including Christo and Jeanne-Claude's *The Gates* in Central Park. (*Courtesy of the City of New York*)

Celebrating New Year's Eve at the annual ball drop in Times Square with Georgina Bloomberg, Diana Taylor, and a member of New York's Finest. (*Courtesy of the City of New York*)

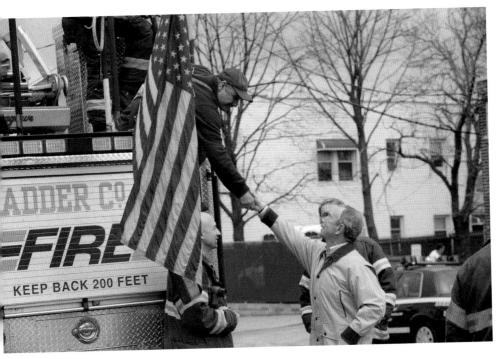

Thanking a firefighter in the Bronx. (*Courtesy of the City of New York*)

Appearing as a special guest on
The Oprah Winfrey Show in Central Park, 2009.
(*Courtesy of the City of New York*)

Commuting to City Hall. (*Courtesy of the City of New York*)

Escorting presidential candidates, Senators Barack Obama and John McCain, and Cindy McCain, through the World Trade Center site, September 11, 2008. (*Courtesy of the City of New York*)

With Bono, who is wearing a campaign button, "Irish for Mike." (*Courtesy of the City of New York*)

Painting a roof white with former Vice President Al Gore in 2009 to launch NYC Cool Roofs. (*Courtesy of the City of New York*)

On Governors Island in 2010, flanked by religious leaders, Mike defends a private developer's plan to build a mosque near the World Trade Center. (*Courtesy of the City of New York*)

Visiting elementary school students with Schools Chancellor Dennis Walcott. (*Courtesy of the City of New York*)

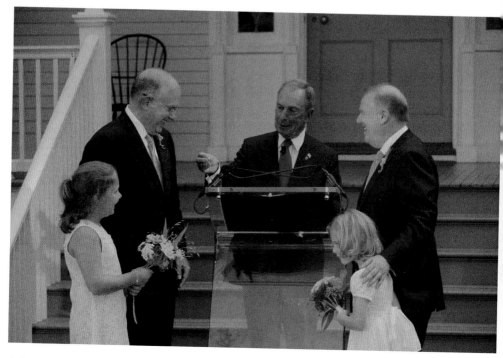

Officiating New York's first same-sex marriage in 2011 for aides Jonathan Mintz and John Feinblatt. (*Courtesy of the City of New York*)

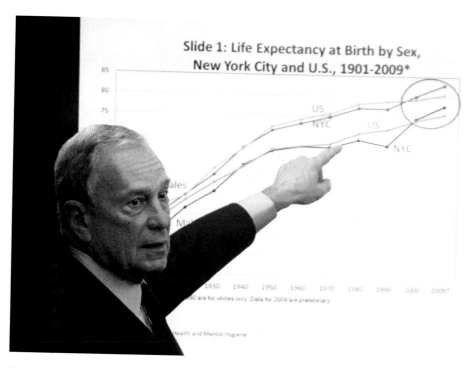

Discussing improvements in life expectancy at City Hall. (*Courtesy of the City of New York*)

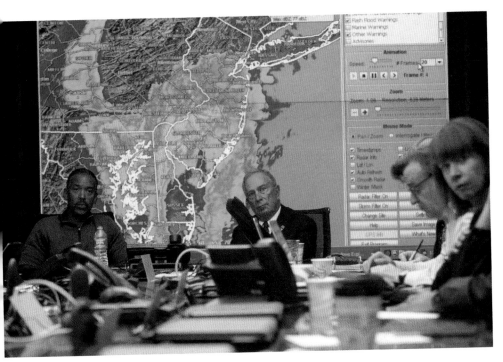

Senior staff meeting at New York City's Office of Emergency Management as Hurricane Sandy approaches, 2012. (*Courtesy of the City of New York*)

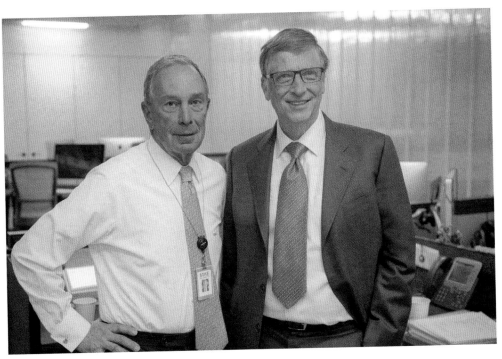

Meeting with Bill Gates at Bloomberg Philanthropies to discuss their work together on public health.

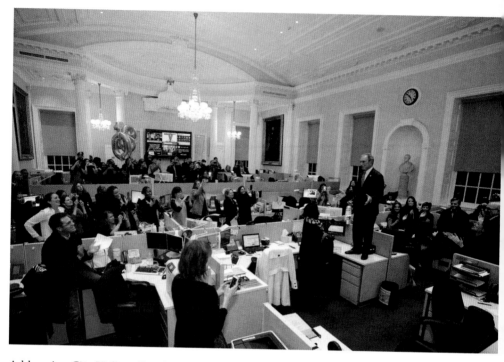

Addressing City Hall staff on his last day as mayor, December 31, 2013. (*Courtesy of the City of New York*)

At the Macy's Thanksgiving Day Parade balloon inflation, an annual tradition, with his daughter Georgina and grandson Jasper.

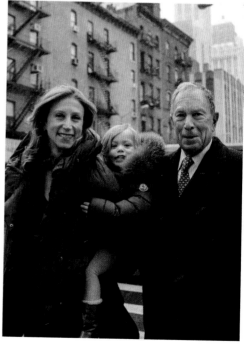

Walking his granddaughter, Zelda, to school with his daughter Emma.

With family—his sister Marjorie, daughter Emma, granddaughter Zelda, and grandniece Charlotte—and the mayors of Boston, Medford, and Cambridge at the Boston Museum of Science Education Center's dedication in honor of his parents, William and Charlotte.

Welcoming Indian Prime Minister Narendra Modi to New York City in January 2016.

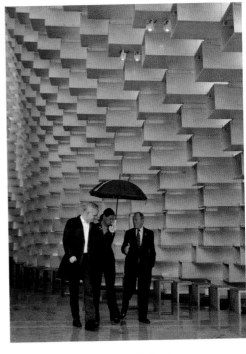

At London's Serpentine Galleries, where Mike has served as chairman.

Mike and Paris Mayor Anne Hidalgo convened more than 400 mayors for the first-ever Climate Summit for Local Leaders in 2015 in Paris.

Greeting Pope Francis at the 9/11 Memorial, 2015.

Visiting with London Mayor Sadiq Khan.

Discussing global trade in the Oval Office with President Obama and other leaders.

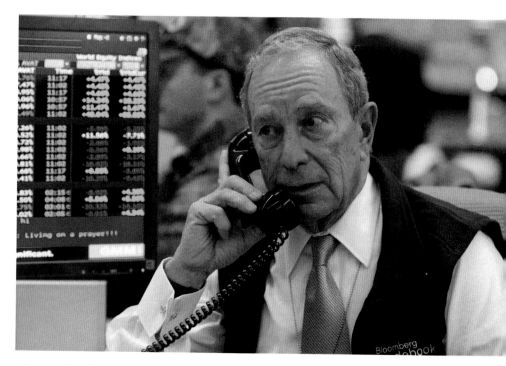

Working the phone on Bloomberg Tradebook Charity Day in 2016.

A 2017 press conference with French President Macron and Paris Mayor Hidalgo
to announce that Mike would help lead an effort to ensure the U.S. meets its commitment
under the Paris climate agreement.

With his daughters, Georgina (left) and Emma (right), at the celebration of the centenary
of the Johns Hopkins Bloomberg School of Public Health in 2017. The School was renamed
in 2001 in honor of Mike's contributions to public health.

Discussing his book, *Climate of Hope*, with co-author Carl Pope on *The Daily Show* with Trevor Noah.

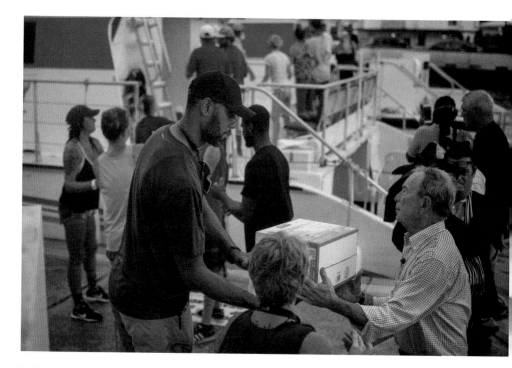

Delivering emergency aid supplies to the hurricane-devastated U.S. Virgin Islands with NBA star Tim Duncan in 2017.

With Alibaba founder Jack Ma at the inaugural Bloomberg Global Business Forum in 2017.

Addressing employees in London at Bloomberg's European headquarters, winner of the UK's prestigious prize for best new building.

Piloting a World War II-era Spitfire airplane over the fields of Cambridgeshire, England, in 2018.

Greeting UN Secretary-General António Guterres, who appointed him to be Special Envoy for Climate Action.

Fish tanks are a signature feature of the Bloomberg office environment. There are hundreds of saltwater and freshwater tanks in Bloomberg offices around the world.

These desktop terminals weren't general-purpose computers; they were just sophisticated successors to the old ticker tape. An electronic screen blinked the last sale, bid, and offer prices for stocks traded on all major U.S. stock exchanges. "We should remove Ultronics and install Quotrons," I told my bosses. Quotron was another brand of terminal just becoming popular, leased by a small, private California company. "Quotrons will work better and connect with our in-house computers directly from the desks. We'll have access to our trading records, be able to retrieve all the publicly available securities indicative data (ratings, call features, P/E ratios, and so on) instantly and effortlessly, and have our own electronic messaging system for fast, reliable internal communication."

I encountered one immediate nontechnical problem in switching terminals, though. The existing vendor, GTE Corporation, was Salomon's only investment banking client of note, and John Gutfreund's personal responsibility.

"You do what's right for your project and don't worry about the rest of the relationship," John said. "Each decision has to stand on its own."

Right on! Supporting one part of your business with another is fine. But not having the independent check of the marketplace is the easiest way I know to fool yourself. "Each tub to its own bottom" is a long-term protection I've always thought as valuable as any short-term cross-subsidization gains. By all means, use skills, data, technology, branding, people, processes, and so on, from elsewhere in your company—but make sure supply/demand can kill what people really don't want.

Another contentious task in building Salomon's in-house sales/ trading system was information control, exemplified by the selection of the central computer that the desktop Quotron terminals would access for pricing and security data. Until then, salespeople and traders were viewed as separate ("stand alone," in computerese) from the staff people, so no one cared what they used. Suddenly, however, these "producers" were about to interface the new desktop Quotrons to minicomputers and, in turn, to the big old bureaucracy-controlled IBM mainframe computers. For the first time, this path would let those generating the firm's data actually access and manipulate it themselves without the staff's oversight.

In those days, bureaucrats never let users have their "own" computers and, more importantly, access to the firm's internal information. The clerical guardians would be terminally (pardon the pun) threatened. If users could see the numbers, they might do something with them independently—thus diminishing their reliance on these gatekeepers. At Salomon, the staff went straight to Billy and John: "You can't let Bloomberg jeopardize the firm's books and records." Their real fears were that others would see how inefficient they really were, and the possibility that a new computer system could replace these mandarins. Naturally, they wanted no part of it.

Just as controversial as the issue of access was buying non-IBM equipment. This the support people considered worse than heresy, and they fought it with great tenacity. In those days, acquiring computers from small start-up technology companies was career-threatening for clerical and technical types at big organizations. The new technologies required less menial support and changed rote jobs into ones requiring thought. To protect their turf, those vulnerable pulled out all stops. Additional dissension was created by outsiders. With IBM's dominance of the data processing business at risk, its salespeople resorted to lashing out at all involved. They went so far as to often insinuate nefarious relationships between users' purchasing agents and minicomputer manufacturers. Questioning the financial health of mongrel manufacturers was their standard operating procedure. The possibility that others' offerings could fill the customers' needs more effectively and efficiently was never considered, which was why IBM eventually got into trouble. Not admitting your problems means you can't fix them. And when the money diverted to these minicomputer manufacturers became substantial, the battle really turned nasty.

Dealings with a large, single-source supplier are always difficult to end. The seller invariably has back-door channels into its customer, which it can use to thwart change. The buyer fears the uncertainty of the new and mentally tries justifying the known devil. People feel threatened by the normal reexamination of practices that vendor-switching invariably instigates: When forced to change one thing, the boss can rationalize other changes as well. The result? Everyone potentially affected bands together and fights viciously to protect their fiefdoms and livelihoods. Given the stakes, no tactic is out of bounds.

At age twenty-eight, I was finding out an eternal truth: Making change is difficult.

*   *   *

Not only was I fighting the front office/minicomputer, back office/ mainframe computer battle, but the interdepartmental computer wars as well. In every organization, each group wants its own automation needs filled independently. Not a competition for resources problem, or even an unwillingness to cooperate, but a "we need it now" issue. Separate development, being more limited, is much faster. Each department fights to go it alone, picks its own computers, writes its own programs, collects its own data, hires its own consultants.

In the short history of computing, this process has played out repeatedly. Users get tired of the formal information-processing department. Those faceless bureaucrats want justification for spending money on hardware ("How dare they?" declare the users). They insist on setting priorities other than "all of the above." ("I don't have time for this detail work. Just do everything!") They ask nasty questions like, "Where will the data come from?" "Who's going to enter it?" "What happens if the needs change?" "What will we do if the computer crashes?" In other words, the experts want to make you confront all the things that have to be faced but you want to avoid because there are no simple, inexpensive, quick, "clean" answers.

Then, along comes the snake-oil salesperson with the PC. The key letter is "P," for "personal." Suddenly, you go to a store and buy a computer on your credit card. You sit down and write simple stand-alone programs that actually do something without all those needless contingency plans the experts want to foist on you. You dispense with backup and expandability. You don't bother using common standards to incorporate others' needs later. You go it alone. Just as you suspected: Those bureaucrats knew nothing.

But a troubling thing happens after a while. Your business gets better and now your simple programs can't handle it. No problem. Hire a few unsupervised programmers to make the software more capable (read complex). Of course, fancier software means bigger computers. Bigger computers mean enhanced operating systems. Enhanced operating systems mean more crashes. Crashes? And we don't have backup? What were we thinking? Who was supervising those programmers? It's not my fault, you say. Blame the bureaucracy. They weren't part of the process? What now? And by the way, we want to merge our data with that of another department. What do you mean it's incompatible? Or that we can't borrow some parts from your computer when ours breaks? We're spending how much? What do I tell the CEO?

So the systems administrators start insisting on budgets and justification for hardware and software expenditures. Unfortunately, no one has yet repealed the laws of gravity or something for nothing. You never get more than you pay for. Usually, you get less. You want more computers? More expense. Will you get more computing? Sometimes.

The new bureaucrats start forcing security and backup and commonality. With the backing of the accountants, lawyers, and consultants, the days of go-it-alone go. All of a sudden, everyone's computers are linked together. The new fashion of the times becomes "networking." So common standards and coordinating software development are a necessity. Each connected PC suddenly can affect all the others in the network. Viruses have to be rooted out, excess traffic banned, database access restricted, staffs supervised, allocations made, hardware acquisitions centralized. Even priorities have to be set since once again there is more to do than the resources available can handle. You've come full circle.

The differences among the three stages of computer evolution are as much human as technical. From the old big mainframes with bureaucratic administration, to limited-function, distributed, "do everything yourself" processing using PCs without any coordination or control, to centrally managed networked resources, no one's ever satisfied. For users, it's politics, not engineering. For the vendors, it's sales. For me at Salomon Brothers, herding all the elephants, trying to get everyone to use a common platform and computer databases, it was a nightmare.

*   *   *

By 1970 at Salomon, we had gotten the salespeople and traders, the debt and equity people, the U.S. and overseas users, the producers and support staffs, to agree on what technology the whole company needed in order to compete. It was *the* great victory needed to build the B Page (and to build any software project, for that matter). And a lot harder to achieve at Salomon than later, when we started Bloomberg in 1981. With our own company, we didn't need to get anyone's acquiescence. We just did what we thought right and that's what our salespeople sold. But this wasn't possible where we were just another group of employees. There we had to ask, convince, or beg.

In the real world, unlike the one used in business school textbook cases, corporate administration often doesn't, and sometimes can't, commit to firmwide projects across specific departments or branches. Individual units may not want a centrally selected product or service that they had no voice in choosing. (Remember, the original thirteen colonies in North America started their revolt against England over the issue of taxation divorced from representation.) It might conflict with something they're already doing. Or cost more. Or take longer to be delivered. In the days of profit-center accounting, some departments may just refuse to pay a share no matter how necessary the product or service is to the long-term overall corporate operation and regardless of "central's" explicit directives.

Salomon back then was no exception. The Executive Committee told us to build for everyone. But it didn't order everyone to cooperate with us, to accept the system, or even to fund it. So we had to cajole, trade, mislead, do anything short of physical violence that worked to get it done. The users on one side of the trading room demanded X to go along. The ones on the other side demanded Y. Thus, we had to deliver (or at least promise to deliver) both X and Y (and for someone else, Z). For some, our incentive was a carrot; for some, it was a stick. With others, we just prayed they'd "die" before we did.

The B Page gave Salomon salespeople and traders proprietary information. But with so many different people having access within Salomon worldwide, security was a big issue. Even today, people who empower others with information face a daunting, no-win task. The only perfect protection for data is to give no one anything. And that's the traditional information-processing management's instinct. But as more and more businesses and functions become data-dependent, those in control have no choice. They are forced to open up, albeit reluctantly.

A big part of our development job at Salomon was information limitation: deciding who had the right to the data as opposed to who had the need. This was exacerbated by our determination to give users the same capabilities overseas as domestically. In those days, letting foreign telephone access into a local office computer was truly revolutionary. Anyone wishing to sidetrack a project could always raise myriad unprovable and irrefutable potential security breaches.

Should one office see business done by another? Should the salespeople see the eventual profit or loss from opportunities they have brought in? Or the trader see a recap of all business transacted firmwide with a specific salesperson's account? These were all policy rather than computer issues that we resolved daily while developing the B Page. And then we re-resolved them the next day when the issue was raised by someone else—invariably, in the opposite direction. And the day after, the same again. Each revision required changes to line after line of computer software. Then the users asked what took so long to deliver the system.

*   *   *

Producing even a small computer program with a reasonable number of "what-if" contingency plans is a decent-size undertaking, with costs and delays. Settling the operational issues is often even tougher. What happens if the software crashes, the hardware fails, or the input data contain errors? Does business stop? Do we close our doors? Writing the computer code isn't the problem. It's identifying possibilities and getting broad concurrence from all users as to what we want the computer to do, every time—and what is an acceptable definition of "every time"? It's convincing people to ask for a reasonable amount of functionality in a manageable set of likely circumstances, and then keeping them from changing their minds during the development process. It's deciding how the computer fits into the rest of your world. The infamous "man-machine interface": That's what's hard.

Much of my battle at Salomon was forcing acceptance of common systems for different products, for debt and equity, for government bonds and for corporate ones, in dollar-denominated areas and in foreign currency ones. Computers like consistency, and when the problem to solve is "show risk across all securities issued by a given company," something has to be used to tie them together. At Salomon, because I insisted on a common syntax (the sequence of keystrokes one enters to ask a question) that applied to all products, calculations written for one area worked everywhere. Then, by convincing the bond traders to use common identifiers, such as T for bonds of American Telephone & Telegraph Company (the same symbol used for the company's stock on the New York Stock Exchange) instead of a historical hodgepodge (TEL, ATT, AT&T, and so on), data from all parts of the company were able to be combined in new and useful ways. Sound like small accomplishments? Try getting a bunch of securities traders to agree on anything! Each always has a million reasons why something should be customized. Of course, if they all got their own way, the company would have collapsed.

Similarly with dates. In America, we write month, day, year. In Europe, it's day, month, year. Is that important? What date is 3/5? March 5th or May 3rd? With numbers, in the United States, we put commas after every three digits going to the left of the decimal point. In many parts of the world, the convention is to use commas rather than periods or "noughts," and in other parts, the decimal point is a comma. That's fine, but we needed one standard globally. What's domestic and what's foreign? Is it 3:00 p.m. or 1500 hours? That dollar-denominated security is in which dollars (U.S., Hong Kong, Canadian, Australian, Singaporian, New Zealand, and so on)? Once again, human issues need standardization to make technology work. Doing business around the world may sound romantic. It may even be lucrative. It's certainly complex.

*   *   *

A rule of thumb in software is that 90 percent of the costs go into building the last 10 percent of the functionality. Successful design and implementation demand the political skills and courage to reconcile the 100 percent specification needed for approval with the slightly-less-deliverables that are possible in the real world. As I found out at Salomon and again with the Bloomberg Terminal, you promise users everything; then you build what you can and what you think they need. It's the only successful strategy for a systems developer. People always say, "I can't do my job without that last little bit." But that last little bit is not only so hard to build, it's invariably so complex to use that no one ever does. Making all settle for a touch less is the job. Management has to reconcile the conflicts between stated needs and what can be delivered, and when that's not possible, to make the decision for everyone, a priori. Companies in the end need direction, not discussion.

Back then, and now, I've always insisted on building a simple "do a few things" version of software up front. Most people are terrible at understanding and enunciating what they actually do day in and day out, and on what basis they make decisions. They're even worse at defining what tools they would use in the future. But if you give them something they can see and touch, then both they and you can get experience as to a program's utility and applicability, or at least have a common basis for enhancements. And chances are, they'll use what you give them up front, forget about anything else that was requested earlier, and think you're a hero for delivering "what they always wanted."

Fortunately, our competitors never work this way. They study. They plan. They work toward getting consensus and approval and closure. They try to define it all up front, even specifying the end game from the beginning. Ridiculous! You can do a six-month software project in twelve months. You can probably do a twelve-month project in two years. You cannot do a two-year project, ever. Humans need to see results in time frames they can handle.

A project takes too long when it consumes so much time to build that no one remembers who requested it, what specifically was ordered, what its purpose was, or even whatever happened to that since-departed person who initiated all this.

At Salomon, we promised everything and set out to build less, but something we could install before new management took over with less enthusiasm for our project. In software, you almost never deliver to the person who ordered it: Because of the time it takes to build and every organization's turnover at the top, you usually deliver to a successor. Besides, who really remembers what he or she asked for a year ago? And who is in a business that still needs what was requested twelve months earlier?

Often, to solve this political problem, managements buy outside services rather than build their own software in-house. This avoids facing the users' demands head-on and, they think, dramatically shortens the time to delivery. (Since we're in the business of providing "turnkey solutions," we obviously think this is a great idea.) But many times, since managements buy technology still under development or insist on radical customization, they're buying essentially a totally new, untried product. The risks and delays turn out to be identical no matter who employs the programmers. This outsourcing strategy often fails for two additional reasons. Traditionally, vendors get paid when they deliver, not when it works. What you order is seldom what you get, and after the check clears, you have little recourse. Then, as with building in-house, once you've already waited for delivery, projected delays always appear shorter than the time it would take to start over.

I've always thought that buyers who "outsource" should find a way to try products as they'll actually use them before they pay the bill and even, if possible, before giving a firm order. The test version, the simulation, the still-in-development scenario is not something I'm comfortable acquiring. The risks attendant with developing technology I think properly belong to the manufacturer or software writer. They get the profits if it works; they should take the grief if it doesn't. It's their business; don't make it yours. My rule is: See it work exactly the way you'll use it (same volume, environment, time of day, and so on) or don't buy it! Demand goods, not promises. And that's exactly what we offer our customers. When we develop new products, we build and deliver a practical working model of what the client can actually use, and then through an iterative development process, we add features and functions that make the product outstanding. In management-speak, this is called MVP: minimal viable product. But for customers, it just means: "Buy what's deliverable, not what could be."

That's what Merrill did with us They had no obligation to take our product until it performed, we guaranteed delivery before the time they could start developing it themselves, and they understood that we would continue to improve it as they used it. I wish all buyers would adopt this practice. Competitors are always contrasting our products with what they say they'll deliver later on. They will do more, better, faster, cheaper, easier, or so they promise. I love the comparison. They compare Bloomberg, an operating F18 jet fighter, with their still-being-developed "witch on a broomstick." Their plane will go faster, fly higher, turn quicker, need less maintenance, and so on, than ours—when they build it. Sure! Anything they say! But our system works today as compared to their laundry list of "pie-in-the-sky" impractical things for tomorrow. It's our off-the-shelf product versus their business plan, their press release. I'll never understand why we don't get 100 percent of everyone's business.

Writing software and implementing data-processing systems isn't just a technical challenge. It takes compromise: Requests are often mutually exclusive. It requires flexibility: Things in practice are invariably different from the plan, and they change with time. It demands imagination: Envisaging future requirements and potential uses is hard to do, yet, because of long development times, that's what you must build for. It also calls for strength: With changing requirements and often the political problem of being a cost center without revenue, staying the course is a challenge. Lastly, it takes leadership: The great system advances are pushed on users, not demanded by them. You can't run governments or companies successfully by polling or asking for suggestions. Someone must have a vision and take others along, not the reverse.

*   *   *

While our Salomon B Page development grew, we delegated responsibilities and included more people. It really became a group effort. As with all projects, those who started it got absorbed by those who took it to the next stage. Some of the people we hired were extraordinarily talented. All worked exceptionally hard. And what we delivered was truly revolutionary. A version of the computer system we built in the early 1970s was still in use at Salomon twenty-five years later—and even then, it was still better than most internally developed market data retrieval and analytical systems being installed at other securities firms. The reason was teamwork.

A manager's primary job is to get those he or she supervises to work together—particularly with technology, where many contribute to any single project. Back at Salomon, and today at Bloomberg, we do that. The resulting cooperation, more than anything, was and is responsible for our ability to deliver useful things. I once sent out an announcement to all the programmers that, henceforth, no one would have a title. I've always thought titles are disruptive at best. They separate, create class distinctions, and inhibit communications. If you don't get a title, you quit. If you do get one, you start thinking other firms may want to pay you more, now that you're officially recognized as superior to what you were previously.

The manure hit the proverbial fan as soon as I did it. The Salomon personnel department manager went ballistic. How could we manage without constantly reminding everyone who they were inferior to? He started screaming that I was out of control—to me, to Gutfreund, and particularly to my nemesis, the new Executive Committee member Dick Rosenthal. People already possessing titles complained. Those hoping to get them soon did too (but a little less strenuously). The results of the policy change? There was no increase in personnel turnover. People worked together better than before.

Another software development practice I started at Salomon (and apply at Bloomberg today) was to insist on an explanation from the programmers of what they were trying to do before I let them do it. I don't have as much technical expertise as even a junior computer whiz, but that's the programmers' problem. They've got to describe it to me in language I can understand. Again and again, if that's what it takes. Describing the "how and when" forces them to face all those things they initially glossed over when they thought about the "what"—utility, cost, maintenance, data quality, redundancy, training, cooperation. They have to satisfy me, a novice.

The information retrieval system we built at Salomon in the early 1970s was rudimentary by later standards, but it made Salomon more productive versus its competitors, and more knowledgeable than its customers. It was designed for internal use only—what was needed then. The last thing Salomon wanted to do in those days was give clients enhanced capabilities and more accurate data. The end of fixed commissions in 1975 had reduced the profit margins in the industry's traditional business. Rather than acting as the customers' agent, firms were making the big money in arbitrage and trading strategies, for which buy-side clients were really competitors. Trading came to rely more on mathematical skills and less on guts. For this, Salomon needed an edge. And that's exactly what having the only useful data retrieval and analytical tool in the industry gave them in the 1970s. With the closed proprietary system we built, Salomon got for a period what no one else had.

Salomon jumped way ahead, and stayed that way for a decade. In a sense, for ten years, when Salomon went to a knife fight, it carried a gun.

By the early 1980s, though, the financial world turned topsy-turvy, in part because the Wall Street broker/dealers lost exclusive control of the information and the ability to manipulate it. Services such as the Bloomberg Terminal eventually became the great levelers, giving everyone access to the same facts and same capabilities. What would have happened had I been allowed to stay at Salomon after the Phibro deal? Would we have stayed ahead of the competition? Would we have given our clients a proprietary B Page to lock them in? Might internal controls have prevented Salomon's Treasury Bond trading scandal in 1991? Would it have stopped the buy side from getting tools to even the fight with the sell side? All useless conjecture (but fun to speculate on nevertheless).

In 1981, after I left Salomon, my successor there told his subordinates that Bloomberg had been wrong. Systems' job was not to give the organization the support it needed. Rather, Systems had to "reduce expectations." (I couldn't make this stuff up, folks!) If he could cut the demand for services, he'd have less of a problem supplying them, he argued. In turn, he'd have less maintenance to provide and lower depreciation expense to explain away, and require fewer difficult-to-manage computer programmers. All this would mean fewer headaches for management in resolving conflicting needs, making unpopular resource allocation decisions, and sometimes having to say "no" to powerful and demanding revenue producers. Of course, if he cut back expectations entirely, the firm wouldn't need him either, but he didn't plan to carry it that far.

While with a lower profile he did manage to survive for a number of years, Salomon almost didn't. In the late 1980s and early 1990s, tragically, Salomon went from having a distinct lead in automation support to being an also-ran. Just when its business required more computerized risk control; right when the competitive landscape for the first time required broker/dealers to provide clients with proprietary technical services or have independents like Bloomberg control the relationship with their clients; simultaneously with Salomon expanding into new markets and more sophisticated products requiring complex analytics—getting less computer support almost bankrupted the firm.

Given that the head of technology can have enormous impact on a company's success, I've always been amazed at who gets picked for this job. Traditionally, the lucky candidate was rarely considered for other jobs in the management structure—typically someone whose career elsewhere in the company was floundering (as was the case with me). Rarely was anyone destined for greater things rotated through this position to gain broader experiences. Given the function's importance, difficulty, and potential for greatness or disaster, you'd have thought the CEO would be smarter in his or her selections. Fortunately, that has changed, at least in some companies.

Systems Areas, Information Processing Departments, Computer Support Divisions—or whatever moniker is fashionable at the time—are typically run by technicians, people whose chief skills are in understanding the internal mechanics of computer hardware. Worse, these senior people have "high-level duties" that invariably keep them from the dirty work of setting priorities, ensuring the suitability of new developments, and giving the common worker incentives. But success requires knowing the company's products, competitive position, and internal workings. That knowledge, along with leadership, business acumen, and hands-on management, is what's needed.

Having the ability to select, manage, and motivate people is the job. Driving the development and operations of support services is the task. Having "the vision thing" is the mission. Companies need people with imagination and energy, particularly with regard to technology. Unbridled enthusiasm and belief that anything's possible may not be the real world, but trying things with low probabilities of success and big payoffs is a lot better than the alternatives. These CIOs have to stay ahead of the curve and take the rest of the organization along. Following or doing the same old thing won't do!

*   *   *

The computerization of Wall Street hasn't always produced the results everyone predicted. Salomon got an advantage with the superior decision-support technology we built, but its earnings were no better than its competitors'. Would Salomon have been worse off without such support? Or do increased capabilities encourage more risky behavior and thus poorer performance? The same questions apply to the entire securities industry. It installed computers to handle transaction processing more efficiently and reduce risk. The volume of shares traded went up, the commission rates per share traded went down, and industry employment grew. But the industry's increases in profits came almost exclusively from new, manually processed products, not the ones the computer helped. And as trading-fraud fiasco after fiasco showed, the risk controls computers promised to bring to the Street never materialized for the poorly run firms. Technology, it turned out, was no substitute for management.

Receiving fewer benefits from computers than promised is not a phenomenon particular to Wall Street. Every parent wants his or her child to be computer literate. People tend to think that those without laptops and tablets in elementary school are doomed to a life of poverty and illiteracy, so we spend millions to equip classrooms with Internet access and state-of-the-art computers. The results have been underwhelming. Too often, technology is used as an excuse not to teach how to think and how to work with others.

Dollars are limited and fungible. Sending them to Silicon Valley means less for teacher compensation (worse instruction) and school construction (larger class sizes).

I've never believed that we need computers in every classroom in the early grades. We should focus on teaching the basic skills of reading, writing, arithmetic, logic, concentration, cooperation, hard work, and leadership. Interaction with a sympathetic, understanding teacher can't be automated, nor can their teaching of the "three Rs." For young children, it's still the best way to teach the basics. It's also the only way to teach the social skills needed to survive in society .

Today, too many of our young people are not learning these basic essentials. About 40 percent of teenagers do not enter college immediately after high school. Some of them graduate from high school. Others don't make it that far. But whether or not they graduate, we haven't given them the skills and training they need to begin a career, and they pay for that for the rest of their lives, in limited opportunities and lost earnings.

At the same time, too many kids who do go to college aren't prepared to succeed there. Partly as a result, the national graduation rate for four-year colleges is only 40 percent. Even after six years, only 60 percent of students who entered graduate. So on the one hand, as evidenced by the low college graduation rate, we are not preparing high school graduates for success in college. And on the other, we effectively treat non-college-bound students as second-class citizens, giving them no preparation for their next steps in life. Bloomberg Philanthropies is working on both of these challenges, and our experience in New York City—where we raised high school graduation and college readiness rates and opened many new schools that focus on career education—shows that progress on both really is possible.

*   *   *

So, from Salomon in 1970 to today, where has technology taken us? One Silicon Valley entrepreneur said, "We wanted flying cars, instead we got 140 characters." It's true that pundits who envisioned computers completely revolutionizing our way of life were wrong. But they weren't all wrong—and cars are a good example.

Today's automobile is a great demonstration of substance over form. A driver put in a time capsule forty years ago could return and drive a brand-new car cross-country without a single instruction. In fact, he or she needs to know less than ever to do so. The steering wheel, brake, and accelerator haven't changed to the eye, nor has how one "interfaces" with them. But no longer does one have to shift gears; computers are all over the engine giving increased efficiency; materials and fuel are used that didn't exist two decades ago; the brakes are computer-controlled so you don't skid; the doors automatically lock when the car hits fifteen miles per hour; the radio mutes when the phone rings; the lights dim and brighten based on oncoming traffic and ambient light; the speakers beep when you approach another large object; and so on. Cars today are more silicon than steel. We don't yet have flying cars, but autonomous ones are already arriving.

The forecasters were right in the sense that matters. We've computerized our automobiles and they're simpler, safer, and more reliable than ever before, thanks to using these devices. The experts simply never envisioned what computers would look like, where they'd go, and what they'd do. The acceptance of technological consumer products depends more on their ability to surreptitiously invade our lives—as they have in so many ways, as the Internet of things infiltrates more and more products and devices in the home—than on their whiz-bang utility. Humans are loath to change and nervous about anything difficult to understand. More capabilities, better efficiency, increased reliability, fewer controls—all are benefits buyers understand and will pay for. They won't accept more complexity, change for change's sake, or so many options that no normal person could possibly remember them without the multilanguage, tiny-print, incomprehensible instruction book on hand. That was part of the genius of the iPhone—it came with no instruction booklet. Apple's message was: The most sophisticated handheld personal computer ever created is intuitively simple and requires no manual.

The junkyards are littered with examples of technology that were introduced simply to highlight the designer's brilliance but ignored the customer's capabilities and needs. And some successful product acceptance has come in spite of its designer's great intellect. Certain well-used innovations don't get employed for the purpose they were produced. When VCRs were popular, most people used them only to play prerecorded tapes, when its original objective was to time-shift over-the-air or cable-delivered TV. That finally became more common with the DVR function on TVs, which is as simple as pressing a button or two. Or, just tell Google or Amazon's Alexa to do it.

With technology and its fast-paced introduction, the key questions are more important than ever: What is the problem? How valuable is the solution? Can we provide it profitably? Where will our competition come from? When I started out with computers, I believed what the manufacturers' promotional materials promised. I grew into a skeptical, nontrusting cynic, but one who believes more than most in the potential technology has to improve our lives. What I learned on the journey was that we are all humans, and technology exists to serve us, not the reverse. The challenge is to resolve people issues, not software ones.

8

Management 101

The Bloomberg Way

W hen you start a company, every obstacle is a challenge. Everyone's out to get you: That's just the way it is, and you work around it. What's available to the big guys isn't available to you, like bank credit. That's an advantage; you develop a low-cost product. What if you can't find anyone to share your vision? Great. When your ship comes in, you won't have any competition. Are the bureaucrats driving you crazy? Fantastic. You'll neutralize them by playing them against one another. Is your company so small you have to do everything yourself? Wait until you're so big you can't. That's worse. I know.

At Bloomberg, we had a major obstacle to overcome after only five years in business: history. As part of our second Terminal sale to Merrill Lynch, we had made an agreement that was limiting our expansion. Merrill had leased more than a thousand of our machines at $1,000 each per month. Simultaneously, they paid $30 million for 30 percent of Bloomberg's equity. We, in turn, agreed not to sell products for five years to their fourteen major competitors (Bankers Trust New York Corp.; Bear, Stearns & Co.; Citicorp; Daiwa Securities Corp.; Drexel Burnham Lambert & Co.; E.F. Hutton & Co.; First Boston Corp.; Goldman Sachs & Co.; J.P. Morgan & Co.; Kidder Peabody & Co.; Lehman Brothers & Co.; Morgan Stanley & Co.; Nomura & Co.; and Salomon Brothers Inc.).

This restrictive term had three more years to run in 1988 when I went to see Merrill's president, Dan Tully. Merrill was enjoying the exclusivity it had negotiated. It gave Merrill the unique conduit to the world's central banks, pension funds, insurance companies, and investment managers that increased Merrill's ability to capture institutional business. Additionally, by using our risk management and trade-processing software, it was saving tens of millions of dollars each year in reduced trading losses and lower clerical expenses. Needless to say, the heads of each of Merrill's units (who were paid on their own department's performance) wanted this competitive advantage to continue.

Tully, on the other hand, had to take a broader view. In addition to the tactical advantages the exclusivity gave Merrill, he had to consider its investment in Bloomberg as a company. That investment would be worth a lot more if everyone could buy Bloomberg subscriptions. And it wasn't just added value arising from the extra Terminals the fourteen embargoed firms would rent. A system used by all financial companies could essentially become an exchange. If everyone had access, then Merrill would have a stake in something much bigger than just a parochial supplier.

After almost a year of discussion, Dan acquiesced to our request to be released from the exclusivity clause. He thought at that point that Merrill had such a significant edge in experience with the Bloomberg Terminal, it would take these other firms years to appreciate the benefits Bloomberg provided in cost reduction and improved controls, to order the Terminals and have them installed, and to train their employees in their use. In the meantime, as long as everyone could participate, institutional clients would come to accept Bloomberg as their preferred conduit to Wall Street. So, for years, even though Merrill wouldn't technically have exclusivity, it would have unique contacts the others could only dream of.

Given the way it turned out, Tully showed himself a master strategist. Three of the restricted firms went out of business

(Drexel, Hutton, and Kidder). The Japanese firms (Daiwa and Nomura) imploded as their penetration of world markets failed to materialize. And the three banks (Bankers Trust, Citicorp, and J.P. Morgan) didn't take over the securities business the way conventional wisdom of the mid-1980s had predicted they would. In the meantime, Merrill kept growing and dominating in every area where it entrusted its processing to Bloomberg, particularly compared to the remaining six formerly embargoed brokerage firms.

*　　　*　　　*

By the late 1980s, Bloomberg had established offices in New York, London, Sydney, and Tokyo, with more than five thousand customers spread over forty countries. We were growing 25 to 30 percent annually and adding staff almost as fast as our business enlarged. This presented new challenges in running our organization.

Companies expanding at that rate are particularly vulnerable to supervisory gridlock and loss of control. Often, the original managers' abilities fall short, as administrative and leadership skills, compared to product knowledge, become key. Letting go and delegating sometimes proves impossible, often with disastrous consequences.

I was, of course, there in the beginning; I too think I can do everything better than anyone else. I believe my design instinct, sales savvy, and management skills are the best around. Still, my ego does allow for the remote possibility that someone might be as good at one or two little things. I've admitted there's a slim chance that ideas coming from others could be valuable as well. In other words, I'm the same as every other entrepreneur. But at least I know what I don't know.

Over the years, as Bloomberg grew, I managed to delegate the running of the established parts of Bloomberg and focus on our new projects. No longer would I make most decisions day to day. My function became more about encouraging others, soliciting new ideas from everyone ("Let's develop a real estate product"), and making sure we allocate resources to new, innovative, and risky development projects ("We need to do something in insurance"). Still today, my job is to ensure that new products come alive at Bloomberg and to integrate them with the rest of our system ("Let's go after the energy market"). I direct customer feedback to the appropriate parties and see that it gets listened to ("What about a corporate-loan database?"). And once a new project is going—once I've added my ten cents—I make sure that we put people in charge who can take it to the next level—and that the rest of us (including me) leave them alone for a while to do their own thing.

At the beginning, I sat with the programmers and watched, learned, and oversaw. Later, I did the same with the salesforce. Then service people got much of my time. At one point, I made myriad phone calls each day to the data-collection group. But as each area developed its own experienced and talented supervisors (almost all our management is "homegrown"), my involvement with that group diminished. Partly, it was a conscious effort to avoid diluting their authority. To some extent, it was just the lack of time that prevented me from micromanaging. Mostly though, it was that the people we put in charge didn't need me anymore. They were the new guys, and as *Forbes* magazine claims I said in the 1990s, "The new guy can do it better." I still believe that.

One growth impediment I still wrestle with personally, however, is our chronic office space problem. Every time we've leased real estate, it's proven to be too small for our needs. Our crowding shows my inability to plan for our rate of growth, but it's also a safety valve: Space available puts a limit on how many people we can hire, and, God forbid, should sales slow, keeps the overhead in check. One time, though, we were so out of space in our New York sales office, a carpenter came in on a Friday night after everyone had gone and cut eighteen inches in width from each desk. We then added new ones of the same type in the reclaimed space. It was hours into Monday morning before anyone figured out why suddenly everyone had a seat. As I always maintain, if you really want to do it, there's a way.

We always have our offices in the best and most expensive parts of town while our competitors look for bargain space in the low-rent districts. It gets back to who you think is more important: your people or outsiders. I believe our people matter. The best for *us*. This is true not only at "headquarters," but everyplace. Our offices around the globe are all at the best locations, with interiors that offer a feeling of luxury and comfort for every employee. Big salt-water fish tanks provide light, white noise, and some relaxation. Glass-walled conference rooms improve interaction. No one has a private office, including me. The waiting area for guests is in the middle of our employees' snack bar: It shows off our people and the normal excitement at our company. If being invisible from your colleagues is what you crave, we're not the right place for you.

I've always believed that management's ability to influence work habits through edict is limited. Ordering something gets it done, perhaps. When you turn your back, though, employees tend to regress to the same old ways. Physical plant, however, has a much more lasting impact. Ours is an open plan layout. People must develop the ability to concentrate, despite myriad distractions. But the good part is, they absorb information peripherally while focusing elsewhere. Openness also constantly puts them in front of their peers, preventing childish fantasies that coworkers are out to get them. As is true with markets, transparency produces fairness. I issue proclamations telling everyone to work together, but it's the lack of walls that really makes them do it. (Of course, this will last only until the next management team brings in the construction company to build barriers, something they inevitably will do the day after my funeral.)

Openness also shows off our most important asset, our people. They are the company. You can replace our technology, data, reputation, and clients, but you cannot duplicate the group we've put together and the culture they've developed. We are a team. Every year, to increase intracompany and interfamily communication, we have a huge company summer picnic with spouses, children, and significant others. (Our kids learn where Mommy and Daddy go during the day and whom they work with.) We constantly encourage one another. (We play sports together, work on charities as a group, teach one another new skills.) Our young people socialize with one another. (We've probably been more effective at introducing people to their future spouses than most dating apps.) We work together. (A number of people have told me that every employee they've seen at Bloomberg has had a smile on his or her face, and that wasn't true elsewhere. I hope they're right.)

Compare us to our competitors. Typically, they have reception areas with deeper carpeting and more wood paneling than elsewhere in their organizations. Their receptionists are chosen for physical attractiveness rather than interpersonal skills. The average employee there is relegated to non-VIP elevators. Clients see only representatives who are sanitized, less human than presentable. What are those companies ashamed of? The fact that your average computer programmer dresses differently from the typical salesperson, or has longer hair, or is shy? That's what programmers are. So what? This is who we are.

In 2017 we opened our new European headquarters in London. It was the first time we constructed our own building. We designed it, with the brilliant British architect Norman Foster, to be a physical manifestation of our company's core values, starting with openness and transparency, which are taken to new level. In the middle of the building, instead of an elevator bank, is a soaring central ramp, where employees and visitors can interact and share ideas. Work stations are circular, to make it easier to interact with others, and they surround communal tables where impromptu meetings can occur. Everything is designed to maximize interaction and collaboration. That's what it's all about. Our goal was to create a building that our employees would be proud of and that our clients would want to come to. And we did that not only through innovative design, but also through art, both inside and outside the building, which excites and inspires people—and serves as a reminder to everyone that we value creativity. The reviews of the building were incredibly positive. One called the building "sexy on the inside and sophisticated all around." Another headline read: "Welcome to the Office of the Future."

Office spaces can say a lot about a company. I like what ours say about us.

*   *   *

We handle perks differently, too. At Bloomberg, as you get promoted and your compensation increases, you aren't expected to work less and take more vacations. Quite the contrary. You're more valuable, you get paid more, and your coworkers should get more out of you. The increase in your compensation is for current and future services, not rewards for past performance. Don't want to commit to that? Then don't accept the promotion and raise. We'll have no hard feelings—and someone else would love the chance.

We have no reserved parking spaces for senior executives. If you want to leave your car right by the door, just come in earlier. Creating class distinctions isn't constructive. That's why I don't believe in executive dining rooms either. The issue isn't fairness. If we constantly remind those people at the bottom that they are not at the top, do you really expect them to be "gung ho" about the company? Remember, remove the bottom 50 percent and half of everyone remaining joins that lower group instantly.

If we expect dedication, cooperation, and performance, we've got to protect, assist, develop, and pay. The social contracts work two ways. The Bible says you reap what you sow. Yes, we expect you to put in long hours. You absolutely must show up for work even on those days when a lay-about seems more attractive. Sure, you sometimes have to work alongside people who aren't your favorites. Of course, you've got to produce rather than lollygag around the water cooler. How else can we pay all employees more each year?

Our company has to do its part. That ranges from physical security to disease and injury prevention programs, and to the most expansive health care plan money can buy. Our company builds employees: Constant training, retraining, coaching, and instruction from on-staff, full-time experts increase everyone's worth. Our company creates opportunities: Management that's promoted from within, transfers to other offices around the world, and chances to move to new areas make us different. Our company shares its financial success: High salaries, significant bonuses, and generous expense reimbursement are part of everyone's package.

Do our employment policies work? Compare us to our competitors or even to any similar-size organization. We have phenomenally low turnover for a company employing many young programmers, salespeople, and reporters, and we attract a pretty diverse labor force. In 2018 the *Columbia Journalism Review* found that Bloomberg has one of the most generous parental leave policies among major media organizations. Our assistance to young graduating students beginning careers is legendary. Almost everyone wants to join us—and only a handful elect to leave.

Loyalty is everything. Our people expect me to have it to them, and vice versa. Be honest, work hard, treat each other fairly and openly. Add a dash of competency, and we'll be together for a long time.

*   *   *

In business, growth is a necessity: You grow or you get out. No company can stay anchored to the status quo, no matter how successful it is. Customers come and go; their needs change with time, and the services that help them do their jobs are always in flux. Woe to the supplier without the best offering. If you're depending on longtime personal relationships, and not the quality of what you provide, start working on your golf game: You have a friendship with the buyer—your competitor already has one with his or her successor!

Nor can a company depend on just the best offerings to carry the day either. They're always transitory or eventually the patent just runs out. Remember Wang's word processor, Prime Computer's mini, or Sony's Beta? Few people do. Consumers have an insatiable appetite for improving their lives—and zero loyalty to past products or brand names. Time may be kind to great literature, art, music, dance, design, or philosophy, but in the commercial world, it's out with the old, in with the new, overnight.

Every day at Bloomberg, we face challenges that jeopardize our comfortable life. We constantly have to fight established competitors trying to take food out of our children's mouths. And then there are the start-ups that want to destroy everything we've built. Stand still and their products will overtake ours. If we're not careful, one day it'll be easier for them to add our features to their products than for us to add theirs to ours. Growth makes us a moving target. No growth makes us a sitting duck.

What makes the challenge even tougher is the threat of being swallowed by industrial giants who covet our business after we establish a market. These interlopers buy their way in and wreck the economics we have built. They hire away our people with preemptory starting salaries, not realizing that few employees of any company are that valuable when stripped of the team doing the blocking and tackling.

And there's another insidious source of competition waiting to get us, one that's particularly galling. Our customers get blasé about our service. If we provide it competently and consistently, they think other companies must be able to do so as well. All of a sudden, these customers start calling in others to make proposals and pressing us to reduce prices. Then they start thinking they can provide the same product or service more cheaply themselves. Perhaps they can even build it and sell it to others as well. So, to survive, we must grow and improve. Any supplier who offers today what it sold yesterday will be out of business tomorrow.

Companies must grow for internal reasons, too. Without the challenge of the new, employees' minds and spirits atrophy. Work devolves from fun to drudgery. Without growth, no new opportunities are created, and employees who work hard to get a promotion have no place to go. If we tried to promote them anyway, we'd push the most productive people into meaningless senior slots. That would neutralize our greatest contributors. So we must grow to create new valuable positions, or watch our best and brightest quit for management jobs elsewhere and dissipate everything we've built over the years.

* * *

Bloomberg grows primarily in the traditional way: We expand our basic product. After all, that's what we do best. As the old western song goes, "Dance with the one that brung ya!"

We make our products global. As our clients, opportunities, and suppliers move to new cities, new countries, even new continents, so do we. Of course, other physical locations require that Bloomberg employees master different languages, understand unconventional conventions in bond calculations, handle unfamiliar customs in client service. We must deal with employment laws inconsistent with those at home, build new relationships with unknown sources, and cope with unknown regulators in everything. We must adapt our product to other markets, other types of securities, other formats, and other terminologies.

We increase our product's functionality. Customers' needs evolve and we provide what they want or lose their business. For example, Bloomberg disseminates information on companies, including earnings statements, balance sheets, press releases, news stories, and government filings. Bloomberg also provides myriad details of the securities these companies sell, such as terms, conditions, restrictions, holders, and transaction prices—as well as information on who runs these companies, who analyzes their prospects, who trades their securities, who invests in their future, their supply chains, competitors, and top holders of debt and equity. And through Bloomberg Intelligence, we provide a research service to clients that capitalizes on the Terminal's extensive data and tools. Our team uses the Terminal to provide in-depth analysis on what is happening at companies and within industries and markets, including both equity and credit markets. We examine their strategies and the factors that could affect them, including government policy and litigation. We publish primers on some 2,000 companies and offer in-depth analysis of about 140 industries to help our customers to shape their decisions. Traditionally, market participants relied on big banks to provide this kind of research, but the potential for conflicts of interest helped create an opening for us. At Bloomberg, our only interest is in providing the best possible data, information, and insights. Plus, the banks faced growing difficulty in getting adequately compensated for their research. So we stepped in to offer research content as the banks continued to move into more personalized research services and more profitable transactions and products. It's been win-win-win for all.

When you add a new product to your company lineup, existing ones usually need modification too. Products are interrelated. Concepts developed by one group of clients are envied by others, particularly fashionable terminology and technology. Your average customer may use only the conventional, but if you lose your reputation as the expert—the guru, the one who's pushing the envelope—you'll lose the loyalty of all those who live by association. Constant "modernization" is just part of the game.

Just growing a product isn't enough to make it succeed, though. Infrastructure must expand too. Backup, contingency planning, reliability, security all become even more important than new offerings. The longer you have clients, the more they depend on you. The more clients you have, the more you have to lose. The more you're viewed as the establishment, the more the old reliable reputation is worth.

Keeping serviceable what you've built is a never-ending process. Every day, something you never thought could go wrong, does. So every day plus one, you fix a problem you previously didn't know you had. Of course, you're locking the barn door after the horse got out—but now the next horse can't escape. Each day, there's one fewer animal potentially running amok. With time, you grow your service record. It gets better and better—never perfect, but more and more acceptable.

*   *   *

Our company standards also grow and evolve. No company's accounting systems adequately accommodate growth without constant enhancement, nor do any company's stated ethics and behavioral practices survive long without modification, particularly as you go worldwide. Practices acceptable here are often taboo in other countries, and vice versa. Disclosure, drug testing, "considerations" (bribes, to an American), harassment, fraternization all have very different meanings in different cultures. What is normal or correct in one place may be blasphemous in another. What is in the public domain here may be a state secret there, with disclosure being a capital offense.

Employment practices—hiring, firing, vacation, maternity, disability, and compensation laws—vary greatly worldwide. Using constant standards can cause no end of confusion and illegality. For any company doing business in two or more countries, it's perfectly possible that a single policy complies with rules in one place and violates the law in another. As a company expands, growth, flexibility, and fresh expertise in the human resources department must occur.

Similarly with security. We fret about losing our intellectual property rights and our wealth, but if we're not vigilant, we could lose things equally as important, our physical well-being and freedom of speech. Not all parts of the world are safe or open. At Bloomberg, we wear identification badges around our necks at work—no exceptions, including me. It's another case of how leadership by example is key.

One area where we haven't changed is our commitment to gender equality. When we decided to open an office in Japan, the two pieces of advice I got from everyone were: get a Japanese partner (satisfying government regulations would be impossible without an insider's help, I was told), and don't send women (Japanese businesswomen in those days wore uniforms and served tea). Bloomberg being Bloomberg, we opened without a local partner (and had no governmental problems) and sent two women to run the place (who were accepted and able to hire men to work under them). So much for convention.

I'd like the company to be 50 percent male and 50 percent female at every level, in every function, in every one of our offices. (Remember, I have two daughters—and I want them to have the same opportunities as your two sons!) Not all of our customers have the same policy. They don't care that the world's population is roughly half women and half men. Sometimes, we would go to high-level meetings where everyone not serving tea was male. Or clients would ignore our female manager and address all conversation to our male representative sitting in the meeting right next to her. Thankfully, that is changing, and more companies are embracing our view of equality.

We've always done what we think right, and we've found that the best way to encourage others to join us is to do what we do best: make accurate data—in this case on gender equality—more broadly available. Investors have noticed that there is some evidence showing that gender equality policies and practices can benefit a company's performance, including its ability to attract and retain talent. And yet there was virtually no information on which companies are leaders on this issue. To change that, we launched the Bloomberg Financial Services Gender Equality Index, and the positive response we received from firms led us to expand the index to cover more industries. Bloomberg has always been dedicated to making markets more transparent, and we've always been dedicated to equality. It's another way we can better serve our customers—and help make the world a more equal place, too.

*   *   *

The other basic way to grow is by product diversification—entering new businesses that are at best only tangential to a company's existing offerings. Companies diversify with a variety of motives. New products look appealing, and management thinks its traditional endeavors have little earnings potential left. The marketplace predicts a period of slow growth (read low price/earnings ratio, thus a low price for the company's stock, thus possible criticism of management). Or maybe the CEO is bored and wants the glamour of being in more trendy industries. Others make the old classic synergy argument that one plus one is worth more than two, like when Scientific Data Systems was bought. (Xerox paid $1 billion in 1969 for this "strategic fit" company—and wrote it down to *zero* only seven years later. A billion dollars was a lot of money in those days.)

Occasionally, product diversification actually benefits the company's employees, stockholders, and customers. Mostly, though, the history of corporate growth through new directions is disappointing. Could it be that, often, no growth in a company's traditional business is caused by poor management, and that lousy supervision and erratic decision making are the real consistent parts of these companies?

When is diversification appropriate? Only when it fits with what you already do. Companies have ethics, talents, and structures suited to specific businesses. Those who think their skills and management abilities are easily transferable aren't being realistic: Generally, they're not. Synergies are seldom more than constructs for consultants' reports. (Apples and oranges are both fruits from trees, but are grown in totally different environments by farmers with differing skills, tools, time frames, and economics. Buying an apple orchard when one already owns an orange grove probably just adds rotting apples and eliminates time to care for the oranges.)

Well-run organizations, whether commercial, political, educational, military, or philanthropic, have conceptual goals stated long in advance. New possibilities are always tested for fit against these predefined objectives. This insistence on a prior specific mission statement against which all proposed actions must be judged tempers the emotions following the "fad of the day." Smart managements plan strategically beforehand, and don't do anything tactical that's not consistent with the plan—particularly in the heat of some once-in-a-lifetime, do-it-now-or-lose-it-forever opportunity brought to you by a breathless investment banker. If it's not your business, it probably shouldn't be.

The same applies to Bloomberg. We've grown dramatically over the years, and our diversification has stayed consistent with our mission statement. Our goal is to provide the information and analytical capabilities serious professionals need to be well-rounded and do their jobs. The focus of our computer Terminal product is clearly for the sophisticated users, as it is for our radio and television programs. The publishing parts of our company target investment professionals or consumers interested in personal finance and markets, or the broader business world and how politics affect it. So far, what we've done fits.

After we look for relevancy versus our strategic objectives, we at Bloomberg look for overlaps with existing products. Will it help what we already do? Can we use the same people? Is the technology required consistent with what we know how to produce? What can we do that our competitors can't? There's no reason to do a copycat product. Consumers can just as easily buy from others. Do we have limitations that would disadvantage us? As a news organization, we have great access, but we can't be seen as a promotional device for our sources. Last, we insist on doing profitable things. I've never believed Bloomberg should be a charitable institution—instead, we give nearly all of our profits to Bloomberg Philanthropies.

*   *   *

We're frequently presented with opportunities to grow or diversify by acquisition. I almost never let a seller's representative send us offering memoranda. If we're not seriously interested in making a bid, it's disingenuous to look; and I really don't care anyway. It may be interesting to know what others have done, but the only thing that matters is what our customers need. Looking would just get us worried and have our practices influenced by managers we'd never hire.

At Bloomberg, we're builders, not buyers. I'd make a terrible venture capitalist; every company I look at seems overpriced. I always think we can create it more cheaply ourselves. Whenever I think goodwill (the accounting treatment for paying too much) is justified, I rush to take a cold shower. What's for sale may be worth it, but why? All these companies appear to me to have problems I'd find difficult to fix, something I'd have to do since, if I ever did buy anything, I'd want to make it my baby and grow it forever. I'm not a seller either.

The real problem with acquisitions is that neither corporate cultures nor technologies mix. The momentary advantage to the buyer adding an existing operation often gets dissipated quickly, and then one's stuck with the reasons it was for sale in the first place. More times than not, when two good companies combine, they stay as separate functional organizations, having contact only through common ownership. When poorly run companies get together, they tend to do it at the operating level, where the worst of both can do the most damage to each other. It's probably inscribed someplace (or should be): Two negatives *always* produce something worse!

In our company's history, we've made only a few major purchases, including *Businessweek*; the Bureau of National Affairs (now Bloomberg BNA), which provides in-depth analysis of legal, regulatory, and tax-related issues; and the Barclays Risk Analytics and Index Solutions, which is highly valued by our customers—and potential customers.

All have worked out, but our modus operandi remains building from within, which avoids the bet-the-store, high-risk gambles that often characterize large takeovers, such as the disastrous TimeWarner-AOL deal. Maybe I'm just not that smart. When I'm looking to expand, I prefer starting with a little capital that we can afford to lose and a few people we can always reassign to other projects. This way, we never feel we're committed to stay with our mistakes, nor are we so overextended we can't handle other additional experimental ventures simultaneously. (Out of deference to our professional service providers, I won't mention the savings in accounting bills, legal charges, and investment banking fees we also get with this build-versus-buy strategy.)

Just as important is the people issue. Growth by building gives us the chance to reward our best employees with newly created management jobs. Growth by buying would just force us to fire a bunch of people I've never met who haven't done anything bad to me. I'm not sure how I'd explain that to my kids, or why at my age I need to give myself that task.

There will be an exception or two that will present themselves in the future—companies with brand identification we'd never replicate, or distribution channels we can't buy, or the opportunity to end a dependency on a supplier we're uncomfortable with. What will we do? You'll see when it happens. (Unfortunately, if we ever seriously looked at acquiring something, our major competitors would probably rush in and outbid us just to stop the process.) All I can guarantee is that if we ever buy another company, it will fit our mission statement and sell at a price I think is lower than the cost of replicating that company's products.

*   *   *

Whether by building or buying, there are dangers in growth you ignore at great peril. We insist on management depth at every position. Lack of it would leave us vulnerable when someone quits or gets hit by a truck. (I want the loss of anyone in the company to hurt us, but not fatally, including the likes of me.) Every job performance review I give my direct-reporting managers includes the question, "Who's your replacement? If you don't have one now, I can't consider you for bigger things. If you don't have one the next time I ask, you may no longer be a direct report."

As we face the issue of growth, we need the best managers we can train—and the best people to build our internal accounting, measurement, and control functions. If we don't stay in control, nothing else matters. We've got to be able to service our clients, pay the bills, collect the revenue, file our tax returns, detect fraud, spot trends, and so on. If there are no controls, there's eventually no company.

Due to their size, our competitors have limited ability to respond to threats. We can't become inhibited in the same way as we grow. Big companies allocate expenses, thereby causing divisiveness in their organizations. We don't run our company with "profit centers." With their focus on cash flow versus earnings (they never consider depreciation a real cost, a stupid assumption given today's pace of obsolescence), they never have the funds available to give the customer the latest and greatest service and technology. We're aggressive with depreciation and assume it's real. They have equipment in the field that, if quickly upgraded to a better product, would cause accounting write-downs and kill their credibility with lenders and Wall Street analysts. We provide new equipment and services to clients when they are available, not when they fit our P&L statement. As a private company, we report to only a few who understand and have a long-term perspective.

Without knocking the value of the accounting profession, it is true that "numbers lie—and liars use numbers." Only with super-human effort can a company keep accounting from being misused as it gets bigger. I can't count the number of times I've watched people incorrectly make decisions that confuse incremental costs with fully allocated ones, or misuse present value calculations. These concepts can be useful tools, but slavish adherence to them can produce cockeyed results. Had the person who invented the wheel used "net present value," we would still be walking!

Size also limits growth by inhibiting (or at least making more difficult) communications, which make sensible controls, not con-stricting policies, all the more necessary. In big companies, meeting after meeting is required to include and inform all concerned before anything happens. Is greater knowledge worth the extra time? I tend to just do my thing and apologize for not posting others after. Secretly, no matter what our rules and procedures, I wish all our people would. Once, I got frustrated at a get-together where each participant read a summary of his or her department's progress for the week, right from the printed notes handed out to all at the meeting's start. The next week I had the chairs removed from the confer-ence room before we started. It's amazing how much quicker and more focused stand-up conferences are. Size also leads to a cover-your-rear mentality that slows down development. Each manager protects his or her own turf, which is particularly true when they can't see what the others are doing. Size hides.

Size's economics of scale are seldom realized. Take the great misconception in our business about software: that maintaining a program is cheaper than developing it. It isn't. The fact is, software needs to be updated constantly to retain value. The inputs to it change. The hardware and communications change. People always need new formats, sorts, fields, and calculations. That's why we constantly hire more programmers. Or what about the belief that hardware is a onetime "capital expense"? People always say something costs N to buy (a cost they "capitalize") and then assume that's the whole cost. I always figure on 40 percent of N *every* year, forever (a cost you expense versus earnings)—10 percent interest, 10 percent maintenance, 20 percent depreciation. That adds up to 40 percent in my book. Don't quibble with details. Use 40 percent. Trust me. Whom do you want to kid? Yourself?

Our greatest challenge today? Fighting the stultifying effects of success, the paralyzing results of growth, the debilitating cancer of entrenchment.

*   *   *

Management must promote growth, while staying within the mission statement's guidelines. Unfortunately, managers are human beings, too, with personal interests, egos, and insecurities similar to those of real people (the people they supervise). There are many examples of an acquisition and/or new initiative begun for noncommercial reasons and justified ex post facto. Fortunately, a more open and competitive world has reduced these abuses. And in all fairness, most managers really do try. The success of American business is ample testimony to their high ethics, hard work, and superior talents. Still, people are people—and managers are human beings first and foremost. What does it take to succeed as a manager?

The primary function of those at the top is the care and feeding of the company's most valuable asset, its employees, including designing and administering a compensation system that encourages cooperation, rewards risk taking, and gives inducements to work hard—Job One for the CEO.

The leverage a great team provides makes management a fantastic investment for a company's stockholders, but phenomenally overpriced when the executives can't get the organization to perform. All the magazine surveys of CEOs' compensation based on earnings growth or stock price performance miss the point. It may be a standard of success harder to measure, but rather than raising stock prices and even generating earnings, building, leading, and motivating the staff a company needs for the future is what managers should be paid for.

Being the spokesperson for the company is an important part of running any organization, and perhaps the hardest to delegate. Everyone wants to hear the top person's views (even if someone else wrote the speech). Guests want to shake the boss's hand (even though no one remembers who was who after the meeting). If you want to exchange business cards or have a picture taken jointly, no one else but the top boss will do. So, while the senior manager may have other pressing duties, he or she has to set a high priority on accessibility to the press, the stockholders, the employees, and the customers. At Bloomberg, I handled all our firm's internal and external public relations until we got so big that I could no longer do it.

Then there's old-fashioned leadership. It's the top person's policies, personal and professional deportment, and working hours that the organization tries to emulate. While the only difference between stubbornness and having the courage of one's convictions may be the results, it's a natural reaction to attribute superior strength, knowledge, and consistency to those we follow. (But the slightest sign of vacillation can kill that image forever.)

Say something as CEO and the organization responds. It may only be by analyzing, criticizing, ridiculing, or specifically deciding to ignore the pronouncement, but notice it they will. You go to the other side of the world and find a nonsensical business policy instituted by your most remote office—perhaps everyone wearing hats indoors. Why? "Well, years ago you said in a memo to keep your head covered." Yes, perhaps you did as a throwaway line, without much thought, outside on a very cold day, applied to a totally unrelated situation you've long since forgotten. But the CEO is the parent, teacher, clergyman, politician. Everyone's watching all the time. Wanting to believe, aching to follow. Are you not comfortable with leading the company twenty-four hours a day, seven days a week? Then step down.

The CEO is also the company's morale officer. He or she must promote an atmosphere in which ordinary people who try new things that fail are encouraged to try again. Projects that succeed always get support and provide their proponents sufficient adulation. It's the failures the timid watch. A belief that trying new things could jeopardize one's career stifles creativity. Lose the contribution of the average employee and you lose the war.

Last, there's the "who's in charge" function. THE BUCK STOPS HERE was a sign President Harry Truman had on his White House desk. He didn't make most decisions, but he did bear responsibility for his staff's actions. (Something modern politicians disgracefully walk away from. "A mistake was made" has become a euphemism for no one taking responsibility.) It's the same with the corporate CEO. He or she can get help, delegate, farm out, get advice, and so on. But in the end, it's one person's decision, one person's responsibility. A major part of the CEO's responsibilities is to be the ultimate risk taker and decision maker. Truman had it right.

Companies that do things correctly for long periods still seem to get in trouble eventually, however. Is it always the CEO's fault? When it's because of the CEO's new game plan every month, you bet. Consistency and predictability are important requirements if an organization is to function well. But the opposite is also true: Let the hierarchy remain static and you get disaster. The good quit for lack of opportunity or out of boredom; the bad entrench themselves. Stirring up the chain of command is another part of the CEO's job. Not easy. Not pleasant. Not even always explainable. Too late to do in bad times, and never thought of in good times. But don't do it—and you'll get killed from within. Or when the inevitable competitor arrives with a better way, the organization previously without a need to improve has grown so lazy it has trouble reacting.

When I look at a company, I pay little attention to its accounting statements. A good accountant with a creative mind can make numbers paint any desired picture. No one understates revenues and profits when they're trying to show off. Presumably, the financial situation is always equal to or worse than stated. A better way to evaluate a company is to talk to the experts. No, I don't mean journalists or analysts. I mean those who *really* know what's going on and what the potential is. First, I call those most knowledgeable, the customers. "Do you plan to buy more or less of this company's product?" I ask. "Are there competitors coming along with better offerings?" Then, I call the other insiders, the headhunters. "Do people want to go to work at this company, or are they trying to leave in droves?" Management, accountants, and other outsiders can say anything they want. Clients and employees rarely lie.

*   *   *

Competition's great—obviously for the consumer, but even for the providers. Every morning when we get up, we relish the day's upcoming battles. They keep us alive, and they keep Bloomberg's corporate family thriving. We can't wait for tomorrow. Who says we can't do that? What do you mean they'll beat us? Have them put on their boxing gloves, and send them into the ring. We're ready!

9

Coming Up Next

America's a Wonderful Country

Periodically, while surrounded by the fruits of our success—the profits, power, notoriety—I get frustrated and dream of starting again. But something stops me. Perhaps I'm too old. Perhaps I'm afraid it was all luck. Or maybe, deep down inside, I really do like the trappings I've accumulated. Nevertheless, when I find we just "cleared it with legal" or had a meeting to "keep others in the loop," or are "justifying" staff versus producers, I want to scream. We used to have the Nike motto attitude: We just did it! Now, there's a "why we can't" lurking in the background. Keeping it from coming out while we grow is our number one management focus today.

In our company, what started simple with time has become complex. Existing contracts have to be honored, so change is difficult. A single straightforward policy has picked up exception after exception over time. Products have grown to overlap. Some have become both redundant and inconsistent, simultaneously. Development, marketing, sales, and support are always in different stages. No one's got an excuse, but everyone's got a reason. Maddening!

Why not just quit then? Chuck it all? Sell the business? Take the money and run? After all, there is a limit to how much you can spend—or prudently leave to your kids. And on the downside, even a reasonably sure double-your-money bet isn't worth a small risk of losing it all, once you've got it. It's one thing to bet the store when the store is worthless, and quite another when you're older and have gotten used to the good life. Cash in, take some money off the table, play it conservatively, relax a little?

Real entrepreneurs never do, though. And I haven't, either. Is "enough" never "enough"? Is it insecurity? What will people say, that when the going got tough, Mike didn't have the right stuff? Or curiosity? Can I get us over the next big plateau? How big can we get? Or lack of alternatives? What would I do if I sold it? Retire?

Generally, real builders are so focused (a.k.a. one-dimensional) and dedicated, they'd have a nervous breakdown after two weeks of sitting around. Their challenge—even their reason for living—would be gone. Why swap fun, influence, challenge, and more money than you could ever spend—for only a multiple of more money than you can ever spend?

In my case, I can't think of anything better than my current situation. It's hard to see how else I could have so much fun and satisfaction. Where else could I create so much? Or help as many young people start careers? Or produce a product our customers actually can't live without? Or have people say, "You're the greatest. You've changed my child's life, helped our family survive, given me a second chance," and mean it? Or, through philanthropy, have such an impact on the world?

Take the company public? And have to answer to more partners, stockholders, and securities analysts? At my age? I know why the investment bankers all want us to issue stock—but why would we want to do it? We're going in the other direction. We've already bought back Merrill's 30 percent investment in our company—the first 10 percent for $200 million in 1996, and the second 20 percent for $4.5 billion in 2008. Not a bad return on their original investment of about $39 million.

Sell? No, thanks. For the moment, answering to essentially no one is the ultimate situation.

So back on the treadmill. Ratchet up the risk. Enter a new medium. Start another software or hardware project. Improve. Develop. Expand. Go for it!

*   *   *

The future holds great promise for Bloomberg the company, and for all of us as individuals. Thanks to agricultural and technological improvements, a smaller percentage of the world's population now goes to bed hungry than ever before in history. That is real progress. In turn, fewer people are illiterate today than in yesteryear. Sure, there's still war and famine and totalitarianism, but less than before.

Better technology and electronic communications exposes alternative political and economic systems to public scrutiny. When you see others doing better, day in and day out, eventually you want the same for your family and yourself. No government, no matter how harsh and repressive, exists without the will of the majority of its citizens. Show the people something better—they'll get it!

From the time civil engineers separated the sewage system from the water supply (causing a big jump in life expectancy), technology has been a boon to humankind. Smallpox has been eradicated worldwide, saving the U.S.—which was the largest donor to the eradication effort—the total of all its contributions every twenty-six days, because we do not have to vaccinate or treat the disease. Now we cure childhood leukemia routinely where before there was no hope. Polio, with its "iron lungs," is nearly in the history books. I've given $125 million to an effort (spearheaded by Bill and Melinda Gates) to eradicate the small pockets of remaining cases, and I'm optimistic we can do it

Most encouragingly, public health programs increasingly prevent disease from attacking the vulnerable. Fluoride in the drinking water has helped generations of Americans avoid tooth decay and cavities. Treating household water through chlorination can reduce diarrheal disease by nearly half. Giving minute doses of vitamin A to children who are deficient would prevent one to three million deaths annually from fatal afflictions, including diarrhea. The great tragedy is that the political will has not kept pace with scientific and technological advances. So much could be done if we cared just a touch more.

That's why I've made public health a major focus of my philanthropy, and specifically, the kinds of noncommunicable diseases—like diabetes and heart disease—that don't get a lot of attention but kill 40 million people every year. In fact, for the first time in human history, more people around the world are dying from noncommunicable diseases than from communicable ones, like malaria and polio. The way we think about mortality, however, has not kept pace. We tend to accept these deaths as unavoidable, but they're not.

In low- and middle-income countries, noncommunicable diseases kill two of every three people, but only 1 percent of global health funding is aimed at stopping them. To draw more attention to this issue, and to encourage more governments to tackle it, I serve as the World Health Organization's Global Ambassador for Noncommunicable Diseases. And our team at Bloomberg Philanthropies works with all levels of government around the world to help them take the kinds of basic steps that can save so many lives, from banning indoor smoking, to taxing the sugary drinks that are one of the leading contributors to obesity, to enacting helmet laws and other road safety measures. We've made a lot of encouraging progress, but there's still so much to do.

New technology also plays an important role in increasing longevity and improving the quality of life. I remember my mother describing how as a girl she traveled by horse-drawn carriage. The Concorde made it possible to fly to Europe in three hours. Growing up, she had gas lamps for illumination. Now, football and baseball games are played outdoors in what's essentially daylight. She hand-delivered messages to her friends as a child. Her grandchildren carry handheld computers (phones) with instant messaging. When she was a teenager, the telephone at the corner store was used only for emergencies. Today, phones are used for countless everyday tasks and communications, most of which don't involve speaking on the phone. Think these "improvements" are trivial? Increasing commerce, comfort, and communication are strong inducement for everyone to avoid World War III.

Tomorrow, things will be even better. Medicine is closing in on cures for cancer, AIDS, strokes. Public health organizations are working to prevent much of the world's famine and pestilence. Small-battery technology is adding mobility to every conceivable kind of electronic device. Global Positioning Systems (GPSs) that use satellite receivers to calculate location and altitude anyplace have changed our world. Soldiers, hikers, flyers, sailors, drivers, even cargo containers have GPSs to tell them where they are. It's a lot harder to get lost than it used to be. Computational ability to create "virtual reality," data retrieval from anywhere in the world, commerce conducted electronically are all here, as is on-demand audio (like podcasts) and video. Whenever you want, watching any program or movie or listening to any kind of news or music has become, "Haven't we always?" People still collect records, but the world's music catalog is now available digitally on your phone.

Amazingly, these advances will be used in the poorer parts of the world only slightly later than in the wealthier areas. The potential for health improvements there is obvious. And one of the great barriers to the deployment of technology is the existence of infrastructure and the financial impact of scrapping it, a problem obviously not felt in places that start with nothing. Wireless phone systems have frequently been installed where previously there were no phones at all, while the large "copper-wire telcos" still fight to keep such systems out of their often poorly serviced "developed" areas.

The same is true with utilities that are threatened by increasingly inexpensive rooftop solar panels. Incumbent businesses always fight to protect their turf—and when they can't win on price in the market, they turn to government to protect them.

*   *   *

Technology is clearly improving our lives, but not all effects prognosticated will prove accurate. Take the prediction that we'll all work from home, for example. Technology makes it possible with connected smartphones and computers. And with the dramatic increase in two-income and single-parent households, there's a need for flexibility to accommodate work and family simultaneously. What's more, the growing service industries (as opposed to the declining manufacturing ones) better allow independent "tasking."

In the 1990s, experts told us these trends would revolutionize the workplace. I never believed it—and I still don't. While working from home is a central tenet of the professional futurist's mantra, there has been only a small increase in office-in-the-home lifestyles. As the competition for employment heats up, people have more need than ever to be where the action is and where the politics are played out, at the office or factory. Tougher, more competitive times are not suited to reduced interaction with fellow workers or more lax supervision. Those arguing that e-mail, chat, and videoconferencing are replacements for gathering around the watercooler must be academics. For a handful of professions, the home is a fine workplace. But for most other occupations, the downsides of lost interaction at the office are substantial. They can be mitigated with frequent visits to the office. But they cannot be eliminated.

Some think computer expertise is required for future success. I don't. Thinking and interpersonal communications skills have been, are, and will be keys to survival. Technology's not going to change that. To prosper, work on your people-to-people relations. Take a psychology course and one on how to use the Scientific Method rather than (or in addition to) a computer science course. We exchange ideas more than information, and we do most of that orally. Having text and visuals to add to understanding is nice. But we're men and women, not machines. Face to face, or over electronic media, we need to transmit and receive sound. When Samuel Morse invented the telegraph, he gave us electronic interactive digital text communication. Nevertheless, we flocked to Alexander Graham Bell's analog voice telephone instead, because it better mirrored the way we live. We talk rather than write to each other—or, as the case is now, we chat. Technology has added to Bell's system the ability to send letters, numbers, pictures—and, of course, emojis. Yes, we type them, but there is a reason it's called chatting: We are having conversations. For all the change this has brought to the way we express ideas—r u ok? lmk ty ☺—it doesn't change the fact that conversations about ideas and information lie at the center of human existence.

Your job will remain to create the what and disseminate it; technology is always monkeying around with the how. It's what you have to say and your ability to present it in cogent, believable terms to yourself, your family, your coworkers, and your community that are important.

While technology is creating broader distribution of information, with enhanced "targeting," it is also causing the size of each audience to become smaller and more knowledgeable. You'll have to be even better prepared in the future to get ahead; the people you'll interact with will be. Alternative delivery systems for news and entertainment mean more choices. And the more choices expand, the smaller audiences become. In turn, this produces much more homogeneity as to age, sex, economics, education, and so on, in those reading, listening, or watching a single specific story or program. Smaller groups, but much more focused ones. Not always great for society, as I explained in Chapter 5, but a marketer's dream, as people are bombarded constantly with ever-more-targeted messages.

The cost of communicating ideas is declining rapidly, and it's an odds-on bet that this will continue for the foreseeable future. For the average person, access to data quickly and affordably, and the ability to compare your ideas to those of others, has surpassed all predictions. More information available, faster and cheaper. Understanding what's important for your job will be paramount.

Nearly all communications systems in today's world are digital. "Digital" is a word that most people use without understanding its meaning. When sending text, sound, still pictures, or full-motion video digitally, technology converts all these media into numbers by turning a series of switches off or on, represented by 0 for off or 1 for on. Fast computers using fancy mathematics take these 0s and 1s and reduce the number of them actually needed to adequately represent the text, sound, or picture. At the receiving end, technology changes these 0s and 1s back into sound, pictures, numbers, and letters for the ear and eye. Important, though, is the fact that until that "reconversion," digital sound, text, and pictures are all exactly the same.

The electronic retrieval and manipulation of data in your home will increase. We've gone from picking up the data via automobile (people used to drive to Blockbuster to rent a VHS tape) to having it delivered by post (e.g., Netflix sent a DVD in the mail) to having it available online and on demand, which has vastly expanded the diversity of alternatives and reduced costs. TV listings, catalogs, and sports scores rather than Shakespeare, serious news, and financial data may be your data fare. That's your choice. How they will be delivered to you continues to evolve, with personal home assistants now providing more and more of it. Those whose jobs are at stake in "legacy" industries don't want to hear it, but the days of "broadcast" as opposed to "request-retrieval" delivery are basically over.

Yet even as industries get more technologically complex, the skills needed in the new economy center far more on critical thinking than technical know-how. In the office or on the production line, tool selection and use is the key, not how each aid is constructed. Being well-rounded, inquisitive, perceptive, logical, and communicative is more valuable than knowing a given sequence of buttons to push. In the future, technical details will matter less—big picture, more.

America is as well-positioned for these trends as any large country could be. We speak English, the closest thing ever to a universal language. We have free internal borders with one currency, so manufacturers in the United States have a single large market for our products, something Europe is still struggling to create—and lately, with Brexit, it has been moving backward. The securities markets of the United States, thanks to strict Securities and Exchange Commission regulations and enforcement, are viewed as open and fair. America's capital availability for industry and start-ups is unmatched anywhere.

Countries that enjoyed double-digit growth through low labor costs often come in for a rude awakening. When your raison d'être is "cheap," no one makes much and anyone more desperate can undercut you anytime. Low wages, low profits, and low taxes where there are high social service demands eventually lead to serious unrest. It is the same in some wealthy countries with a tradition of confrontational and inflexible management/labor relations. Much strife lies ahead.

By comparison, American workers have aspirations to advance and improve their situation. Over time, and sometimes with great pain to individuals, the United States has refocused away from the old smokestacks and toward the future's technology, advanced manufacturing, entertainment, and service economies. America's concentration on value-added industries puts it in a position to maintain margins and salaries and generate the capital to reinvest in innovative new tools and technology.

America's competitive position in the global economy remains strong, despite the federal government's failure to take the steps needed (on education, immigration, infrastructure, trade, and many other issues) to position us for a new century of growth.

*   *   *

In predicting the future, we all unconsciously slant our prognostications toward a brighter world for ourselves. It's really too terrible to contemplate a scenario that terminates our ability to earn a living or predicts the destruction of our assets. No one has enough intellectual honesty to do so anyway. We always assume that "it will all work out"—and politicians never want to deliver the hard news. Some trends, however, are so certain, they're coming no matter what, and we'll just have to learn to live with them and adjust our behavior accordingly.

Positioning ourselves to respond is what competition is all about. Since Bloomberg was always up against companies many times our size, we had to enter each commercial fight with an advantage. I don't believe that business battles should be even. Remember the math: The chance of coming out ahead in a fair contest is one in two. In consecutive tests, that chance becomes one in four, one in eight, one in sixteen, and so on. In other words, the likelihood that we will prevail five times in a row in a fair fight is only about 3 percent. At Bloomberg, we don't want fair fights. We want to go into contests with an advantage.

Working harder and being smarter give us a head start. So does thinking clearly about what we want and which compromises are acceptable before we make business decisions. Quicker decision making, less self-delusion about our capabilities and limitations, and the discipline of sticking to what we do well all give us a leg-up advantage over our rivals.

So does generous compensation throughout the company. Compensating top management appropriately influences how hard everyone works together and how well a company does. How much to pay the CEO? Try roughly the amount other competent managers make in other fields. Management skills generally are fungible across industries. The argument that someone is worth tens of millions of dollars in compensation per year because his or her company's market value went up many times is so ludicrous that I've always been amazed anyone can espouse it as fair with a straight face. No one suggests the CEO reimburse the owners when the stock goes down. Nor does anyone actually believe that a major company would collapse if the CEO got hit by a truck (whether driven by a stranger or a representative of the board), or that he or she could have done it without the stockholders' money.

Most companies, most of the time, grow and contract with the market they're in. Management often makes the difference only at the margin. Changing executives periodically almost always improves results, no matter how entrenched the CEO is. Mythology to the contrary, no one's irreplaceable and there are few revelations in business. The corporate change that works is *evolutionary* change, not *revolutionary* change: The quick fix, like buying a competitor or growth through acquisition, usually boosts earnings only for a short while. Corporate fixes through public relations and industry analyst "stroking" aren't worth much either: Stock P/E ratios go with the group, which is why they call it the herd instinct.

As a private company, we don't have a stock price to worry about. But we do have to give employees the incentive to go in the same direction as the owners. All our staff get a salary commensurate with what the local market pays for their specialty and experience. Additionally though, they all share in the success of the company, through bonuses. The system works well and fairly. We have a complex product; people buy it for a variety of reasons. Sometimes it's the salesperson's demonstration skills and ability to meet objections. Sometimes it's because of our service people's help, or a useful news story written by our journalists, or the data and the ability to analyze them as categorized and interpreted by our collection and research and development people. Often, it's because of those who are our first line of offense and defense—the people who answer the phone when you call, or greet you when you walk into our offices. Everyone contributes. Everyone is valued. And everyone benefits when we succeed.

10

Out of the Office

Character and Consistency

There are defining moments in one's life, discrete events we all remember as turning points: graduation, marriage, births, deaths, career changes. But even more lasting impact comes from experiences that stretch over long time periods. Like one's home life. From my years growing up to my family life today, I've been shaped by the people around me. And I've tried to live that life with a sense of adventure—not just in my work life but in my private life as well.

I was born in Medford, Massachusetts, on Valentine's Day in 1942. My father, William, was a bookkeeper for a local dairy company and worked six or seven days a week all his life. My mother, Charlotte, stayed home as a housewife until he died. Then she went out and became the breadwinner. She taught me you've got to do what you've got to do, and to do it without complaining. I remember her making us wait every night for my father's return from the office to have dinner together as a family. We ate in the dining room with a linen tablecloth, linen napkins, and the family silverware. The food didn't come out in pots; only serving dishes came to the table. She insisted the best should be for the most important people, our family, and she did for us what my friends' mothers did only for guests. We've got to take care of each other was her message. No one else will.

My younger sister, Marjorie, and I would sit across from each other, with my parents at opposite ends of the table. My father described what he did at work that day. (One of his jobs was to buy actual tank cars full of milk for the dairy to make into cheese and, once in a while, he'd even resell them when they had too much inventory. I think he thought of himself as a great commodities trader. Perhaps that's the source of my interest in Wall Street.) And each of us around the table in turn did likewise. It wasn't a formal thing; we just all were interested in each other's activities and, as a family, shared them.

I didn't play baseball with my father or do crossword puzzles with my mother (I'm a so-so athlete and a terrible speller), but we did other things together: driving to New Jersey for a family vacation, sightseeing, going to a movie, dining at a local inexpensive family restaurant. Never did my parents argue (at least not in front of my sister and me). Never did anyone say "mine" as opposed to "ours." It really was a cohesive, happy, sharing unit. If I screw up my life, I can't blame my mother, father, or sister.

Our family always got together for the traditional annual events of Passover in the spring and Thanksgiving in the fall, along with the occasional birth, bar mitzvah, wedding, or funeral. School vacations seemed to split the family rather than the reverse. Some went skiing. Others went to the sun. Still, we always kept in touch. Until she died at age 102, I called my mother first thing in the morning when I got to work.

Taking care of your family when I was a kid was a given, something I hope my own children have learned. Similarly, I preach again and again at work that everyone in our company is family, that we must take care of one another. We really are related in both an emotional and a fiscal sense. Anyone who goes through life successfully receives the help of others. And no organization succeeds without most of its members contributing.

Having outsiders you can depend on in a time of crisis is helpful—as when my niece, Rachel, was arrested in Egypt. (As I have reminded her, we now have a "criminal" in the family.) While Sue and I were in England attending my father-in-law's funeral in 1996, Rachel went sightseeing across the Israeli border into Egypt. When she came out of the ladies' room at a bus stop, the police arrested her, claiming they had found a gun in the bathroom. The protocol of this standard shakedown was to "confess" instantly and pay a bribe on the spot. Rachel, being Rachel, refused. We had to get Bloomberg's Jerusalem reporter, our London bureau chief, the Cairo bureau of another news organization, and a family friend in the State Department to prod the United States embassy for help. Such scams happen all the time. After she was released, an American diplomat warned my sister, "Now, don't tell anybody about this. It would hurt our relationship with Egypt." Of all the dumb things. Who on earth is our guy protecting? How will other parents know to warn their kids? Talk about misplaced priorities. That diplomat never learned my mother's lesson of taking care of "us" before "them."

*   *   *

The day my acceptance to Harvard Business School arrived, I called my mother, knowing she'd be pleased.

"Don't let it go to your head," she said. That's how she reacted to everything.

The person who would have been really thrilled was my father, who had died a year earlier. For Dad, an average working-class guy from Chelsea, Massachusetts, Harvard was a rarefied and almost unattainable waypoint on the trail to the great American dream. The B School, the Salomon partnership, and our notoriety today, all would have meant even more to him than to me. My mother, while she was certainly proud of her son, put it more into perspective. Sometimes, when people asked if she was related to *the* Bloomberg, she would say no just to avoid the conversation. My father would have said, "Absolutely! That's my boy. Let me tell you what else he's done."

They were always two different kinds of people. His was a less wealthy upbringing than hers. Dad's immediate family immigrated from Eastern Europe as children and never had much money. My mother's parents were born here and had done better financially. Perhaps that economic disparity, combined with the fact that one was first generation and one second, explains their different personalities. I remember my grandmother on my mother's side as very American, but my grandfather on my father's side was more Old World.

I'm proud of both families. Remembering your roots is important. Still, if you were to ask me who I am, I would say American. I wouldn't think of saying Russian American, white American, or male American. For me, no modifier is necessary. Is it that I am assimilated? It just never occurs to me to think I need to be. I am part of this country. Where my parents came from, my lineage, doesn't define me. As far as I'm concerned, I came from Saint Elizabeth's Hospital in Brighton, Massachusetts, where I was born.

Beginning in the 1990s, it became fashionable to describe the United States as a mosaic rather than a melting pot. I've always thought that was a mistake. The separatism it creates is not good for our society. Remembering and being proud of where you came from is something to celebrate—and nowhere are the celebrations and parades bigger than in New York. But it's also important to remember and be proud that we're all part of a great big family, the American one. And as in the traditional smaller families, we have to live together, communicate among ourselves, and help one another to survive.

My father's death came as a surprise to me, even though it shouldn't have. He'd had rheumatic fever as a child. In those days, that disease severely damaged your heart and dramatically shortened your life span. I remember once playing with his white metal World War II air-raid warden's helmet and asking, "Why didn't you join the Army?" "Too old," he said. But I never bothered to do the math myself. Had I thought about it, I would have realized he wasn't too old; his bad heart kept him out of the military. So until I was a junior in college in the spring of 1963 and got a call from my mother, due to my intellectual laziness I didn't know the true state of my father's health. She told me about his problem, that he was in the hospital and not doing well, and that I should get on the next train from Baltimore. He was unconscious when I got to Boston. The doctor told me he wasn't going to live. Today, he could have survived; medicine wasn't as capable then as it is now. They didn't know how many days he had left, so my mother and I agreed I'd go back to school. Forty-eight hours later, my uncle called to tell me to come back. I returned that night for the funeral. Today, fifty-five years later, I still miss him.

My sister was then a student at Antioch College and about to enter one of the on-the-job training phases of its work-study program. She selected a job in Boston to be closer to home. "You can come back to Boston if you want, but you're not going to live at home. A young college girl should be living outside and building a life of her own," my mother said. And that's what Marjorie did. She worked the next six months in Boston but lived in a rented apartment. Forcing your children and protégés to go solo—and leaving them alone while they struggle as adolescents with relatively simple problems—is something parents and mentors must do. It's not easy, but it's necessary if they're to survive later on their own.

My mother was a very practical person. When my father went into the hospital, she read the instruction manual on how to operate the gear shift in the new family car. Until then, she'd only driven an automobile with an automatic transmission. After practicing by herself on the local streets, she started chauffeuring the visiting family back and forth to the hospital.

She didn't get upset when things were beyond her control. She never complained. I think I inherited that "just do what you can do and go on to the next thing" approach. Still, I'm a bit of a screw-up who does much spontaneously. By contrast, my sister is focused and deliberate. My father was direct and to the point as well. Had you asked him, "How are you?" he would have told you. Ask my sister, she does the same. Ask my mother, she'd always say "fine." Ask me, a little of both, depending on my mood, I suppose.

* * *

I had close friends in high school, but after graduating in 1960, we all went our separate ways and didn't stay in touch. In college, I had two real pals. One took exactly the same courses as I did for years. We'd sit on the steps of his or my fraternity house each night and talk until 3:00 in the morning. We argued sports and politics and civics, and so on. When I went to Harvard Business School, he went to work for the government as an engineer.

Years later, I went to visit him for a weekend. He had been one of my best friends, but after a decade apart, we had little in common. He'd been working for the military, and I'd been in graduate school and then gone to Wall Street. He was married with young children and lived in a small apartment. I'd been dating, burning both ends of the candle, and traveling around the globe. We'd moved into very different worlds. I never saw him again until our thirty-year college reunion. A great guy, but a lot of friendship is built on common experience. End the commonality and you tend to drift apart.

My friendship with the other guy, Jack Galotto, who was a year ahead of me in school, withstood the test of time. He went into medicine, I went into business. He stayed in Maryland, I moved to Manhattan. What was the difference in the two friendships? Why did one last while the other didn't? Perhaps because I was also friendly with Jack's wife, Mary Kay? Or that Jack traveled and socialized in similar circles? Or that both Galotto children worked summers for Bloomberg? Or that he and I had actually lived together in our fraternity house while in school? Though Hopkins was a serious place, and very competitive scholastically, we did drink and party a lot together. Maybe that bonded us for good.

I was the first Jew to be admitted to the Phi Kappa Psi fraternity. After I graduated, the same local chapter admitted the first African American in its history. In those days, all fraternities were either predominantly Jewish or Christian. I joined one of the latter just because I liked Jack and wanted to be in his. (He was assigned to "rush" me as a prospective brother and stayed with me morning, noon, and night during the four weeks of rush. I don't think I ever had a chance to see another fraternity for comparison. It certainly wasn't a mistake, though. For four years, I loved it.) I always seem to be going a little against the mainstream.

Today, I've come to believe schools shouldn't tolerate campus organizations or living/eating arrangements that favor one religion or race. Education's purpose is to give students the broadest experience practical. Adults can associate with whomever they want after graduation—that's what freedom is all about. Still, teachers should require young people to try the unfamiliar so their future choices are intelligent, well-reasoned, and based on knowledge, not hearsay. Our bill of rights may apply to all, but it doesn't prevent us from forcing our youth to learn.

After school was finished, my first ten years working in New York were "play hard/work hard" times. As a bachelor who traveled with a big expense account, I had a girlfriend in every city, skied in every resort, ate in every four-star restaurant, and never missed a Broadway play. Nor did I ever pass up a chance to have one more business dinner with a visiting client, tour one more customer's office, or make that next overseas call in the middle of the night. With bachelor friends like Hugh Lowenstein and Michael Charles, I set new records in "burning the candle at both ends." There was never enough time in the day to do it all—but I always did.

Even now, decades later and a bit wiser, I still think the perfect day is one in which I'm hopelessly overscheduled. Exercise early in the morning and get to work by 7:00 a.m.; a series of rushed meetings; phone call after phone call; e-mails demanding a reply; a hurried business lunch between myriad meetings to solve firm, personnel, financial, and policy problems; perhaps give an interview to a news outlet about a Bloomberg Philanthropies initiative; constantly welcome visiting clients; participate in a Q&A at a client's big event; make a speech about one of the issues that our foundation is working on; an early dinner event with customers or for a charitable organization we support, followed by a second dinner with friends (where I actually get a chance to stop talking and eat); fall into bed, exhausted but satisfied with the day's accomplishments, maybe trying to make a dent in the magazines piled up on the nightstand. That's the best weekday one could ever have!

*　　*　　*

In 1973, I started dating Susan Brown, a loyal subject of the British Crown who'd just moved to New York. As she's stated publicly, over the next three years our dates progressed from Monday night inexpensive Mexican food to Saturday night fancy French cuisine—and there was nothing else to do but fall in love and get married. We had two daughters, Emma in 1979 and Georgina (George to everyone) in 1983. At first, Sue was uncomfortable traveling with me on business or entertaining clients. She grew to enjoy it just at the time I got pushed out of Equities at Salomon Brothers and into Systems Development, where there were many fewer nighttime or out-of-town activities. With two children to raise by that time, it was just as well.

While Sue certainly knew a lot about what I did at work on a conceptual level, other than on the most general terms we never talked business. ("How was your day?" "Fine.") I never brought the company's politics home. No matter how absorbing and consuming professional life can be, I've always felt it important not to make my business dominate the family conversation. To do so wouldn't be fair to my family—or to those at work expecting me to treat their problems in confidence. The company's business is the company's business, and I tried to keep the worlds separate; leave work problems at work, and home problems at home.

The concept of "corporate wife" or "first spouse" really turns me off. No one actually needs to know the inner workings of their spouse's place of employment, nor should he or she have a ceremonial role representing the company, or even our government. This remnant of feudalism is a fiction perpetuated by sycophants. Nepotism of any kind has no place in business or politics. Jobs should be available to all, and allocated on merit, not given as a reward to someone because of whom they are sleeping with. If the spouse wants a job, he or she should apply for it. (Or run in the next election!)

When leaving Salomon Brothers, I said to Sue, "I'd like to start a business. It'll mean I'll have to work a lot harder than I've ever worked before." (Which was difficult to do, given I was working six days a week.) "Are you okay with that?" And she responded, "Yes." Years later, she would say, "You're working so much, you're never with the family," and I replied, "I told you it would require a commitment. This is what we agreed." Of course, that's my version of the conversation.

Having a business career and raising a family create inherent conflicts. Investment of time is the primary controllable determinant of success in both. The one constant in life, however, is the clock. You can only do so much. So Sue and I always worked it out. Generally speaking, I always tried to be home for family dinner on weekdays. Every weekend and vacation I spent with our daughters on the competitive horse show circuit or at our country house.

When it comes to managing my time, there are things I do to mitigate the everything-at-once conflict. I sleep less, combine my social life with business entertaining, and make my commute to work short. I create an agenda of what I want to accomplish each day and I stick to it. And a thousand other time-saving strategies. In other words, I focus more, combine activities, and attempt to become more efficient.

Still, as you balance work and family, the inevitable either/or will invariably arise: the hockey game or the board meeting, the horse show or the sales call. Raising the family and earning an income to support it. Professional child psychologists (and most of the ones I know either have no normal children or are bizarre themselves) won't understand the conflict, or the resolution: Sometimes you go to one and sometimes to the other. Nothing and nobody's perfect! Doing this has resulted in raising two children who've grown into caring, thoughtful, and hardworking adults who have made me so proud.

We had a great marriage for a long period of time, but in 1993, Sue and I decided to divorce. Over the years, we had gradually drifted apart. We developed different interests, and as our daughters became more independent, the differences became more apparent. I liked skiing; she didn't. She liked movies; I didn't. She liked to stay at home at night; I liked to go out. I liked to travel to certain places while she liked to travel to others. Business was a very important part of my life; she almost never came to visit my office. Nothing went wrong per se. We just developed separate lives doing different things. One day, we looked back and found things had changed. It was a slow evolution, but it happened.

As was true with my parents, Sue and I never argued or fought. When we disagreed, we worked it out, or one of us simply stepped back and went along in the interest of harmony; it's been the same since we split. We didn't battle then, and we're certainly not going to do so now. People think our relationship is strange. "Your divorce is so civilized," we're told. When you have children to raise and you care about each other, how can you let it be otherwise? Sue's a wonderful person and a great friend, and to this day, we still do things with the kids as a unit, like weekend horse shows and holiday dinners together.

* * *

I've always thought much of my early career success wouldn't have been possible if I had been married at the time. Without the family responsibilities, I was able to channel my efforts toward business. Today, I've got a similar situation. The kids are grown with families of their own, and the choice of playing or working is often strictly up to me. Right now, while I'm writing this page, for example, the sun is shining and my friends are out playing tennis, golfing, flying, lying on a beach. I could join them, or do this. Obviously, I've made my selection—the same one I did long ago, when I was starting to work at Salomon Brothers. Life's a compromise. Will the satisfaction derived outweigh the sacrifices required? Of course. I never look back.

* * *

Ever since college, I've been engaged with independent projects and adventure, on my own terms. I've never been a spectator. I've always preferred doing things myself to watching other people do them, which is why I'm not much of a sports or movie fan. I'll never throw a football like Tom Brady, hit like Aaron Judge, skate like Wayne Gretzky, or shoot like LeBron James. But I'd rather try than just watch and daydream, even with sports our generation never had. When I saw kids snowboard or rollerblade by, I had to give it a whirl.

The same with skiing and flying. Almost as soon as I joined Salomon, I learned to fly—airplanes, helicopters, you name it. It's been fun, it's been a challenge, and it has taught me a lot.

One Monday, in January 1976, a Salomon partner came into work waving a story from a small local newspaper. "You crashed your helicopter this weekend, huh?" he said loudly in the partners' dining room—calling attention to a newsflash I had conveniently "forgotten" to mention that morning.

I'd been flying a rented helicopter all by myself off the coastline of Connecticut that Saturday when suddenly BANG. As I found out later, a defective piston rod had broken and smashed through the engine casing. The crankcase oil then spilled out onto the hot manifold cover and caught fire. All I knew then, however, was that I'd lost power and thick black smoke was starting to billow into the cockpit. I've always had a habit, when going over water, of staying high enough to make land in an emergency. I also always monitor an active airport radio tower. With the noise of the explosion, I wasn't sure what was going on in the engine compartment behind me, but I certainly knew I was falling and couldn't breathe. I was going down. The only question was whether I'd walk away once I got there.

Fortunately, all helicopter pilots practice something called autorotation, where you can land softly without an engine. Without thinking about it—because you don't have time in the ten seconds left aloft to reason or panic—I hit the "push to talk" button and said to the local tower, "Helicopter 9272 going down, small island off Norwalk." And I heard the controller say, "Understand, Helicopter 9272 . . ." By then I was below the horizon and I couldn't receive the signal. But I knew they'd heard me and would send help.

I was falling fast. I disconnected the engine from the transmission to let the overhead rotor spin free and build up kinetic energy. Then, a few feet above ground, I changed the pitch of the blades to generate lift. This stopped the fall just before the helicopter contacted the surface. I'd practiced autorotation again and again, and it worked. When I gently touched land, I had the helicopter skids firmly on the island and the tail over the water. The blades were just skimming the tree in front of me. Grabbing the fire extinguisher, I opened the engine compartment and extinguished the flames. It smoked for a while, but I was safe.

There were ice floes all around and some duck hunters in boats nearby. One rowed close and asked if I was injured. I would have been more than "injured" if I had gone into the frozen water. But I hadn't, so off they rowed. Was I scared? Well, there'd been no time for any emotion when I was in the air, and on the ground I was safe. So the answer is *no*—unless of course you count the internal shaking I couldn't stop for the rest of the day.

Fifteen minutes later, an Army Reserve helicopter showed up. They landed and offered me a ride back to Westchester. I asked for transportation to Teterboro Airport in New Jersey, where I'd rented the chopper and left my car. They didn't have time as they had to get back to their base in Albany, but they told me a rescue helicopter was on the way and would take me anyplace. So like the duck hunters, off they went, too.

Shortly thereafter, the Coast Guard arrived. Looking up at the giant white machine hovering overhead, I knew it was much too big to land on the small island. They opened the door and held out a blackboard with the words, "Do you need assistance?"

There I am, standing by a smoking aircraft in the middle of winter on a postage-stamp-size island with nothing but ice floes for miles around—they're asking me if I need help? They lowered the rescue basket with instructions taped to the ends. I got in, hooked my feet under one restraint and grabbed a handhold on the other. They winched me fifty feet up in the air, banging me against the bottom of the helicopter for effect while they aligned the basket with the door, right in the fierce rotor downdraft with the deafening engine noise. But finally, I was up and in.

"What happened?" they asked.

"Engine quit."

"Where do you want to go?"

At Teterboro, my instructor was standing on the tarmac waiting for me, furious, because I was now two hours late. Somebody else had the helicopter rented after me and was screaming about his reservation. Then, instead of coming back in the little rented Enstrom F-28 helicopter, I showed up in an enormous Coast Guard rescue craft from Sikorsky. Surprise!

I've always valued practice. There are occasions when there just isn't time to figure out survival procedures, no matter how smart you are. Repetition builds instinct. I'm living proof. And preparation. I subscribe to the expression, "Stay ahead of the plane." It basically means, "Do things now while you have the time, so you don't have to later when you're rushed." I try that, not just in the air, but on the ground as well. You never know when an unexpected demand will prevent you from addressing something important you could have seen to earlier but didn't. If I'd not kept altitude or monitored an active airport tower, history might have been different.

*   *   *

I was tested in a similar way in 1995. I had a propeller fail while I was flying my nephew, Benjamin, on a tour around Manhattan. We had taken off from Westchester Airport, and since it was bumpy, I had asked Departure Control for clearance to a high, hopefully calm altitude. We were climbing through fifteen hundred feet above the ground when all of a sudden POP. The engine was going around fine, but I had no thrust! Instantly, we went from a very powerful airplane to a very heavy glider.

High-performance propeller-driven airplanes run the engine at a constant speed no matter how much thrust is needed. To get more or less "push" (really "pull"), you change the pitch of the propeller blades. In my case, the governor in the propeller failed, and the oil pressure it controls suddenly couldn't keep the prop at an angle. Instead, the blades flattened, which gave us no forward drive whatsoever, no matter how fast they were going around.

My instrument gauges went crazy. The engine was running, but it might as well have been dead. (At least with a dead engine, it's quieter.) I had no time to play amateur mechanic. We were going down. Instantly, I started a 180-degree turn and called Air Traffic Control (ATC): "Departure, November five zero four Mike Bravo." That was my plane's call sign. "Emergency. Engine problem. Going back to Westchester."

"Contact tower, one nineteen seven. Will advise." The response from ATC was instantaneous.

Switching frequencies to 119.7 MHz with one hand while flying with the other, I said to the controller, "Westchester, four Mike Bravo back with you." Departure had already briefed the tower controller over their land line.

"Clearing all runways. Your choice. I've scrambled the equipment." That meant he had called out the fire engines.

"I'll take three four," I said as I carefully and methodically went through my prelanding checklist.

Turning to a heading of 340 degrees magnetic, I had just enough height to glide down, lower the landing gear, land on Runway 34, and roll off onto a taxiway to a dead, and I mean dead, stop. If I had been at a lower altitude, I wouldn't have made it back. Who knows where I could've put the plane down. The Hudson River? Landing in the water wasn't on my "to do" list. But I was lucky. Or, you could say my safety habit of always gaining altitude as fast as practicable had paid off. It's always the little things that buy you a slight extra margin, that in turn saves your rear (or your life). And if you never need it, that's even better.

My private, unprovable theory is: Nothing's going to happen to me in an airplane or helicopter from now on because, while the likelihood of one accident is small and the likelihood of two minuscule, there are no measurable odds on the likelihood of three happening to a single person. (Unfortunately, this isn't true in reality. Each is an independent event, so I'd better continue to take care. Still, it's somewhat comforting.)

I don't think Ben quite understood what was going on at the time. As I went into the turn, I said, "Ben, there's something that needs adjusting. We're just going back for a quick check." The engine was running, so as far as he knew the plane was fine. After I made the turn, he could see the airport ahead. And when the controller in the tower said he had "scrambled the equipment," Ben didn't know what that meant. As we landed, fire engines converged on us from all sides, at which point Ben figured out what was happening, but from a nicely safe vantage point on the ground. The lesson I suppose is: Don't panic. Do what you were trained to do. No more. No less.

My sister wasn't thrilled when she heard what had happened. But as I told her later, any landing you walk away from is a good one. Of less importance, there was no damage to the plane except that I overboosted the engine when I lost power and had to get it overhauled. That made the day an expensive tour of Manhattan that Ben never had.

Why fly? I like it when you have to do what you say you're going to do. You must "walk the walk," not just "talk the talk." Instrument pilots make a formal agreement with Air Traffic Control as to what they'll do under all circumstances. Everyone else in the clouds has done the same. You take off, go into a storm that's just three hundred feet above the ground, fly for two hours, and come out of the clouds just above the treetops, perfectly lined up for a runway hundreds of miles from where you started. This works even when you lose all your radios on the way. There's something about arriving safely that's very satisfying. You must do exactly what you agree to do or you might die. You apply all those rules and concepts you learned. You use those numbers, techniques, gizmos, and gadgets on the instrument panel; they really mean something.

There's no hypocrisy, no "fudging." What you say is what you do! All pilots learn to make a commitment and stick to it, follow the book, and depend on others to do the same. Those who don't, don't survive. Consistency in thought and conduct in the aviation world is required to live. In our everyday life, it's important for success as well.

*   *   *

My lessons and adventures also happen on the ground. Once I was skiing from a helicopter with some friends in British Columbia, Canada. The snow was unstable and our guide told us to stay far apart in case of an avalanche. He went down the hill first, followed by an old friend from California, Bob Brandt. Then my friend Eric Borgen fell. Another friend, Tom Weisel, and I stopped to give him a hand. Everybody else got stuck behind us. As we were ready to start again, somebody screamed, "Look, it's moving!" The snow right in front of where we were standing was moving downhill at an ever-increasing rate. The guide saw the avalanche coming, and skied up onto an outcropping. Brandt, unfortunately, looked over his shoulder, then tripped and fell—and the snow just covered him.

Suddenly, as the slide stopped moving, there was deathly silence. We realized that a human being who was there a second ago wasn't there now.

When you ski in back country like the uninhabited Bugaboo mountains, everyone wears transmitters under their clothing. If you need to, you can turn these transmitters into receivers. Then, as you go near somebody who's buried, their transmissions from under the snow will get louder and louder. As you get farther away, quieter and quieter. So you go back and forth in one direction until you figure out where the person is on that line. Then you go up and down 90 degrees in the other direction until you pinpoint your fellow skier, who should lie beneath the point where the lines cross.

We all skied down next to the avalanche and took off our skis. Everybody stopped above a large ice formation. But Bob couldn't have been above it. I didn't know how avalanches work, but I was sure they didn't carry you up the glacier, and I remembered Bob falling after he had passed that point. So I stopped a little farther down, took off my skis, and walked onto the hard snow with my beeper turned to "receive." Instantly, I picked up his signal. "He's down here!" I shouted.

"No, no. He's up here. We have him." They were clustering around each other digging like mad with their hands.

I knew right away what had happened: In the general panic, somebody up the hill had not turned his or her "transmit" to "receive." Their receivers were listening to a signal from someone in their own group instead of from somebody buried. Except for me. I was a hundred yards down the hill and there was only me above the snow. And I was hearing something. I didn't have any question whatsoever that I was right.

The guide had panicked along with everyone else. He should have stopped and checked, particularly when I was down there insisting they were wrong. His behavior was an example of believing what you want to, irrespective of possibilities raised by inconsistent facts.

He did do one thing right, however. He called the helicopter that had been ferrying us to the mountaintops. This helicopter was servicing multiple groups of skiers. It dropped one off, and while they skied down, it took the others up. When the helicopter brought in the second group to help with the search, their guide had time to make sure everybody was on "receive." While they were flying, he gave them shovels and calmly explained to them what they should do when they got on the mountain. They tried to land where I was, on a flat area that made a great helipad. But I wouldn't budge. I just kept signaling them to back off. The pilot kept gesturing wildly and trying to push me away. I refused to move, so the helicopter had no choice but to land below me and balance on a precipice during unloading. Everybody jumped out, furious with me for being stubborn and slowing them down. But as they came up the hill, I yelled, "I have the guy here. They must be doing something wrong above. Listen carefully as you come by."

Sure enough, as they came up the hill in a line with their receivers on, there was no question that I was standing right on top of Bob Brandt. They could detect him, too. When we dug him out, he said he could hear me the whole time, but I couldn't hear him screaming for his life. Maybe it was the wind, or maybe the snow muffled the sound. He wasn't harmed, just panicked. Later that year, he came down with colon cancer, had an operation, and was 100 percent cured. So, twice in twelve months, he cheated death. And he certainly didn't mind that I was a bit stubborn.

People accept things as gospel even when they don't understand them. They don't sit back and say, "Explain that to me." "Say it again." "Does that make sense?" I find it annoying when people talk freely about the XYZ—some acronym representing something or other—and when I ask, "What does XYZ stand for?" they don't have a clue. Too often, people do things automatically, thoughtlessly. It has nothing to do with their inherent intelligence. It has everything to do with their inquisitiveness. Our schools too often fail to teach logic and skepticism. We are taught facts and techniques, not concepts and thoughts; we learn to accept, not question. This terrible failing in our educational system penalizes students for the rest of their lives.

Lack of consistency is another common failing that hurts us. People say, "We'll always go in this direction," but when they are faced with a real-life situation, they often act independently of their previous plans. Either their original resolution wasn't well thought out, or they just don't have the intellectual honesty to do what they said they'd do. Picture an airline pilot. When there's a fire in engine No. 3, do you really want him or her playing amateur aeronautical engineer? No! He or she should follow the instructions arrived at much earlier in a controlled environment by aviation and safety experts: Take out the book marked "Fire in Engine No. 3" and follow the checklist, slowly, deliberately, and carefully. That's what will save the plane and its passengers. We should all do the same in our daily pursuits when relationships and careers are at stake. Think. Prepare. Plan in advance when there's no time pressure. Then, in real life, do what you said.

*   *   *

There are many reasons why some succeed and others don't, why some just continue to grow and others spurt up and, as quickly, collapse. Three things usually separate the winners from the losers over the long term: time invested, interpersonal skills, and plain old-fashioned luck.

You are born with a certain genetic intelligence level. Given the current state of medical science, you're probably stuck with whatever God gave you. Nor can you change much of your environment in any practical sense. But does that mean you should give up? Sit back and just accept the hand you've been dealt? No, of course not. Ambition and hard work, mixed with luck, can carry you a long way.

Most fortunes are built by entrepreneurs who started with nothing and generally got fired once or twice in their careers. And throughout history, the vast majority of great writers, artists, musicians, dancers, jurists, and athletes have come from the less financially secure families. The CEOs of many Fortune 500 companies went to State U rather than Ivy League schools. Could it be that good "prenatal intelligence" (the ability to pick the right parents) is possessed by those born into poor families as opposed to those who are children of the rich? Or that the traditional prerequisites of success are not terribly important today?

The rewards almost always go to those who outwork the others. You've got to come in early, stay late, lunch at your desk, take projects home nights and weekends. The time you put in is the single most important controllable variable determining your future. You can try to beat the system by winning the lottery, but the odds are terrible. You can hope the government tries to equalize with Robin Hood tax policies and throws some money your way. The

Communists tried to eliminate any form of meritocracy for seventy years and, in addition to wrecking their economies, they starved millions of people to death in the process.

If you put in the time, you aren't guaranteed success. But if you don't, I'm reasonably sure of the results.

Still, the Socialists had at least one thing right. No one does it alone. We can't each have our own army to protect our freedoms. Insurance only works if we spread the risks. It's in everyone's interest to educate all the children who will run our society when we're in our dotage. Only pooled resources can cure diseases we haven't gotten ourselves (yet!). Society is a collection of individuals: Our ability to act alone at a microlevel is provided by sharing certain responsibilities at the macrolevel. Even animals band together for companionship, protection, and food. We're better positioned to control our own lives than ever before in history, and simultaneously, in a nuclear world, we're less able to go it alone.

*   *   *

I've worked hard. You bet! But time after time, even sometimes when I didn't know it was happening, my destiny has been determined by others. Among those influencing my fate were my parents, sister, wife, kids, teachers, friends, and coworkers. Those who counseled me, those who comforted me, those who lent and shared and stood aside so that I could advance—all of them contributed to my well-being. There are other ways to say thanks to them (the best being by my conduct in life rather than my words on this page), but no other context is as good as this book to publicly state their importance. Plain and simple, my success is theirs, too.

The selfish loner who phrases everything as "I" or "me" will never go the limit. Not one of the businessmen and businesswomen at the top really deep down inside thinks that he or she did it alone. The more successful you are, the more likely it is that "you" is a group. To win big, you must have an ability to leverage your work by identifying, including, convincing, and inspiring others to follow your vision. Then share the praise, or they won't be there for very long to help, and soon there'll be little for you to talk about.

If you work hard and cooperate with others, are you guaranteed to be a billionaire, win a Nobel Prize, raise great kids, and become a household name? Not always. There's that other component: luck. I know people who have done all the right things and still don't come out on top. Some who by chance have been part of organizations where some idiot wrecked everything they built. Some who went into a business where unforecastable changes in technology, war, disease, or taste obsoleted, eliminated, or made unfashionable their product. Some whose health gave out at much too early an age, and others whose family needs kept them from trying something new. Any of a thousand other unfortunate, unforeseeable, and probably unpreventable obstacles can arise.

If I had not gotten thrown out of Salomon Brothers, I'd never have founded our company. If I'd been thrown out later, the opportunity to compete against those distracted growing giants would have been less, and our success would probably have been diminished. Suppose I hadn't been accepted at Johns Hopkins or Harvard Business School, or met Sue, or found just the right people to work at Bloomberg, or had the same college friends, or safely landed that helicopter or that plane. My life would be very different.

Work hard. Share. Be lucky. Then couple that with absolute honesty. People are much more inclined to accept and support someone they think is "on the level." We all will forgive if we don't question the intent. And never forget the biblical admonition, "Do unto others as . . ."

11

Wealth, Wisdom, and Work

Philanthropy and Public Service

On October 1, 1981, I began the entrepreneurial phase of my life. That Thursday, my prospects for future success were uncertain (unless you count the $10 million I was receiving for my stake in the sale of Salomon Brothers). I'd just been fired, and no one was offering me gainful employment. I was starting a new company to compete with corporate giants that had decades of history, hundreds of offices, thousands of workers, millions of customers, and billions of dollars of assets. I wasn't broke, but I was going against the odds.

Fifteen years later, on October 1, 1996, I sent a multimillion-dollar check to the Johns Hopkins University as part of a $55 million contribution I'd made to this great institution's capital fundraising campaign (which I was chairing). In the previous twelve months, I had made two other seven-figure gifts to cultural and educational organizations. The years between had been good to me—and now I was going to give some of it back. Within a few years, I was giving away $200 million a year. Within a few more, I had created a foundation, Bloomberg Philanthropies, that was giving away far more: $702 million in 2017. I've now given more than $6 billion, with $1.5 billion going to Hopkins, including $300 million to create the Bloomberg American Health Initiative, which aims to reverse the declining health and life expectancy that many U.S. communities are experiencing.

From the beginning, I've been committed to giving away the vast majority of my wealth during my lifetime. When Bill Gates and Warren Buffett organized the Giving Pledge in 2010 to convince billionaires to give away at least half of their wealth during their lifetime, I gladly signed on. I've always believed that the ultimate in financial planning is to bounce the check to the undertaker.

There are few people as lucky as I have been. Depending on your perspective, I deserve it or I don't. No matter which, I have it. And rather than complain about this world, rather than watch the less fortunate suffer, rather than miss the opportunity to leave my kids a better world, I've been using my time and wealth to improve it.

*   *   *

My first exposure to public service was as a Cub Scout when I was seven or eight years old. Each year, on Election Day, we volunteered to escort the elderly from their buses or cars to the voting booths. Wearing our uniforms, with every badge and medal we'd earned, and (of course) the American flag sewn on our shirts, we beamed with self-importance as we played what we were told was a "critical part" in the democratic process. Allowed the freedom to cross the police crowd-control barriers at will, we felt power and privilege. With banners flying, police standing about, campaign workers handing out campaign literature, we were overcome with pride and excitement, just like in a Norman Rockwell painting.

Twice, I had the privilege of escorting the town's most renowned citizen, the mother of the lost aviator Amelia Earhart. She must have been in her eighties then and needed to hold tightly to my arm as we walked. Everyone cleared the way and showed great deference to her as we moved slowly, step by step, to the polls. Being the center of attention (or at least next to the star) was heady stuff. I was impressed with myself, even if no one else was.

Around the Korean War period, Americans expressed their patriotism openly. On Patriot's Day, every April 18, hundreds of adults would gather in the town center for the reading of the Henry Wadsworth Longfellow poem "Paul Revere's Ride," celebrating the start of the American Revolution. A mounted rider in period attire would retrace the famous rebel messenger's historic route from Boston to Lexington and on to Concord. To the delight of the children lining the sidewalks, he'd scream, "The British are coming, the British are coming," as he galloped by.

Perhaps the proudest moment of my early life was being chosen one year to read this famous rhyme on the raised platform overlooking the assembled revelers. With "Paul" on his prancing horse in front of me, the high school band playing John Philip Sousa marches, and newspaper photographers snapping away, I read aloud into a real live microphone the famous poem: "Listen, my children, and you shall hear/Of the midnight ride of Paul Revere/ On the eighteenth of April, in Seventy-five/Hardly a man is now alive/Who remembers that famous day and year . . . /One, if by land, and two, if by sea/And I on the opposite shore will be . . . / And yet, through the gloom and the light/the fate of a nation was riding that night . . ." I can remember it still.

Memorial Day, honoring those fallen in defense of our country, was another big celebration in Medford. Back then, all towns had parades and wreath-laying ceremonies at the local cemetery. The police on motorcycles; the firefighters in their trucks; the fraternal organizations, churches, and veterans' groups with flags and bands; and the regional branch of the National Guard, with rifles at the ready, all marched. From school, we filed two by two in orderly rows to the parade finish at the town's war memorial. There we would stand at attention very solemnly pledging allegiance "to the flag of the United States of America and to the Republic for which it stands, one nation under God, indivisible, with liberty and justice for all." Then the lone bugler played "Taps," and the jolting firing of the Honor Guards' guns in salute closed the proceedings.

I was friendly with a girl whose father had been killed in World War II; his name was engraved on a bronze plaque at a nearby traffic circle. She was the first person of my generation I knew who had lost a parent. Once, we were chosen together to carry the school's Memorial Day wreath to the monument as everybody looked on. It was quite a responsibility for children. Our classmates, the parade participants, and the elected officials all watched as we moved slowly in step to the drummers' cadence. Heaven forbid we would trip, cough, sneeze, or otherwise break the solemnity of the occasion. It was an honor to participate, and it made those carefully listed rights and privileges we studied in civics class somehow more real and important.

I grew up holding great respect for police officers and firefighters, too. We played on the fire trucks when visiting the fire station to pet the traditional firehouse Dalmatian. We talked and joked with the police officers handling traffic at the corner school crossing each morning. While officers' uniforms create fear in many parts of the world, the familiarity born of constant interaction always left me feeling the wearers were employees of "we the citizens" and there to protect and serve.

Long before I became mayor, one of my favorite philanthropic causes became the New York City Police and Fire Widows' and Children's Benefit Fund, which provides funds to the widows of fallen officers and firefighters who died protecting us. Unfortunately, the list of beneficiaries grows longer each year. Today, I still never walk by an officer in the street without reaching out my hand to say thank you.

*　　　*　　　*

Maybe my childhood experiences kindled my passion for public service later in life. In the late 1990s, after I had become wealthier than I ever imagined, I began thinking about how I could most effectively give back. I was still in my 50s, and the idea of a third career (after being a Wall Street trader and tech entrepreneur) began to take hold.

I never had any interest in being a legislator. The pace, the focus, and the compromises don't appeal to me. The legislative process is so slow that I'd last for all of five minutes as a senator or a congressman. I knew that if I ever ran, it would be for a job in the executive branch of government—mayor, governor, or president. All three are executive jobs that mirrored my experience and skill set. That's why I ran for mayor and have considered running for president.

It still amazes me how many people presenting themselves as candidates for high office have an interest in running for any position they can get elected to, with no thought of what their skills are, or whether they'd be better at administration or strategic thought. When considering candidates for an executive job, we shouldn't think that serving in a legislative position prepares that person for the totally different responsibilities of an executive. In the real (commercial) world, where performance is the only thing that counts, these people would never be considered for promotion to positions requiring totally different talents.

Politics, no matter what the cynics say, is a noble profession. What a shame that some who hear the call to run for office ruin what's so good in America—and make promises they know they can't keep. We should insist that officials deliver after the election what they promised during the campaign and uphold the highest ethical standards. It's a sin that some of our highest elected officials come up so short.

A year or so into my first year in office, we released a progress report telling the public which campaign promises were kept and which were still in progress. And when we came to believe that an idea no longer made sense, we owned up to it and told the public. Full transparency—imagine that! Unfortunately, few others have followed our example.

In a democracy, we need good, smart, hardworking people with management experience to run for executive office and run the government. Society is too complex for us to run things ourselves. Somebody has to bring us to a centrist consensus acceptable to most, with minimal imposition on those at the fringes. That's what politics is all about. It's hard to think of a tougher challenge or a more needed service—or, in my experience, a more satisfying occupation.

Serving as mayor of New York for twelve years was one of the most rewarding experiences of my life. Today, people ask me what I'm most proud of from my time in office. It's a hard question. Improving schools, so that more children have a chance to pursue their dreams. Driving down crime to record lows. Expanding public parks. Investing in infrastructure improvements, which will lay the foundation for job growth for decades to come. Revitalizing the waterfront with new parks, jobs, housing, and art and culture. Reducing the city's carbon footprint by nearly 20 percent, which also helped give the city its cleanest air quality in more than fifty years. Standing up against xenophobic and nativistic sentiments at a time when so many others did not. There's a lot we did that I'm proud of. But the one accomplishment that might sum it up best is a single number: three years. That's how long life expectancy increased on our watch, far outpacing the increase in the rest of the country. Helping people live longer, healthier lives—that's one of government's most basic responsibilities.

*   *   *

In addition to giving me a sense of public service, my family taught me about private philanthropy when I was very young. I have never forgotten seeing my father write out a check for $25 or $50—which was a lot of money for us—to the NAACP. I asked him why he was giving to that group, and he explained that discrimination against one group is discrimination against all groups. Tolerate it for another race or religion, and expect it for your own. His donation was a gift—not only to the NAACP but also to me.

I learned from my father another important lesson about philanthropy and what drives it. Every year, he received a publication listing contributors to a charity he supported. During dinner, he would look down each page for familiar names and remark on the size of the gift made by people he knew, or the complete absence of other names from the list. What his acquaintances gave certainly influenced my father in deciding on contributions for the following year. Peer pressure: Its impact in the philanthropic world is hard to overstate. People are very conscious of their place in any pecking order. Contributor lists, grouped by amount donated, very often get donors to stretch to the next highest level. When soliciting for donations, always ask for more than you think you'll receive. You may be wrong and get it. The potential contributors will be flattered that you thought they could give that much. And they certainly will give more than they previously planned, when confronted with the bigger target. Competition works. In the 1990s, I gave my first large gift to Harvard—and a few months later, someone else donated three times that amount for a similar purpose, citing my gift as the impetus.

When asked for a major contribution, if I'm interested in the cause, my first question to the solicitor is, "What did the organization's board members and you personally give?" If they don't support the cause, at whatever level they can afford, maybe it doesn't deserve my help. Conversely, when I ask others for donations to an effort or organization, I always start the conversation by describing how and why I'm supporting it. Those I'm asking have a right to know, and I'm proud of what we do.

Asking other folks for money is difficult, and some find it distasteful. But you have two choices: Don't ask and don't help as much as you can, or ask and maximize assistance to your favorite causes. Do you care enough to swallow your pride, summon up your courage, commit your resources, and take the time to pick up the phone? Those who do follow through don't necessarily find it easier than those who can't bear to make the call—they just care more about helping.

When the National September 11 Memorial & Museum was in development, construction costs had ballooned to the point where fundraising had stalled, because people stopped believing it would ever get built. I was serving as mayor at the time, and while I wasn't looking for another job, building the memorial and museum was so important to our city—and to all who had lost loved ones in the attacks. We owed it to them to build a powerful and inspiring memorial that would stand the test of time. And so I agreed to become chairman of the board. Immediately, we enlisted construction experts to help us bring costs back down to earth, and I began calling and meeting with potential donors. We committed to opening the memorial by the 10th anniversary of the attacks and to raising $450 million. With a lot of great work from many people, we met both goals. Fundraising is never easy. But if you believe in a cause enough to donate your own hard-earned money, why not ask others to help?

The reality of great wealth is that you can't spend it all and you can't take it with you. All you can do is give it to other individuals (with large gift or inheritance taxes to *pay*), or give it to philanthropic organizations (usually with large income tax credits to *receive*). The issues left to your discretion are only to whom, how much, and when to give.

So, after you've gotten used to having more money than you can spend, what do you do?

First, forget worrying over taxes. More people do more stupid things trying to avoid the inevitable than they can count. Our country gave you the opportunity—now pay back your share and get on with it.

Second, don't spoil your family—or try to control them after you are gone. I've watched family after family destroyed by excessive and unequal distributions to descendants, and by family patriarchs' and matriarchs' attempts to control others' behavior from the grave. If a fortune pits sister against brother, or causes self-destructive behavior, having given your hard-earned wealth to them turns out to have been the worst thing you could have done.

Third, be selfish! Buy yourself enormous pleasure: Give most of your wealth to charity! And encourage your children and theirs to be generous, too.

I've created trusts for my children, and for the rest of their lives, they'll have the ability to distribute grants through their own foundation to worthy institutions and creative individuals needing support. Every so often, they get together and approve grants. They also sit on the board of Bloomberg Philanthropies, where they help guide its work and funding, which in 2017 topped $700 million. But they don't work at Philanthropies or at the company. I've never believed in nepotism and have always wanted them to have their own lives and careers, based on their own interests. It's been wonderful to see them follow their own passions, and I'm very proud that both have taken a deep interest in philanthropy. If your kids understand the importance of helping others, you've done something right.

*　　　*　　　*

In the early days of my philanthropy, I gave to worthy causes and bought tables of tickets at fundraising dinners for organizations doing important work. But as the checks got bigger and I became more involved in public policy issues, I realized that to have the largest possible impact a more systematic approach was required. In the 2000s, with help from Patti Harris—who had managed philanthropy at Bloomberg for seven years until I appointed her as deputy mayor in 2001—we set up an umbrella organization with a board of directors, Bloomberg Philanthropies, to oversee all my giving. The organization allows us to do more than write checks. It allows us to identify what we consider to be the most pressing challenges and make long-term commitments to them—not only in terms of funding but also in terms of strategy and goals. Patti oversees the foundation's work and has built a talented team that is constantly pushing harder and reaching higher.

In deciding where to focus our giving, two experiences have had a profound impact on me.

The first was my time chairing the board of my alma mater, Johns Hopkins, beginning in the 1990s. Until then, while I loved science, I had no particular interest in public health policy. But after spending some time with the dean of the School of Public Health, Al Sommer, I began developing a passion for it. Medicine can save one life at a time. Public health policy can save millions at a time. Small policy interventions—like putting warning labels on tobacco products—can make all the difference and save an enormous number of lives. The trouble is, philanthropists have often given far more of their wealth to hospitals that might one day save their lives. Traditionally, there wasn't much philanthropic money in public health. As I became more active in philanthropy, I made sure that we focused on unmet needs that others—both in foundations and government—tended to overlook, because that's where we could have the greatest impact.

The second experience that shaped my approach to philanthropy was the twelve years I spent as mayor of New York City. I had always seen donations from the perspective of a donor or a nonprofit institution, so I understood the need that donations filled. But in government, I also got to see the opportunities they opened up—and the potential for innovation they created.

The simple fact is, the public sector traditionally has not innovated very well. And I think that's true for two reasons. First, there are powerful disincentives working against government innovation, because innovation involves risk, and risk involves the potential for failure. And if there's one thing that scares politicians—not to mention their political advisors—it's failure. Plus, the media magnifies failure and opponents exploit it. So, politicians play it safe and avoid taking risks. That may win you reelection, but it's not going to help you solve problems, which is what you get elected to do.

The second disincentive working against innovation in government is more understandable: fiduciary duty. As an elected official, you are responsible for spending taxpayers' dollars wisely, and it can be hard to justify spending the public's money on an untested idea, especially when budgets are already stretched thin. That's where philanthropy comes in.

Elected officials who are willing to risk failure can raise private money to test ideas, reducing the downside of experimentation. In so many areas, governments represent our best hope for making the broad-based societal changes that philanthropic organizations are devoted to bringing about. Governments have the scale of broad-based policy and regulatory authority that allows them to drive change in ways that philanthropic organizations cannot. But by forming partnerships with government, philanthropic organizations can help push those changes forward.

In other words, philanthropists have resources that governments need for innovation, and governments have powers that philanthropists need for solving problems. It's a perfect match—and from our experience in New York City, these public-private partnerships can be incredibly powerful.

Take our antipoverty work. We wanted to tackle the obstacles facing many young people, particularly young black and Latino men—but it was the middle of the Great Recession and the city's budget was already stretched thin. I had agreed to make a $30 million contribution to create what we called the Young Men's Initiative. But that wasn't enough. So, I invited George Soros to lunch and asked him to chip in $30 million, too. I'm not sure he was expecting such an expensive lunch—but to his great credit, he agreed. And after we demonstrated the potential, the Obama administration launched a nationwide program modeled in part on ours.

In just about every area of city government, we formed public-private partnerships to tackle challenges with new ideas. Over twelve years, we raised $1.4 billion in philanthropic contributions that made possible a wide variety of programs, from a new leadership academy to train high school principals, to innovative new initiatives to tackle poverty, to hundreds of public art installations.

Encouraging innovation in government is now a core part of the work that our foundation does. We run a competition called the Mayors Challenge that incentivizes cities to come up with creative new ideas for tackling common challenges. We pick the best of them and provide funding to help cities implement them. Providence, Rhode Island, won our first Mayors Challenge with a program to increase the number of words that toddlers are exposed to. The program has gotten a lot of attention because it's novel and it's fairly simple: It counts the number of unique words that parents, guardians, and caregivers speak to their children. By increasing the number, they can help spur a child's cognitive development. Or at least, that's the idea—and other cities have already begun adapting it. Adaptability is actually part of the competition criteria: We look for the most promising ideas that have the potential to be replicated, so we can spur change not just in one city but around the world.

Philanthropy has traditionally been thought of as an alternative to government—and in some cases, it is. But I also see it as a way to embolden government. That idea lies at the heart of the work that Bloomberg Philanthropies does in all of the five major areas we focus on: public health, education, the environment, the arts, and government innovation.

Through advocacy aimed at elected and appointed officials, and through partnerships with them, philanthropic organizations can accomplish far more than they could by acting alone.

*   *   *

We have a simple goal at Bloomberg Philanthropies: helping the greatest number of people around the world live better and longer lives. To reach it, we apply some of the lessons I've learned in both business and government about problem solving.

Lead from the front. Special interest lobbying and campaign contributions—and reelection considerations—too often set the agenda in politics, and as a result, the public is not well served. Philanthropy can lead where elected officials fear to tread. For example, our work to eliminate coal-fired power plants isn't politically popular in some coal-producing states, but it is saving lives in those regions—and around the country. We've given $180 million to support a partnership led by the Sierra Club, called Beyond Coal, that has succeeded in closing or phasing out more than half of the coal-fired power plants in the United States. As a result, we've cut the number of Americans dying from coal pollution to 7,500 each year, from 13,000, while also substantially cutting our country's carbon emissions. A story in *Politico* described it as perhaps the most effective campaign in the history of the environmental movement.

Some politicians are still insisting that government can put coal miners back to work. But the truth is that advanced technology and cheaper and cleaner sources of energy have been putting coal miners out of work for decades. The question isn't whether that trend can be reversed; it can't. The question is whether we're going to be honest with people who live in coal regions and work with their communities to spur new industries and jobs—a challenge the federal government has never embraced. Bloomberg Philanthropies is among those trying to fill the void, through small-scale pilot programs that support local economic development and job-training programs.

Look for unmet needs. Sometimes the biggest opportunities haven't gotten the attention and funding they deserve. Take road safety. Every year some 1.3 million people are killed in road crashes around the world, and another 50 million are injured. Adopting

223

and enforcing basic safety laws—like requiring helmets to be worn on motorcycles, and seat belts and air bags to be standard in cars and trucks—can prevent many of those deaths and injuries. In the United States, we often take these safety features for granted. But in much of the world, they don't exist. By galvanizing public support for these kinds of policies, along with infrastructure upgrades that design streets for safety, philanthropic organizations can save countless lives and prevent even more injuries.

Spread solutions that work. There's no one-size-fits-all solution to every problem, and every city and country is different. But when a wheel turns smoothly, don't try to reinvent it. In New York City, we were never shy about borrowing good ideas, and we were happy to see other cities and countries borrow ours. Bloomberg Philanthropies works to identify strategies and policies that are both effective and replicable—and then spread them around the world.

Follow the data. Accurate and reliable data is the driving force behind Bloomberg, and our foundation is no different. We have a saying: "In God we trust; everyone else bring data." Our work is driven by reliable data, and we follow it wherever it leads. We use it to identify problems and opportunities others have overlooked—and to target our resources, measure our success, and adjust our strategies. For instance: Believe it or not, half of all deaths in the world go unrecorded. There's no death certificate, so governments don't have reliable data on what people are dying from. Without that data, they don't know where to focus their efforts to save and improve lives, and they have no way to measure whether those efforts are effective. Working with partners, we've helped twenty countries that are home to more than one billion people improve their death-record collections, which will pinpoint causes of death and disease and provide a better understanding of the best ways to prevent them. It's not the sexiest issue by a long shot, but it has the potential to save a lot of lives.

Data doesn't give us all the answers: that requires creativity and innovative problem solving. But data and facts anchor our thinking to reality at a time when political debate is increasingly untethered from it—especially at a time when "alternative facts" have become popular.

Focus on cities. Unlike those in Washington, mayors and other local officials cannot get away with ignoring proven facts in favor of personal opinions. They are the officials most directly responsible for the services people depend on, and their success is measured in real time: whether streets are safe, the air is clean, roads are in good condition, and students are graduating from school. When a child suffers from asthma caused by dirty air, parents call the mayor, not their member of Congress. Local leaders have no incentive to build policies based on misinformation, because they have nowhere to hide from bad results.

Because they are held accountable, local leaders also tend to be more willing to work with members of other political parties, and to experiment with bold new ideas—wherever they come from. That makes city halls more nimble, more pragmatic, more responsive to public concerns, more open to experimentation, and more committed to using data than national governments. It also makes them great partners for foundations.

Cities around the world are a major focus of our work. We provide funding for mayors to hire what we call i-Teams, shorthand for Innovation Teams. The teams help cities bring different agencies together to find new solutions to problems, and they help mayors generate and implement big ideas. We've also assembled a collection of all-stars from our time in City Hall and created a pro bono consultancy, Bloomberg Associates. Their expertise is much in demand by mayors, and they receive far more requests for help than they can take.

In 2017, we launched the $200 million Bloomberg American Cities Initiative, the largest-ever philanthropic effort to support mayors and city halls. The timing is not coincidental. We need cities, and data-driven mayors, more than ever.

Form partnerships. The challenges we face in America and around the world are increasingly complex, and neither the private nor the public sector can solve them alone. Public-private partnerships were critical to my time in City Hall, and they lie at the heart of our work at Bloomberg Philanthropies. A great example of this is our work on climate change. When President Trump announced his intention to withdraw from the Paris Climate Agreement in 2017, I worked with California governor Jerry Brown to organize a coalition of states, cities, and businesses that remain committed to driving down emissions and upholding our end of the bargain. We call the group America's Pledge, and if it were its own country, it would be the third largest economy in the world, behind only the overall United States and China. The fact is, bottom-up partnerships that are aligned to market trends—like the declining price of renewable energy—have driven far more progress on climate change than top-down mandates. That's why I believe the United States will meet its commitment under the Paris agreement, no matter what obstacles Washington throws in the way.

Empower advocates. Special interests often hold sway over governments, but countries and communities can fight back and win. We work to help them do that on a broad range of issues, particularly where industries spread money liberally in lobbying, campaign contributions, and often deceptive advertising. We help organizations be effective advocates in mobilizing public support and moving government officials to act. For instance, we support groups that are pushing their governments to adopt tobacco control measures that are proven to have an impact, such as tobacco tax increases, graphic health warnings on tobacco products, and smoke-free laws. Today, cigarette sales are declining globally for the first time in history, and that's saving lives. Advocacy is also critical to our work on other public health issues, including obesity, opioids, road safety, and maternal and reproductive health, as well as in education and the environment.

I've given $1 billion to combat tobacco use, which will kill one billion people this century if we do nothing. But my first big contribution to the fight against tobacco was not a check I wrote but a bill I signed back in 2002. The law that we adopted in New York City banning smoking in bars, restaurants, and all indoor workplaces set in motion a wave of change that has spread around the world. Nations in Europe and South America—where smoking was such an ingrained part of the culture—adopted similar laws, as did states around the U.S. By proving that the law could work in New York City, we helped start a global movement. That experience informed my approach to philanthropy—and it's why we focus much of our tobacco control work on helping local grassroots organizations around the world change their government's policies.

*   *   *

Helping others is also good for business—and at Bloomberg, it's always been a big part of our culture.

We have offices around the world, and in each one, we encourage our employees to get involved in community service. We also match their donations to the many charities that Bloomberg supports. And some of our philanthropic work we do in partnership with clients: We've teamed up with Citi and the YMCA to build bikes for low-income kids. Other work we do builds on the expertise of our employees: We have been long-time supporters of the FIRST Robotics Competition. We sponsor teams composed of hundreds of high school students (from mostly low-income areas) who are interested in science and engineering, and we pair them with Bloomberg employees who volunteer to mentor the teams and guide them through the six-week competition that centers on building an industrial-size robot. It's a great learning experience for the kids—something I would've loved to have done as a teenager. It fosters a spirit of teamwork among our employees. And it also gives us exposure to talented kids who, someday, we may be recruiting.

Our employees also participate in a mentoring and tutoring program we call Bloomberg Startup. More than 3,500 employees—almost 20 percent of our workforce—participated last year. Tutoring and mentoring has always been a focus of my philanthropy. One of our earliest projects involving our employees was our school-painting activity. Working with Publicolor, a New York–based nonprofit, our staff donates their time on weekends to apply colorful paints to the walls of a school building, usually in a low-income neighborhood. Together, we transform the learning environment of thousands of kids, while also entering into mentoring relationships with them.

We've long supported another organization, Prep for Prep, which sends the brightest low-income kids to private schools they could not otherwise afford to attend. And every year we hire hundreds of summer interns, many from low-income families. Getting the most productive workforce requires attracting the broadest possible spectrum of candidates, across gender, religious, sexual orientation, socioeconomic, and racial lines. Having a diverse workforce increases the likelihood that the next great idea will be born here, not at some other company—and the intern program is one way we can improve our odds. We try hard to make their experience for the few months they work with us as meaningful as possible. Young people get to see what our company and the business world are like, and we create an experience that aims to prepare them to be leaders in whatever field they choose. In a few years, we'll be in competition with other firms for these same kids or their friends. Hopefully, based on their familiarity with Bloomberg, they'll choose us—and many have.

Helping kids has always been a passion for me, and education has long been a focus of my philanthropy. Years ago, I served on the board of the Institute for Advanced Study, at Princeton, New Jersey, a think tank for postdoctoral students working on the more theoretical problems in the social and natural sciences. Who knows what great advances will come from its members? (Albert Einstein was one of the institute's first faculty members.) I've also given back to Harvard and other schools. But my educational giving has been primarily focused on the school that first gave me a chance, Johns Hopkins. When a Hopkins researcher makes a breakthrough discovery, or an alumnus diplomat helps spread peace, or a writer inspires creative expression, I share a little bit of the reward—the knowledge of making a difference.

The same is true with watching an undergrad go on to do great things. We endowed needs-based scholarships that allow high school seniors (who otherwise could not afford it) to attend Hopkins—without taking out loans. The truth is, when kids who have earned their way into top colleges don't attend because of family finances, not only do they lose out—so do the colleges. And so does our country.

In recent years, our foundation has created programs aimed at increasing the number of high-achieving, low-income students who attend top colleges—not just Hopkins but schools across the country. Right now, only one half of 1 percent of children in the bottom 20 percent of family income attend one of the nation's top 200 colleges. If we really believe America is a meritocracy, we cannot accept that statistic. Our foundation has enlisted about 100 college presidents who have committed to enrolling more of these qualified students, through a program we developed called the American Talent Initiative. We also created a high school counseling program, called College Point. It aims to give high-achieving, low-income students guidance through the college application and financial aid process so that more of them attend high-caliber colleges that match their abilities. Together, the two programs help increase the supply of spots for qualified low-income applicants *and* the demand for them by students.

Helping to give more children access to the American dream is one of the most satisfying things I can do—and one of the most important for our country.

Our company has also worked to spread opportunity further and wider on college campuses, through partnerships with historically black colleges and universities. There have always been too few African American business journalists, and so we have had relationships with a number of these colleges and universities dating back to the 1990s. More recently, Matt Winkler created a journalism program with the University of North Carolina at Chapel Hill. It's designed for aspiring journalists from diverse backgrounds, and it has led to new Bloomberg interns, some of whom have become full-time employees. Partnerships with other colleges, including Hampton, Morgan State, and Appalachian State, have also helped us increase diversity in business journalism.

We support aspiring journalists overseas, too, particularly in regions without deep histories in business reporting. The Bloomberg Media Initiative–Africa has worked with universities in Kenya, Nigeria, South Africa, and other African nations to train journalists to analyze and report on economic data and to improve the quality and availability of that data. We also support business journalism programs at universities in China, India, and the Middle East. Reliable data and excellent business journalism can help inform international investors about opportunities in these regions, lifting living standards and benefitting global growth. It's another example of how doing good is good business.

*   *   *

Those opposed to private contributions to support public aims argue that they eliminate the rightful role of government. Those opponents miss two points. First, the government can't do everything. Second, the government doesn't do everything well. Both of those truths became especially clear to me during my time in

City Hall, and some of our company's philanthropic work has grown out of that experience. For instance, we are the top coat donor to the largest winter coat drive in New York, and we offer a twelve-week work experience for graduates of a program run by the Fortune Society, which works to help those who were incarcerated get their lives back on track.

My experience in City Hall also made me acutely aware of the power of public support at a time of crisis. The world's response to the attacks of September 11, 2001, lifted our city's spirits and helped us begin the process of recovering and rebuilding. That morning was primary Election Day—my first election as a candidate for mayor. I immediately suspended the campaign and spoke with family members who feared the worst. Our employees routinely visited clients in the World Trade Center, and tragically, three of our team members there that day did not make it out alive: Peter Alderman, William Kelly, and Paul Ortiz. As we mourned, we did whatever we could to help, by opening up our offices in Lower Manhattan to rescue and recovery workers and offering our support. Weeks later, I was elected mayor—winning the opportunity, and awesome responsibility, to begin healing our city and leading it out of the darkness.

The incredible support New York City received from around the world left me with a special appreciation of the need to help those suffering through a crisis. When back-to-back major hurricanes struck the Caribbean in 2017, Tom Secunda, who has a house on St. John in the U.S. Virgin Islands, called to tell me how devastating the storms were. But much of the federal government's attention was focused on more populous areas hit by the storms, including Houston. So we immediately mobilized a disaster relief effort, flying down emergency medical supplies from Johns Hopkins, along with doctors and nurses, plus food and other essential items. We also did something just as important: We lent members of our team who, through their time in City Hall, had experience dealing with

Hurricane Sandy in 2012. Together with Tom, they worked closely with the local government to assist in the recovery effort and help them navigate the Federal Emergency Management Agency and its regulations. When much of the recovery work was done, Tom and our team continued to support the government's efforts to make the island more resilient in future storms, which—given climate change—are likely to grow worse. Hopefully, our work can serve as a model for other places that experience devastating storms.

Companies, of course, have a legal responsibility to maximize the assets of stockholders. Nowhere is there relief from that objective (nor, given the potential for abuse, should there be). Activities not furthering that cause are generally prohibited. Just because management thinks something's worthwhile from society's point of view, they can't (or shouldn't) give away the stockholders' assets. Companies have an obligation to distribute dividends and let the individual shareholders do what they see fit. Likewise in the conduct of their affairs. If it doesn't further the corporate purpose, it's outlawed.

Still, when helping others helps the company, it couldn't be more in the stockholders' interests or more appropriate as a corporate activity. Private companies, like individuals, enjoy greater freedom than public corporations to do what they think is right. We refused to enter the South African market during apartheid. We adopted this policy before many U.S. municipalities required it for their suppliers. Sometimes, you just have to do what you think is best for society, even when it's not popular or profitable.

Today, Bloomberg is a leader in sustainability, partly because it's good business (it saves us money), partly because it's the right thing to do (lower emissions improves public health and fights climate change), and partly because it helps us attract employees who want to work for a company that cares about the environment. Young people, especially, expect companies to do their part on climate change. Being a leader helps give us an edge on other companies that may be recruiting them. Our headquarters in New York is a LEED-certified building, and our new European headquarters in London, which we opened in 2017, is the world's most sustainably designed office building. If you want your employees to look forward to coming to work every day, you need to design an environment that inspires them—and then treat them well.

Through support for cultural organizations, we're able to offer our employees, along with their families, free access to some of the world's greatest museums, theaters, galleries, and performing arts centers. And to enhance everyone's experience—our employees and all visitors—Bloomberg Philanthropies has worked with a number of cultural organizations on a program called Bloomberg Connects. It provides visitors with digital tools that allow them to have the kind of expert, tailored, curated experiences that VIPs get when they visit.

For a relatively small cost, we can give employees and their families a benefit that they value—and that they'd miss if they left. It's a great way to build loyalty, while also supporting the arts organizations that add so much life to the cities where our company is located. We want to be known as a company that not only takes care of our employees but is also generous to our community. It all helps the bottom line. Companies that don't understand that don't do as well as they could. Give something back and you'll wind up with more.

Of course, no company can get involved in every issue or solve every problem. But where we think we can make the biggest difference, we don't hesitate to jump in. And since we're Bloomberg, we like to tell our story of service with data. In 2017, Bloomberg employees planted 73,059 trees, built 1,521 bikes, cleaned 75 local parks, donated 2,500 hours of coaching for small business owners, gave 20,884 articles of clothing to charity, assembled 35,408 emergency hygiene kits and care packages for those displaced by natural disasters, prepared or served 1,861,699 meals to families in need—and the list goes on. Since I've always believed in leading by example, I pitch in too: I've painted schools and planted trees and donated blood, something I've been doing for ages. The best way to encourage employees to donate their time and energy is to do it yourself. Inspiration works better than dictation.

* * *

I give out of a sense of responsibility to help others, but I also have a less altruistic reason: Giving back is just about the most rewarding thing you can do. By making gifts when we're still around, we can get the greatest satisfaction available for cash today: watching the process of helping others unfold.

Both Johns Hopkins University and Yale University had benefactors who experienced this firsthand. Zanvyl Krieger, a Baltimore lawyer with a great feeling for humanity, had planned to leave the magnificent sum of $50 million to Hopkins after his death. Then, in 1992, he asked himself, on second thought, "Why wait?" Why let another generation go without an education? Why let some cure for a disease be discovered after more have died? So he gave the money then, rather than leave it in his will. Were the adulation, recognition, respect, and pleasure received worth it? His response said it all: "Should have done it even earlier."

Lee Bass had a different experience, a less pleasant one, but another reason to make gifts when you are alive rather than as a bequest. He gave $20 million to Yale for a particular program. For a variety of reasons, they could never get it going. So he took his money back (and gave it away to some other equally worthwhile cause). Had he done it by bequest, he'd have had no second chance.

Giving now, rather than after you die, also allows you to share the satisfaction with others, by giving in their names. Years ago, in honor of my mother's seventy-fifth birthday, I endowed a professorship in the study of art history at Hopkins. It's something she was interested in and the school needed. For the remainder of her years, she took great pleasure knowing the Charlotte Bloomberg Professor is teaching, researching, and enhancing our culture. My mother, my sister, and I annually awarded grants to people contributing to Jewish causes, another of my mother's great loves. The Charlotte Bloomberg Awards and the yearly awards ceremony were something she looked forward to each winter. You could see it in her eyes as she helped to select the winners and bestow the honorarium.

I've also endowed a professorship/fellowship at Harvard University to study and research philanthropic and volunteer policies and practices, named in honor of my late father. Every two years, this "chair" passes from one school at Harvard to another (Divinity, Education, Law, Government, the College, and of course, my alma mater, Business). And so, every twenty-four months, a new person studies, teaches, researches, and writes from a new perspective about my interest, philanthropy.

Making donations in the name of my parents is a way not only to honor them, but also to honor the values they passed down to my sister and me and to our children. The Charlotte R. Bloomberg Children's Center at Johns Hopkins is a state-of-the-art hospital that we designed with beautiful art installations to create a peaceful and inspiring environment conducive to healing. In Jerusalem, we worked with the emergency medical service provider, Magen David Adom, to create the William H. Bloomberg MDA Jerusalem Station, which serves all people—Jewish, Muslim, Christian, or otherwise—in need. And it was a special moment for me when we dedicated the William and Charlotte Bloomberg Science Education Center at the Boston Museum of Science. After my parents, the museum was my greatest teacher. What better way to honor both? I've also dedicated buildings at my daughters' alma maters, Princeton and New York University, and given other gifts in honor of them and their children. Through philanthropy, I can pass on the lesson my father taught me all those years ago while writing a check to the NAACP: We all have a responsibility to help others.

That responsibility is one reason I'm opposed to eliminating the inheritance tax, as some want to do. Dynastic fortunes are not healthy for a democracy, and the inheritance tax is one way to limit them—and thankfully, the wealthiest individuals have traditionally limited them on their own, by distributing their largesse wisely. The Carnegie, Ford, Mellon, Rockefeller, and Duke fortunes were largely given back to society by their makers and heirs, creating institutions that have had much more lasting impact than the politicians would ever have delivered by taking that same money through income and inheritance taxes. The original fortune builder, and one or two of their successor generations, may have lived well, but most contributed more than they took. America, and the world, is much better off because of them.

Are today's wealthy families as generous as those who came before? The Bloomberg Billionaires Index contains extremely generous benefactors—and some who are not as generous. But from the "robber barons" before World War I to today's philanthropic giants, those who achieve much for themselves are generally those who give the most—and they are in good company. Americans give wealth away in record amounts to help others, and our willingness to share success is unique. The number of nonprofit institutions has skyrocketed. We may have more than others—but we give more help to those who have less. Where else are there as many privately funded universities, museums, symphonies, hospitals, churches, and so on? Think other places are fairer, more egalitarian, more generous, offering a better life to average persons (particularly for those traditionally discriminated against)? Get serious. When people vote with their feet, they *always* come in this direction.

*　　　*　　　*

Private philanthropy is an American tradition—one of our unique contributions to humanity, and one of the reasons for our country's great success. And you don't have to have great wealth to make a difference. Small gifts add up and do great things collectively—and technology has made it easier than ever to organize a fundraising drive, as Kickstarter and other online fundraising platforms have shown. After the 2017 mass shooting in Las Vegas that killed fifty-eight people, I announced via Twitter that I would match all donations to Everytown for Gun Safety, a group we founded to support laws that help keep guns out of the hands of criminals, the mentally ill, and other dangerous people. In just a few short days, donations poured in. The American people can achieve far more than wealthy individuals, but wealth can help incentivize and organize public actions.

However much people contribute, and whatever it is they give, I've always respected those who try to change the world for the better rather than just complain about it. Some devote their time, some their money. Some focus on philanthropy, some on government. I've been lucky to do both. And I have tried to do it in the way I think does the most good. That's the most valuable inheritance I'm leaving my daughters and grandchildren: trying to do my part to make their world better, safer, fairer, and healthier. It's also the best gift I can give myself—nothing is more rewarding. Is there more I could be doing? Sure—we all could do more, and I'm always looking for new opportunities to make a difference. But I don't have any trouble sleeping at night. And I still believe that tomorrow will be the best day I've ever had.

Index

Alexander, Hank, 49–50
Allen, Stuart, 17
American Talent Initiative, 229
America's Pledge, 227
Analysis process, 44–45
Asano, Osamu, 102–03
Associated Press (AP), 71, 73, 74, 96,
    98–99, 100
Aubert, John, 56–57

Bank for International Settlements, 59
Bank of England, 58
Barnes, Mac, 48, 56
Bear Stearns, 18, 26, 153
Becher, Henry, 115
Bell, Stuart, 48
Beyond Coal, 223
Birnbaum, Jeffrey, 94, 95–97
Bloomberg, Charlotte (mother),
    9, 16, 189–90, 191–92, 193–94,
    234–35
Bloomberg, Emma, 8, 196, 219
Bloomberg, Marjorie, 190, 193, 195, 204
Bloomberg, Georgina, 41, 115, 196, 219
Bloomberg, Michael
    childhood of, 9–12
    college experience of, 12, 195
    decision to become an entrepreneur
        by, 39–43
    decision to join Wall Street by, 15–17
    draft classification of, 14–15
    early work and social experiences of,
        195–96
    enjoyment of job by, 40, 59, 67, 178,
        199
    family background of, 9, 16, 28,
        189–94
    flying and skiing hobbies of,
        199–208
    Goldman Sachs interview of, 17, 18
    Harvard Business School experience
        of, 13–14, 23, 29–30, 37, 191
    marriage of, 196–99
    others influencing destiny of,
        209–10
    planning for future by, 30–32
    Salomon career of. See Salomon
        Brothers
    starting time and working hours of,
        29, 30, 32, 41, 67, 190, 196
    time management strategies of,
        197–98
    work as big part of life of, 40–41
Bloomberg, Susan Brown "Sue," 7–8,
    46, 191, 196–97, 198–199
Bloomberg, William (father), 9, 16,
    189–90, 191–93, 195, 217–18, 235
Bloomberg American Cities Initiative,
    225–26
Bloomberg American Health Initiative,
    211–12
Bloomberg Associates, 225
Bloomberg Business News (television
    show), 117
Bloomberg Connects, 233
Bloomberg Intelligence, 126, 163

Bloomberg LP, 39–67
  acquisitions policy of, 123, 168–69
  analysis and planning process before
    opening, 43–45
  art in offices of, 18
  Bloomberg's multiple jobs in early
    years of, 60
  Bloomberg's role at, 155–56
  building not buying approach of,
    80–81, 116, 123, 142, 168–69
  building product first planning ap-
    proach in, 44
  business philosophy of, 62–65
  compensation in, 187–88
  competitors of, 115–16, 161–62
  consultants compared with employ-
    ees of, 61
  daily Treasury prices supplied by,
    71–72, 74
  data-collection process at, 56–57
  decision to become entrepreneur
    with, 39–43
  design process at, 51–52
  doing things differently approach at,
    65–66
  early clients of, 58–59
  early consulting work of, 48–49
  employment policies of, 159–60,
    164–65, 169, 190
  firing from Salomon and starting of,
    8, 38, 197
  first employees recruited for, 46–48
  first office of, 45–46, 47
  first programmers and technical staff
    hired by, 48
  first sale to Merrill by, 48–51, 54–56,
    57–58, 59, 143
  gender equality at, 165–66
  growth approaches of, 160–64,
    166–69
  growth drawbacks and, 170–72
  Help Desk at, 120
  importance of employees of, 157–58
  initial service and installation pro-
    cess for sales made by, 59–60
  Merrill's investment in, 80, 97, 178

  mission of, 107–08
  moving from "hands-on" to "hands-
    off" management in, 60–61
  as multimedia company, 126–27
  naming of, 114–15
  news carried on Terminals of, 78–79
  office space issues at, 156–59
  philanthropy and community ser-
    vice at, 227–34
  planning and successes at, 31–32
  pricing policy of, 66–67
  product diversification at, 166–67
  radio and television broadcasting
    expansion of, 116–20, 124–25
  Terminals developed at, 51–54, 57–78
  working style at, 50–51
Bloomberg Media Initiative-Africa, 230
Bloomberg News, 69–112
  algorithms for stories at, 84–85
  competitors of, 69, 87–88, 89, 90–92
  credentials needed by, 93–99
  decision to begin, 78–83
  Dow Jones and, 86–89
  Japanese news organizations and,
    101–06
  mission of, 107–08
  mobile phone access to, 108–09
  newspaper publication of stories
    from, 99–101
  success of, 106–07
  supply and demand and, 111–12
  technology changes and, 109–11
  Terminal functions used with, 86–87
  uniqueness of, 83–84
  Winkler at, 86, 94, 95, 99–100,
    102–04, 126
Bloomberg Philanthropies
  cultural organizations and, 233
  guidelines in, 223–26
  management of, 219–20
  New York City causes and, 230–31
  public health focus of, 180, 211–12
Bloomberg Personal (news magazine),
    121–23
Bloomberg Startup, 228
Bloomberg Terminals

building rather than buying policy and, 50, 51, 53, 58, 80–81, 141
companies and reasons for using, 53–54
data-collection process for, 57
Dow Jones competition and, 86–89
financial data supplied on, 70–72, 74, 75, 146, 163, 167
first sale to Merrill of, 48–51, 54–56, 57–58, 59, 143
Google comparison with, 54
Help Desk on, 120
Merrill's help in selling, 72–73
Merrill's contract renegotiation and, 153–55
New York Times request for, 99–100
news dissemination using, 69, 78–81, 82, 86, 96, 96, 119, 123, 126
pricing policy for, 66–67
Boston Museum of Science, 11–12, 235
Boy Scouts, 10–11
Bradley, Robert, 26
Brandt, Bob, 205–07
Brenner, Elliot, 97–99
Brown, Jerry, 226
Brown, Rodney, 48
Brown, Susan "Sue," 7–8, 46, 191, 196, 197, 198–199
Buffett, Warren, 212
Burks, Ron, 15
Businessweek, 123–24, 169
Butts, Dave, 102–04

Charlotte Bloomberg Awards, 235
Citicorp, 91, 153, 155
Clark, Ginny, 27
Computerization projects, 129–51
Salomon's B Page project example of, 129–46, 148
software development and, 141–42, 145
technology systems head and, 146–48
Cutis, Mark, 70

Darwin, Charles, 20
Delaney, Jack, 58

DeScherer, Dick, 51
Dow Jones & Co., 107, 114, 115
Bloomberg data compared with, 88–89
Bloomberg News and, 69, 73, 78, 83, 86–89, 90
Telerate terminals used by, 72, 76–77, 91
Winkler at, 70, 72, 95, 99
Dow Jones Industrial Index, 84–85
Draft classifications, 14–15

Education, philanthropy in, 228–30, 234–35
Eisen, Harvey, 114
Eli, Gerry, 48
Elsas, Jay, 24
Entrepreneurs
analysis and planning process of, 43–45
decision to become, 39–43
family life affected by, 197–98
Environmental movement, 216, 223, 227, 232
Everytown for Gun Safety, 237

Failla, Nick, 48
Federal Reserve Bank of New York, 71, 76
Federal Reserve Banks, 59
Fenster, Steve, 15–16, 17
Feuerstein, Don, 34
Financial News Network (FNN), 116–17
FIRST Robotics Competition, 227–28
Ford, Henry, 63
Fram, Jon, 116–17
Frankel, Max, 100
Franklin, Susette, 48

Galotto, Jack, 194–95
Gates, Bill, 27, 212
Geller, Marty, 51
Gender equality, 165–66
Gerstel, Jessy, 132

Giving Pledge, 212
Goldman Sachs, 15, 17, 18, 26, 39
Gutfreund, John, 29, 113
  Blomberg's firing and departure
    from Salomon and, 1, 2, 4, 6
  Blomberg's interview and hiring by,
    18, 19
  leadership style of, 22–23, 24–25, 26, 27
  mentoring by, 7
  working relationship with, 5, 36, 38,
    130–31, 133, 134, 145

Hackett, Bruce, 27
Harris, Patti, 219, 220
Harris, Ron, 50
Harvard Business School (HBS), 24, 235
  education at, 13–14, 18, 37, 191
  summer job during, 29–30
Harvard University, 217, 229, 235
Health, philanthropy in, 179–80,
  211–12, 220
Healy, David, 26
House/Senate Standing Committee of
  Correspondents, 94–99, 109
Hunter, Sam, 48

IBM, 37, 131, 134–35

Japan
  Bloomberg News in, 101–06
  Bloomberg's office in, 165
Johnny Tremain (Forbes), 10
Johns Hopkins University, 12, 21, 195,
  229, 231, 234–35
Jones, Clay, 102

Kaufman, Henry, 1, 2, 4, 7
Kenney, Jerry, 48
Kertess, Hans, 26
Kirkland, David, 26
Kisha clubs, 101–02, 104–06
Kuhn, Loeb & Co., 19
Lectman, Ira, 24–15
Leverone, Bob, 117
Levitt, Ted, 91

Levy, Gustav "Gus," 17, 20, 27
Lewis, Cy, 18, 20, 26, 27
Lewis, Sandy, 18–19
Lombard, Joe, 131

MacMillan, Duncan, 46, 47, 51, 55
Management
  Bloomberg expansion and, 155–56
  compensation for, 187
  factors leading to success by, 172–75
  moving from "hands-on" to "hands-
    off" approach in, 60–61
  new projects and selection of, 120–21
  promoting from within for, 160
  succession planning and, 170
  technology systems head and, 146–48
Maniatty, Connie, 24
Massey, James, 27
Mayors Challenge, 222
McCollough, Brett, 48
McCool, Curtis, 48
McCue, Mary, 94
McGraw-Hill, 83, 91, 123
McLuhan, Marshall, 107
Meehan, Michael, 26
Memorial Day celebration, 213–14
Merrill Lynch & Co., 70, 80
  Bloomberg investment of, 80, 97, 178
  Bloomberg News and, 88–89
  Bloomberg's alliance with, 72–74, 89,
    97, 178
  Bloomberg's first sale to, 48–51,
    54–56, 57–58, 59, 114, 143
  Bloomberg's contract renegotiation
    with, 153–55
Menschel, Dick, 18
Meyers, Jack, 58
Micklethwait, John, 126
Miller, Michael, 73–75
Mitchell, Fred, 48
Morgan Stanley, 16, 19
Moriarty, Ed, 49–50
Murakami, Yoshio, 103–04, 105
Murphy, Vince, 131
Museum of Science, 11–12, 235

NAACP, 217–18, 235
National September 11 Memorial & Museum, 218
National Press Club, 106
Neff, Tom, 48
Nelson, Harry, 18
Neuman, Dana, 48
New York Times, 82, 99–100
New York City
   Bloomberg as mayor of, 214–16, 67, 218, 220, 230
   philanthropy in, 214, 220, 230–31
   public-private partnerships in, 220–22, 226
New York City Police and Fire Widows' and Children's Benefit Fund, 214
Newspapers, expansion into. *See* Bloomberg News

Obama, Barack, 222
Osborn, Dave, 28
Ostrow, Bob, 48

Patriot's Day celebration, 213
Perry, Jay, 25, 26, 27, 34, 35–36, 37, 38
Phibro Corporation, 2–4, 5, 6
Philanthropy, 214, 216–19, 228–37
   asking for money in, 217–18
   cultural organizations and, 233
   education and, 228–30, 234–35
   father's example in, 216–17, 235
   guidelines in, 223–26
   honoring parents in, 234–35
   New York City causes and, 220, 230–31
   public health focus of, 180, 211–12, 220
   reasons behind, 218–19
Philipp Brothers, 5
Planning process, 43–45
Product diversification, 166–67
Public health, 179–80, 181, 211–12, 220
Public-private partnerships, 220–22, 226

Public service
   childhood exposure to, 212–14
   as New York City mayor, 67, 214–16, 218, 220, 230–31
   public-private partnerships in, 220–22
Publicolor, 228
Publishers and Editors Association, Japan, 102–05, 109
Punturieri, John, 48
Purdy, Mark, 48

Quotron, 91, 133–34

Radio, expansion into, 109, 116–19, 124–25, 126
Real estate company, summer job at, 29–30
Reuters, 78, 83, 90, 91, 105, 107, 115
Rieger, James, 48
Rockefeller, John D., 27
Rosenthal, Dick, 35, 36, 37–38, 145

Salomon, Robert "Bob", 4
Salomon, William R. "Billy," 4
   Bloomberg's hiring interview with, 17
   Bloomberg's selection as general partner and, 34–35
   Bloomberg's working relationship with, 5, 26, 29, 36, 130, 134
   Salomon culture and leadership of, 6, 7, 19, 21–22, 27, 35, 115
Salomon Brothers, 1–8, 9, 12, 15–38, 199–200
   battle over use of common computer systems at, 139–40
   Billy Salomon's leadership and culture of, 19, 21–22, 27, 35, 36
   block-trading position at, 25–27, 131
   Bloomberg's B Page computerization project at, 129–46, 148
   business started after departure from, 8, 41–42, 197

Salomon Brothers   (*Continued*)
chief-of-staff proposal at, 22–23
debt to mentors at, 7
decision to apply to, 15–16
enjoyment of working at, 32, 33, 38, 67
firing from, 1–2, 4–5, 7, 8, 38, 39
first summer at, 23
fit with culture of, 19–20
Gutfreund's leadership style at,
   22–23, 24–25, 26, 27, 29, 36
Information Systems position at, 36–37
interview and hiring at, 17–19
last day at, 8
loss of partners at, 6
Phibro merger of, 2–4, 5, 6
planning for future while working
   at, 30–32
Purchase and Sales (P&S) Department promotion of, 23–24
roller-coaster life at, 35–36
Rosenthal-Bloomberg warfare at,
   37–38
selection as general partner at, 33–35
social life and fun activities balanced
   with work at, 30
software development at, 141–42, 145
staying for long term at, 32–33
technology systems head at, 146–48
Utilities Desk trading position of,
   24–25
Wall Street lifestyle and, 27–29
wife's reaction to departure from, 7–8
working environment at, 20–23
Salomon Inc., 5
Secunda, Tom, 46, 47, 51, 231, 232
Seeff, Laurence, 48
Seirup, Lynn, 48
Selective Service System, and draft
   classifications, 14–15
Sierra Club, 223
Smith, Robert, 75–76
Software development, 141–44,
   145, 172
Sommer, Al, 220
Soros, George, 221–22

Standing Committee of
   Correspondents, 94–99, 109

Technology change, 129–51, 180–81
drawbacks to, 182–85
evolutionary aspect of, 187
Salomon's B Page computerization
   project and, 129–46, 148
software development and, 141–42,
   145
technology systems head and,
   146–48
Telerate terminals, 72, 73, 74, 76–77,
   87, 91
Television, expansion into, 116–17,
   118–20, 126
Tiven, Benjamin, 202, 203–04
Tiven, Marjorie Bloomberg, 190, 193, 204
Tully, Dan, 154

Vatican, 58
Venture capitalists, 43
Vietnam War, 14, 15

Wall Street Journal, 29, 82, 87, 94, 129
Bloomberg article in, 69–70, 74–77
Bloomberg data supplied to, 96
Walton, Sam, 27
Weinberg, Janet, 117
Wilson, Margarette, 34–35
Winkler, Matt, 74–82, 86, 94, 96, 102–03,
   126, 230
Bloomberg article by, 69–70, 74–77
Bloomberg-Merrill alliance and,
   69–72, 73–74
Bloomberg News career of, 78–81,
   82, 86, 94, 95, 99–100, 102–04, 126
WNEW, 117–18
World Bank, 59
World Health Organization, 180
Wu, Andy, 48

Young Men's Initiative, 221–22

Zegar, Chuck, 46, 47, 50–51